Domestic Heating Design Guide

ISBN (print)   978-1-912034-88-8
ISBN (PDF)   978-1-912034-89-5

Domestic Heating Design Guide 10th Edition

Illustrations www.Robertburkeillustration.co.uk

Printed and bound by Tewkesbury Printing Company, UK

Contents

0   Introduction **0-1**

0.1   Contents 0-2

0.2   Version Control 0-3

0.3   DBSP Committee Member Organisations 0-4

0.4   Foreword 0-5

    0.4.1   Brexit 0-5

0.5   Domestic Heating Design Guide Introduction 0-7

    0.5.1   Objective 0-7

    0.5.2   Scope 0-7

    0.5.3   How to Use this Guide 0-7

1   System Information **1-1**

1.1   Contents 1-2

1.2   Version Control 1-3

1.3   Relevant Regulations, Standards and Documents 1-4

1.4   Introduction 1-6

1.5   Energy Efficiency and Carbon Emissions 1-7

    1.5.1   What Energy Efficiency Means 1-7

    1.5.2   Environmental Impact 1-8

    1.5.3   Primary and Delivered Energy 1-8

    1.5.4   Why Energy Efficiency is Important 1-9

    1.5.5   Home Energy Ratings and Energy Performance Certificates 1-10

    1.5.6   Heat Generator Efficiency 1-10

    1.5.7   Hot Water Storage Efficiency 1-11

    1.5.8   Controls 1-11

1.6   Heat Generator Considerations 1-12

    1.6.1   Heat Generator Efficiency and Performance Standards 1-12

    1.6.2   Gas Boilers 1-13

    1.6.3   Liquid Fuel Boilers 1-18

    1.6.4   Biomass Fuel 1-20

    1.6.5   Heat Pumps 1-23

    1.6.6   Electric Heating 1-28

    1.6.7   Solar Heating 1-32

    1.6.8   Heat Networks and Heat Interface Units 1-32

1.7   Ventilation 1-33

    1.7.1   Ventilation in Living Space 1-33

    1.7.2   Combustion Air and Safe Operation of Flues 1-34

2   Customer Liaison **2-1**

2.1   Contents 2-2

2.2   Version Control 2-3

2.3   Introduction 2-4

2.4   Pre-Installation Documentation 2-5

    2.4.1   The Specification 2-5

    2.4.2   The Quotation 2-7

2.5   Post-installation Documentation 2-11

    2.5.1   Commissioning 2-11

    2.5.2   Handover 2-14

    2.5.3   Maintenance 2-15

2.6   Appendix 2-16

    2.6.1   Sample Survey Checklist – Blank 2-16

    2.6.2   Sample Quotation Sheet – Blank 2-18

3   System Design (Heat Loss) **3-1**

3.1   Contents 3-2

3.2   Version Control 3-3

3.3   System Design (Heat Loss) – Introduction 3-4

3.4   Heat Loss Calculation – Principles 3-5

    3.4.1   Ventilation and Natural Infiltration Heat Loss . . 3-5

    3.4.2   Calculation of Fabric Heat Loss 3-5

3.5   Heat Loss Calculation – Considerations 3-7

    3.5.1   Surface Area of a Building 3-7

    3.5.2   U-values 3-8

    3.5.3   Design Temperatures 3-14

    3.5.4   Ventilation 3-20

    3.5.5   Intermittent Heating 3-22

3.6   Annual Energy Estimation 3-25

3.7   Heat Loss Procedures 3-26

3.8   System Design (Heat Loss) – Appendix 3-27

    3.8.1   Thermal Conductivity Table 3-27

    3.8.2   U-value Tables 3-29

    3.8.3   Worksheet A – Heat Losses – Blank 3-42

    3.8.4   Worksheet A – Heat Losses – Instructions 3-44

4   System Design (Domestic Hot Water) **4-1**

4.1   Contents 4-2

4.2   Version Control 4-3

4.3   System Design (Domestic Hot Water) – Introduction . . 4-4

4.4 Hot Water Sources 4-6

    4.4.1 Hot Water Storage Cylinders 4-6

    4.4.2 Combination Boilers 4-12

    4.4.3 Thermal Stores 4-14

4.5 Other Hot Water Considerations 4-15

    4.5.1 Bacteria (*Legionella*) Protection 4-15

    4.5.2 Scalding Prevention 4-16

    4.5.3 Secondary Circulation. 4-17

    4.5.4 Hard Water 4-17

    4.5.5 Hot Water Supply Pipework 4-18

    4.5.6 Wastewater Heat Recovery. 4-18

5 System Design (Heating) 5-1

5.1 Contents. 5-2

5.2 Version Control 5-4

5.3 Introduction. 5-5

5.4 System Layout. 5-6

    5.4.1 Typical System Layout. 5-6

    5.4.2 Y-Plan Configuration 5-7

    5.4.3 Primary Circuit Radiator 5-8

    5.4.4 Open-Vented Systems 5-9

    5.4.5 One-Pipe Circuits 5-9

    5.4.6 Reverse-Return Layout 5-10

    5.4.7 Reverse Circulation 5-11

5.5 Heat Emitters 5-13

    5.5.1 General. 5-13

    5.5.2 Heating System Water Temperature. 5-13

    5.5.3 Exposed Pipework Emissions. 5-14

    5.5.4 Output Emission Factors 5-15

    5.5.5 Radiator Selection. 5-19

    5.5.6 Underfloor Heating 5-19

5.6 Pipework 5-21

    5.6.1 Pipework Sizing Strategy 5-21

    5.6.2 Pipework Sizing Strategy – Approximation 5-21

    5.6.3 Pipe Sizing Design: Fluid Velocity 5-24

    5.6.4 Pipe Sizing Design: Frictional Resistance 5-31

5.7 Sizing the Heat Source 5-36

    5.7.1 Heat Generator/Boiler Sizing Method. .5-36

5.8 Circulators. 5-38

5.8.1   Circulator Selection 5-38

5.8.2   Circulator Position. 5-38

5.8.3   Circulator Sizing 5-39

5.8.4   Isolating Valves 5-41

5.8.5   Integral Circulators 5-41

5.8.6   Circulator Fault Diagnosis. 5-41

5.9   Fluid Expansion Compensation 5-44

5.9.1   Sealed Heating Systems. 5-44

5.9.2   Open-Vented Systems 5-54

5.10   Low-Loss Headers and Manifolds 5-57

5.10.1   Low-Loss Headers. 5-57

5.10.2   Manifolds 5-57

5.11   System Controls. 5-60

5.11.1   Introduction 5-60

5.11.2   Control functions – Inputs 5-61

5.11.3   Control functions – Outputs 5-66

5.11.4   Control Functions – Controller 5-73

5.11.5   Zoned Heating 5-75

5.11.6   Recommended Control Systems .5-77

5.12   Pipework Insulation 5-79

5.12.1   Insulation of Heating System Pipework 5-79

5.12.2   Insulation of Domestic Hot Water Pipework 5-80

5.12.3   Insulation in Unheated Areas 5-80

5.12.4   Insulation of Condensate Pipework 5-81

5.12.5   Installation of Insulation 5-81

5.13   Water Treatment 5-82

5.13.1   Debris, Corrosion and Limescale. .5-82

5.13.2   Antifreeze 5-83

5.13.3   Microbiological Contamination 5-83

5.14   Heat Storage and Buffering 5-84

5.15   System Integration 5-85

5.16   Appendix 5-86

5.16.1   Worksheet B – Heat Emitters and Pipework – Blank 5-86

5.16.2   Worksheet B – Heat Emitters and Pipework – Instructions 5-88

5.16.3   Worksheet C – Water Content of System – Blank. 5-90

5.16.4   Worksheet C – Water Content of System – Instructions 5-92

0 Introduction

0.1 Contents

0.1   Contents. 0-2

0.2   Version Control 0-3

0.3   DBSP Committee Member Organisations. 0-4

0.4   Foreword 0-5

    0.4.1   Brexit 0-5

0.5   Domestic Heating Design Guide Introduction 0-7

    0.5.1   Objective. 0-7

    0.5.2   Scope. 0-7

    0.5.3   How to Use this Guide 0-7

0.2 Version Control

Version number	Changes	Date
10.01	Initial version	10-Nov-2020

The Domestic Building Service Panel Guide reporting tool can be used to notify the panel of any suggested corrections, or comments. These will be collated and used as the basis for review of forthcoming updates. Please feel free to use the tool, which is located at https://www.dbsp.co.uk/reporting-tool

0.3 DBSP Committee Member Organisations

Organisation	Acronym
Domestic Building Services Panel (Guide Author) – https://www.dbsp.co.uk	**DBSP**
BEAMA – https://www.beama.org.uk	**BEAMA**
Building Engineering Services Association – https://www.thebesa.com	**BESA**
Building Research Establishment – https://www.bregroup.com	**BRE**
Chartered Institution of Building Services Engineers – https://www.cibse.org	**CIBSE**
Chartered Institute of Plumbing and Heating Engineering – https://www.ciphe.org.uk	**CIPHE**
City & Guilds – https://www.cityandguilds.com	**C&G**
Electrical Contractors' Association – https://www.eca.co.uk	**ECA**
Heating Equipment Testing and Approval Scheme – https://www.hetas.co.uk	**HETAS**
Heating & Hotwater Industry Council – https://www.hhic.org.uk	**HHIC**
Heat Pump Association – https://www.heatpumps.org.uk	**HPA**
Hot Water Association – https://www.hotwater.org.uk	**HWA**
Oil Firing Technical Association – https://www.oftec.org	**OFTEC**
Scottish and Northern Ireland Plumbing Employers' Federation – https://www.snipef.org	**SNIPEF**

0.4 Foreword

This publication is the work of the Domestic Building Services Panel (https://www.dbsp.co.uk), a joint initiative of the heating industry in collaboration with the Chartered Institution of Building Services Engineers (CIBSE).

The panel was created as an initiative of the then Department of the Environment in the late 1990s. This edition builds on earlier publications, and includes many recent revisions, as well as a major reorganisation and improvements to the layout. The aim has been to keep pace with the changes in products, appliances, controls and client expectations, together with higher performance standards imposed by regulations and the longer-term ambition of the legally binding target set by the Climate Change Act 2008. The latter requires the UK to be zero carbon by 2050, and provides to mitigate climate change by decarbonisation of energy supplies.

On 19 January 2021 the government confirmed a fundamental shift from gas fuelled heating appliances to electric heating, in particular heat pumps, in new homes from 2025. The Future Homes Standard 2025 will be set so 'that new homes will not be built with fossil fuel heating, such as a natural gas boiler. A low carbon heating system will be integral to the specification of the Future Homes Standard and we anticipate that heat pumps will become the primary heating technology for new homes'.[1] This will have a very significant impact on the design and installation of domestic heating systems and on those who design and install them, marking the greatest upheaval in the market since the transition to natural gas some 50 years ago.

0.4.1 Brexit

The UK left the European Union (EU) on 31 January 2020 and the Withdrawal Agreement transition period ended on 31 December 2020. The UK and the EU concluded a trade and co-operation agreement with a zero tariff deal in the trade of goods and provisions to support trade in services.

At the time of publication, the detailed arrangements relating to trade are still emerging. The rules for trade in construction products, including lifts and escalators, have now changed. It is also important to note that as a part of the wider package of changes to building safety legislation, the government has announced that the Office of Product Standards and Safety is to take responsibility for safety and standards of construction products, including the testing and certification regime. This new regime is very likely to cover many of the products included in this Guide. Users of this guidance should therefore be aware that the regulations referenced here that relate to the UK may be affected by these emerging policies.

The following summarises what is known at the time of publication. Readers are advised to check official sources current at the time of reading this guidance.

The language of regulation is likely to change, for example:

- EU Directives and Regulations that applied to the UK on 31 December 2020 are now part of UK or devolved administration regulations, which will be the sole source of statutory requirements in the UK.
- The CE mark system will continue unchanged in the UK during the transition period. The UKCA (UK Conformity Assessed) mark is intended to replace the CE mark. UK regulations currently set out a further 'time-limited period' during which CE marking and UKCA marking will co-exist, after which it is expected that UKCA marking will be required for products being placed on the UK market. Most products that are currently CE marked will fall under the scope of UKCA marking.

---

[1] *The Future Homes Standard: 2019 Consultation on Changes to Part L (Conservation of Fuel and Power) and Part F (Ventilation) of the Building Regulations for New Dwellings – Summary of Responses Received and Government Response.* https://www.gov.uk/government/consultations/the-future-homes-standard-changes-to-part-l-and-part-f-of-the-building-regulations-for-new-dwellings

Note: EU Notified Bodies will be replaced by UK Approved Bodies, which will be responsible for third-party conformity testing, where this is required for UKCA marking. EU Declarations of Conformity will be replaced by a UK Declaration of Conformity, and EU-type examinations, certificates, etc., will be replaced by UK-type examinations, certificates, etc.

UK-based Notified Bodies are affected significantly. They are no longer established in the EU, and their notified status ended on 31 January 2020. Certificates allowing products to be placed on the EU single market will be limited to products for the UK market. Some Notified Bodies have established operations in an EU member state to enable the subsidiary to continue to operate within the EU single market.

These changes clearly affect those parties involved in the movement of goods and services.

The UK national standards body, the British Standards Institution (BSI), remains a member of the European standardisation organisations (ESOs), the European Committee for Standardization (CEN) and the European Committee for Electrotechnical Standardization (CENELEC), until at least the end of 2021. The ESOs are not institutions of the EU, and are not directly affected by the UK leaving the EU. The current ambition is for the ESOs to update their statutes to enable the BSI to remain a full member even though the UK is no longer a member of the EU.

Under the rules of the ESOs, when a standard is adopted by CEN or CENELEC it is adopted by the standards body of each EU member state. This will continue, and is not affected by the UK leaving the EU. This also means that, when a standard is harmonised by the EU, the BSI will adopt the harmonised standard as a British standard.

The UK government has announced that, for the purposes of the UKCA mark, it will designate standards against which products may be UKCA marked.

0.5 Domestic Heating Design Guide Introduction

0.5.1 Objective

This *Domestic Heating Design Guide* has been produced to assist specifiers and designers of 'wet' central heating systems for single family and multiple occupancy buildings, and covers both new and existing dwellings. Wet central heating systems are low-pressure hot water (LPHW) systems for distributing heat throughout a building; they are sometimes called 'hydronic' systems. The Guide is also intended for practitioners who want to gain a better understanding of the principles and methods underlying the design process, and it offers a method for reaching agreement with a client as to what is needed and will be provided.

0.5.2 Scope

This Guide covers the most widely used system designs, but contains sufficient information to inform a more general design process when the standard approach is not suitable.

The Guide is intended:

- To be used in conjunction with other publications. Reference must always be made to relevant building and other regulations and standards. Associated statutory guidance should also be consulted. All references to legislation, guidance and standards are only correct at the time of publication.
- To aid in the design and specification of LPHW space- and water-heating systems connected to an automatically controlled heat source. This includes open-vented and unvented/sealed heating and domestic hot water heating systems.
- For use in The British Isles.

This Guide is *not* intended to cover:

- The design and regulatory requirements for the heat generators themselves. Specific requirements for the installation of gas, solid fuel, wood or biomass, liquid fuel fired and electrical heating equipment, including fuel storage where applicable, are provided in other publications. Only outline details and the implications of the LPHW system for the heat source are given in this Guide (see section 1.6).
- The design of hot and cold water system draw-off pipework or sanitary appliances.
- Installation work.

0.5.3 How to Use this Guide

This Guide has been restructured from previous editions to show the design stages more clearly and to help the reader find the parts needed. Below are two flow diagrams, one for the first-time reader and one for those looking to design a system using this Guide. These flow diagrams can be used to more easily navigate around the Guide.

0.5.3.1 First-Time Reader Flow Diagram

If you are new to this Guide, it is recommended that you work through the following path to understand the background information behind this Guide:

Introduction	Guide introduction – section 0
System information	Introduction – section 1.4 Energy-efficiency considerations – section 1.5 Heat source considerations – section 1.6
Customer liaison	Introduction – section 2.3
Heat loss	Introduction – section 3.3
System design (domestic hot water)	Introduction – section 4.3
System design (heating)	Introduction – section 5.3

0.5.3.2 System Design Flow Diagram
The following is a flow diagram to guide readers through the process of designing a system with this document:

Note: Sections 2 through 5 regularly refer to section 1 (System Information) for more details on any topic that crosses the boundary between multiple sections

Customer liaison

Specification – section 2.4.1
Quotation – section 2.4.2

System design (heat loss)

Heat loss calculation – section 3.4
Heat loss calculation considerations – section 3.5

System design (domestic hot water)

Hot water system selection – section 4.4
Hot water considerations – section 4.5

System design (heating)

System layout – section 5.4
Heat emitter selection and design – section 5.5
Pipe sizing – section 5.6
Sizing the heat generator – section 5.7
Circulators – section 5.8
Fluid expansion compensation – section 5.9
System controls – section 5.11
Pipework insulation – section 5.12
Water treatment – section 5.13

Customer liaison

Commissioning – section 2.5.1
Handover – section 2.5.2
Maintenance – section 2.5.3

1 System Information

1.1 Contents

1.1   Contents 1-2

1.2   Version Control 1-3

1.3   Relevant Regulations, Standards and Documents 1-4

1.4   Introduction 1-6

1.5   Energy Efficiency and Carbon Emissions 1-7

    1.5.1   What Energy Efficiency Means 1-7

    1.5.2   Environmental Impact 1-8

    1.5.3   Primary and Delivered Energy 1-8

    1.5.4   Why Energy Efficiency is Important 1-9

    1.5.5   Home Energy Ratings and Energy Performance Certificates . . . 1-10

    1.5.6   Heat Generator Efficiency 1-10

    1.5.7   Hot Water Storage Efficiency 1-11

    1.5.8   Controls 1-11

1.6   Heat Generator Considerations 1-12

    1.6.1   Heat Generator Efficiency and Performance Standards 1-12

    1.6.2   Gas Boilers 1-13

    1.6.3   Liquid Fuel Boilers 1-18

    1.6.4   Biomass Fuel 1-20

    1.6.5   Heat Pumps 1-23

    1.6.6   Electric Heating 1-28

    1.6.7   Solar Heating 1-32

    1.6.8   Heat Networks and Heat Interface Units 1-32

1.7   Ventilation 1-33

    1.7.1   Ventilation in Living Space 1-33

    1.7.2   Combustion Air and Safe Operation of Flues 1-34

1.2 Version Control

Version number	Changes	Date
10.01	Initial version	10-Nov-2020

The Domestic Building Service Panel Guide reporting tool can be used to notify the panel of any suggested corrections, or comments. These will be collated and used as the basis for review of forthcoming updates. Please feel free to use the tool, which is located at https://www.dbsp.co.uk/reporting-tool

1.3 Relevant Regulations, Standards and Documents

Statutory guidance. Building regulations and standards relevant to the country where the installation is to occur should be followed; see Table 1.1.

Table 1.1 Building regulations and standards relevant to each country

Subjects covered	England	Wales	Scotland	Northern Ireland	Republic of Ireland
Thermal insulation of building fabric, hot water storage and pipework, control of heating systems	Part L – The conservation of fuel and power	Part L – The conservation of fuel and power	Section 6 – Energy	Part F – The conservation of fuel and power	Part L – The conservation of fuel and energy
Provision of adequate ventilation for building occupants and control of condensation	Part F – Ventilation	Part F – Ventilation	Section 3 – Environment Section 6 – Energy	Part K – Ventilation	Part F – Ventilation
Heat-producing appliances; fuel storage systems	Part J – Heat producing appliances	Part J – Heat producing appliances	Section 3 – Environment Section 6 – Energy	Part L – Heat producing appliances and liquefied petroleum gas installations	Part J – Heat producing appliances
Unvented hot water storage	Part G – Sanitation, hot water safety and water efficiency	Part G – Sanitation, hot water safety and water efficiency	Section 3 – Environment	Part P – Sanitary appliances and hot water storage systems	Part G – Hygiene (unvented hot water storage is effectively prohibited, as only the cold water supply to the kitchen sink may be connected directly to the mains water supply)
Domestic building services compliance					Heating and Domestic Hot Water Systems for Dwellings Achieving Compliance with Part L 2008

Gas safety legislation. All gas appliances and other gas fittings must be installed in accordance with the Gas Safety (Installation and Use) Regulations 1998, which apply in England, Northern Ireland, Scotland and Wales. In particular, it is required that all businesses, whether employers or self-employed persons, that undertake work on fittings supplied by natural gas be registered with a body approved by the Health and Safety Executive (HSE). The Gas Safe Register was approved by the HSE for this purpose. In the Republic of Ireland, gas heating installations are regulated by the Register of Gas Installers of Ireland (RGII) and the Irish standard IS 813:2012 (Domestic gas installation).

Water legislation. Equipment connected directly to public water supplies in England and Wales must comply with the Water Supply (Water Fittings) Regulations 1999. Similar regulations apply in Northern Ireland, the Republic of Ireland and Scotland, through water by-laws.

Boiler efficiency legislation (see section 1.6.1). Boiler efficiency is controlled by the Boiler (Efficiency) Regulations 1993, and the Boiler (Efficiency) (Amendment) Regulations 2006, which introduced combination boilers (also known as 'combi' boilers). The European legislation is Council Directive 92/42/EEC of 21 May 1992 (Efficiency requirements for new hot-water boilers fired with liquid or gaseous fuels). Also refer to the Framework Directive for the Eco-design of Energy Using Products (EuP).

Electric heating (see section 1.6.6). This is covered by BS 7671:2018+A1:2020 (Requirements for Electrical Installations). In the Republic of Ireland the standard IS 10101:2020 and the Electricity Regulation Act 1999 apply. The Commission for Regulation of Utilities (CRU) regulates the safety of electrical installations, and the Electrical Safety Supervisory Body (ESSB) is the safety supervisory body responsible for the inspection and monitoring of the certification process through the Safe Electric Scheme. The National Standards Authority of Ireland (NSAI) is responsible for providing a comprehensive set of standards for the electrical industry. See section 1.6.6.

1.4 Introduction

As well as the more technical tasks involved in the design of a heating system – heat loss calculations (section 3), specifying the hot water system (section 4) and specifying the heating system (section 5) – there are a number of other important considerations that need to be taken into account. This section runs through these considerations, and is referred back to throughout the rest of the Guide, as many of the considerations span multiple sections.

Topics covered in this section include:

- Energy efficiency – considerations that should be made to reduce the installation and running costs of the system, as well as reducing its carbon emissions, are discussed in section 1.5.
- Heat generators – while the specification of heat generators is beyond the scope of this Guide, some of the considerations that will affect the design of the heating system according to the type of heat generator are discussed in section 1.6.
- Ventilation – similarly, the specification of ventilation and flues is also outside the scope of this Guide, but some of the implications are discussed in section 1.7.

1.5 Energy Efficiency and Carbon Emissions

1.5.1 What Energy Efficiency Means

The energy efficiency of a dwelling depends on its level of insulation and ventilation, how the heating is controlled, as well as the efficiency with which its heating and hot water systems can convert fuel or power into heat.

The fabric of the dwelling has a large influence on the amount of energy required to keep it thermally comfortable. If the building is badly insulated, even the most efficient heating system will require a great deal of energy to keep it warm. Overall, an energy-efficient dwelling is one that is well insulated, draught-proof, has an efficient heating system and has good heating controls. In newer housing, which is built to much higher insulation standards, ventilation is likely to be the greater cause of heat losses.

Although it may not always be possible to improve building fabric insulation, the heating installer should be aware of opportunities to improve insulation and draught-proofing, and bring these to the client's attention. Better insulation will generally improve comfort and client satisfaction, and may lead to opportunities for a more competitive quotation.

Hot water systems should always be insulated to minimise heat loss from storage cylinders and primary circuits; the heat output from these may contribute to space-heating requirements in the winter, but in summer it is wasted and may make the house uncomfortably warm.

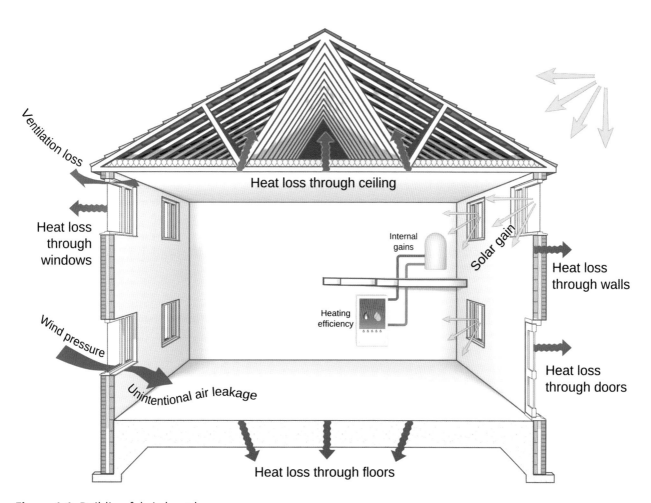

Figure 1.1 Building fabric heat loss

1.5.2 Environmental Impact

The burning of fossil fuels, such as gas, oil and coal, is responsible for a large proportion of all carbon dioxide (CO_2) emissions to the atmosphere. The concentration of CO_2 in the global atmosphere has been rising at an increasing rate since the start of the industrial revolution. Climatologists and others have formed a consensus view that the 'greenhouse effect' arising from CO_2 and other gases produced by humans in the atmosphere is likely to increase global warming, with consequent changes to climates around the world. This has led to agreements reached under the auspices of the United Nations to limit further emissions of greenhouse gases.

The UK has committed to reducing its greenhouse gas emissions to zero by 2050,[1] which requires a reduction in the energy demand for space and water heating and eliminating the combustion of fossil fuels to supply it. Energy-efficiency measures applied to homes are expected to contribute a significant proportion of the necessary reductions. Reductions will be achieved by better insulation, lower air leakage in cold weather, more efficient and better controlled heating systems, and improvements to lighting and electrical appliances.

1.5.3 Primary and Delivered Energy

The energy supply to a house is obtained either by connection to a mains network or in bulk, requiring a local fuel store. In either case, it is possible to express the energy content of the fuel in common units such as kilowatt hours (kW h). The energy content of fuel delivered to the house is known as 'delivered energy'.

Metered supplies of electricity and gas are sold to the consumer in kW h. Gas is measured by volume in cubic metres (cubic feet on older gas meters). One cubic metre of natural gas from the public supply produces about 11 kW h; this can be calculated from the calorific value of the fuel, which is shown on gas bills in units of megajoules per cubic metre (MJ/m^3). Fuels supplied in bulk are sold by weight or volume, but the units used for sale can readily be converted to kW h by using the calorific value of the fuel. For example, a litre of heating oil has an energy content of 10.35 kW h.

Not all forms of delivered energy are equally useful. Electricity has many uses, as it can be converted to heat with 100% efficiency when used in direct electric heating (or higher with the use of a heat pump), and can also operate motors, lights and electronic circuits. Consideration needs to be given to the fact that electricity has traditionally been generated from fuel consumed at power stations, with an average efficiency of around 40%. The energy at the power station used to provide a household with 1 kW h of delivered electricity was therefore considerably greater at around 2.5 kW h. This is known as 'primary energy'. However, this has changed rapidly, due to the growth in renewable generation technologies and the substitution of coal power plants by more efficient combined cycle gas turbine power plants. Consequently, the primary energy factor (the ratio between the primary energy and the energy delivered to the building) for electricity in the UK has fallen from about 2.5 to 1.5.[2] There are also energy overheads associated with the production, refining and distribution of fuels, and these are reflected in the primary energy factors, although they are much smaller than for electricity, being typically around 5%.

The distinction between delivered and primary energy is important when considering the energy running cost and environmental impact, both of which are more closely related to primary than delivered energy. Electricity is clearly a premium source of energy, and is more versatile at the point of use than other forms of energy. In 2010, UK electricity generally relied on coal for 34% of its energy input. By 2018, coal usage had fallen to less than 1%, while the proportion of renewables used had risen from less than 10% to more than 40%.[3] All this has led to improved generation efficiency and reduced CO_2 emissions per unit

---

[1] The Climate Change Act 2008 (2050 Target Amendment) Order 2019. https://www.legislation.gov.uk/ukdsi/2019/9780111187654

[2] Department for Business, Energy and Industrial Strategy (2019) *The Government's Standard Assessment Procedure for Energy Rating of Dwellings*, version 10.1. https://www.bregroup.com/wp-content/uploads/2019/11/SAP-10.1-08-11-2019_1.pdf

[3] Department for Business, Energy and Industrial Strategy (2019) *Updated Energy and Emissions Projections: 2018. Annex J: Total Electricity Generation by Source.* https://www.gov.uk/government/publications/updated-energy-and-emissions-projections-2018

of delivered electricity. Further growth in renewable sources (such as solar photovoltaic (PV), onshore and offshore wind) is expected to completely decarbonise electrical power by 2030.

The price of electricity remains high, with a cost per kW h about 4–5 times that of natural gas at on-peak rates and about twice that at off-peak rates. However, CO_2 emissions per unit of delivered electricity have dropped significantly over the last decade, to a level considerably lower than gas, which has led to a widespread interest in the electrification of heating systems in order to decarbonise buildings.

1.5.4 Why Energy Efficiency is Important

Energy efficiency produces benefits for individual householders and for the environment.

For households, the benefits are lower fuel bills and more comfortable living conditions. A well-insulated airtight house needs less heat to bring it up to a comfortable temperature, and it cools down more slowly when the heating system is turned off. An efficient, well-controlled heating system uses less fuel to produce a given amount of heat. Good insulation and a well-controlled system combine to reduce the total amount of fuel needed, and hence the cost. Affordable heating is of particular importance in the social housing sector, which caters for households with low incomes. Consequently, contractors working for housing associations and local authorities need to pay particular attention to energy efficiency.

The environmental benefits of energy efficiency are discussed in section 1.5.2. Energy efficiency contributes to reduced environmental impact through the use of less fuel. It is also important to take account of the difference in carbon emissions between fuels. Replacing one type of heating system with another that uses a different fuel will affect the CO_2 emissions. Table 1.2 gives CO_2e (CO_2 equivalent[4]) emissions per unit of delivered energy for electricity and heating fuels in the UK, and primary energy factors, taken from the Government's Standard Assessment Procedure for Energy Rating of Dwellings (SAP) (see section 1.5.5) in October 2013.

Note: SAP 10.1 uses new emissions and primary energy factors, which for electricity are substantially lower. than previous versions The figures were published in November 2019 and are detailed on p. 171 of the SAP 10.1 specification.[5]

Table 1.2 CO_2e emission factors and primary energy factors for delivered energy in the UK (SAP 2012, October 2013; SAP 10.1, November 2019)

Fuel	CO_2e emissions (kg/kW h)		Primary energy factor	
	SAP 2012	SAP 10.1	SAP 2012	SAP 10.1
Electricity	0.519	0.136	3.07	1.5
Mains gas	0.216	0.21	1.22	1.13
Liquid petroleum gas (LPG)	0.241	0.241	1.09	1.41
Heating oil	0.298	0.298	1.10	1.18
Coal	0.394	0.395	1.00	1.06
Woody biomass	0.016–0.039	0.023–0.053	1.04–1.26	1.05–1.33

---

[4] CO_2 equivalent (CO_2e) emissions include gases other than CO_2, with a weighting factor to equate their environmental harm to that of CO_2.
[5] The Government's Standard Assessment Procedure for Energy Rating of Dwellings: Version 10.1.
https://www.bregroup.com/wp-content/uploads/2019/11/SAP-10.1-08-11-2019_1.pdf

1.5.5 Home Energy Ratings and Energy Performance Certificates

Energy assessment is calculated using the Government's Standard Assessment Procedure for Energy Rating of Dwellings (SAP). SAP is used mainly for new dwellings, and a simplified version, the Reduced Data SAP (RdSAP), is used mainly for existing dwellings when a complete set of building data is usually not available. In the Republic of Ireland, the Dwelling Energy Assessment Procedure (DEAP) is used for the same purpose. These methods are also used to produce Energy Performance Certificates (EPCs), which are required for all new housing and existing housing when it is sold or first let to tenants. The SAP and DEAP produce energy ratings that are based on running costs for space and water heating, and depend on the form of the building, its thermal insulation, which fuel is used and the performance of the heating system.

Ratings are expressed as a value in the range of 1 to 100 or more; the higher the value the better, with 100 representing zero net energy cost. Higher than 100 would mean that the dwelling exports more energy to the supply grid than it receives, which may be possible if, for example, solar PV panels and wind turbines have been installed. Ratings allow comparisons of energy efficiency to be made, and can show the likely effect of improvements to a dwelling in terms of energy use. Using energy ratings, designers, developers, house-builders and home owners can take energy-efficiency factors into consideration, both for new dwellings and when refurbishing existing ones. Energy ratings can be used at the design stage as a guide to energy efficiency and the reduction of future fuel bills. The SAP also generates a TER (Target CO_2 Emission Rate) for a new dwelling to achieve, and a DER (Dwelling CO_2 Emission Rate) for the dwelling as designed and constructed. To comply with building regulations the DER must be equal to, or less than, the TER. For existing dwellings that change ownership or tenancy, an Energy Performance Certificate can be produced by the reduced data version of the SAP (the RdSAP), which uses the same calculation methods but requires less input data.

The heating designer has an opportunity to influence the SAP or DEAP rating of buildings by selecting a high-efficiency heat generator, the choice of fuel and specifying good controls. For boilers, SEDBUK (see section 1.6.1.2) was specifically designed to provide values for boiler efficiency use in SAP calculations, and has been used in SAP assessments since 2001.

1.5.6 Heat Generator Efficiency

The efficiency of the heat generator is the main factor affecting the overall energy efficiency of central heating systems. It is important because it determines how much fuel or electricity is used to provide the householder's requirements for space and water heating. Minimum standards of efficiency for most types of heat generator are imposed by national building regulations and the European ecodesign requirements.

The selection of specific heat generators is outside the scope of this Guide, but it is important to note that the decisions made by the designer and specifier of a heating system will affect the heat generator efficiency. For example, heat generator efficiency depends on the type of product and operating conditions, and how well matched the generator is to the demand for heat. The demand for heating varies greatly throughout the year, and the heat generator efficiency varies too. It is important to distinguish between instantaneous values (e.g. those obtained by measurements in a laboratory under carefully specified and controlled test conditions) and the annual average obtained after installation of the heat generator in a particular building. It is a mistake to compare the efficiencies of products or systems unless they have been measured in the same way under the same test conditions.

Other factors include:

- the power output of the heat generator in relation to its design heat load and radiator sizes – see sections 1.6 and 5.7
- whether the heat generator is providing space heating or water heating, or both
- the flow and return water temperatures (these may vary throughout the day) – see section 5.5.2
- if it is a condensing boiler, the extent to which it runs in condensing mode – see section 1.6.2.3
- the heating system controls – see section 5.11.

All of these, and more, are at least in part within the control of the specifier and designer, while installation and commissioning are important to the realisation of the designer's intentions. Lower water temperature raises efficiency, although radiator sizes have to be increased to achieve the same overall heat output. Regular servicing and maintenance are needed to ensure that efficiency is sustained, particularly for liquid fuel fired boilers.

Information on the efficiency of domestic gas and liquid fuel boilers, new and old, in the UK can be obtained from the Product Characteristics Database (PCDB) used by the SAP, which can be accessed at http://www.ncm-pcdb.org.uk (see section 1.6.1.2).

Note: Section 1.6 of this Guide discusses more specifically some of the specific heating and hot water system design considerations for a number of different types of heat generator.

1.5.7 Hot Water Storage Efficiency

Many new installations have combination boilers, which produce instantaneous hot water on demand, and so a separate hot water storage cylinder is not needed. Hot water storage cylinders still have some advantages, however, and their energy performance is dominated by their insulation and the size of the heat exchanger.

Firstly, cylinders should be well insulated, as heat lost to the surroundings cannot contribute usefully to space heating requirements when no heat is required in summer and may cause uncomfortably high temperatures. Insulation is especially important if the cylinder is installed in an unheated space.

Secondly, the heat exchangers within cylinders should have sufficient capacity to provide rapid warm-up. Poor heat exchanger performance causes the boiler to run for long periods at low loads. Apart from providing poor service to the household, this reduces boiler efficiency and increases heat losses from the primary circuit.

As a minimum, the designer should always specify hot water cylinders that comply with BS 1566, BS 3198:1981 or BS EN 12897:2016. 'High performance' cylinders, which have fast recovery heat exchangers that are usually better insulated, are recommended.

It is a good control strategy to aim for water heating at separate times from space heating, especially if space heating has been designed to operate at lower water temperatures.

Note: Section 4 of this Guide discusses hot water storage and hot water production in detail.

1.5.8 Controls

The output required from a heating system varies considerably, particularly in response to external temperature. Controls are needed to ensure that the system provides the right output for all conditions, including those where little or no additional heat is required. Controls contribute significantly to the efficient operation of a heating system, by preventing overheating and allowing the desired temperatures to be achieved in each room only at the times required. The selection of suitable controls also plays a key part in the overall running costs of a heating system.

Basic controls for time and temperature should be regarded as essential, and in any case are a requirement of building regulations. Upgrading controls on older heating systems can save a worthwhile margin on energy bills. More advanced controls are becoming more common, allowing features such as remote control of a building from a computer or smartphone, or artificial intelligence to learn occupancy patterns. These may give rise to further savings where the building is occupied irregularly and the occupant does not engage with their heating controls.

Note: Section 5.11 of this Guide discusses the operation of the principal types of control and specifies appropriate packages of controls for different types of system.

1.6 Heat Generator Considerations

While the selection of a specific heat generator is outside the scope of this Guide, various decisions that the designer of a hot water or heating system must make will be driven by the type of heat generator that supplies the system. Therefore this section provides an overview of various heat generator types, their advantages and disadvantages, and their specific requirements from a heating system.

This section also continues from section 1.5, and highlights some of the energy-efficiency requirements and considerations surrounding each type of heat generator. Selection of heat generators needs to consider the move away from fossil fuel appliances and their replacement by heat pumps and other electric appliances.

1.6.1 Heat Generator Efficiency and Performance Standards

1.6.1.1 Ecodesign

In 2009, EU legislation was introduced to improve the energy efficiency of products and reduce energy and resource consumption. The Ecodesign Directive (Directive 2009/125/EC of 21 October 2009) provides a consistent EU-wide set of rules for improving the environmental performance of products, such as household appliances and information and communication technologies or engineering, by setting out minimum mandatory requirements for the energy efficiency of these products.

Additionally, the Energy Labelling Regulation of 2010 (Directive 2010/30/EU of 19 May 2010) complements the Ecodesign Directive by requiring labelling of these products, in order to give information about their energy and environmental performance to consumers. A typical energy label for a heat pump is given in Figure 1.2. It shows the energy rating at two water temperatures, the noise level and figures for three climate zones.

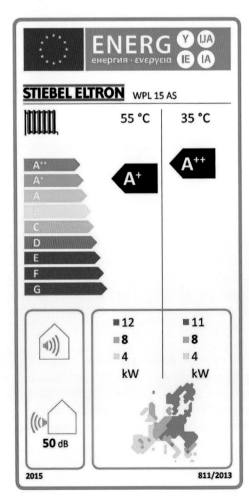

Figure 1.2 EU energy label for a heat pump

In 2013, the EU published ecodesign and energy labelling regulations for space heaters (Regulation 813/201) which established minimum energy efficiency requirements for all space and combination heaters with a rated heat output lower than 400 kW. Most types of combustion boilers (except biomass and solid fuel), heat pumps and electric boilers lie within the scope of these regulations. The requirements came into force in September 2015, and the declaration of the energy rating needs to take place at the point of placing the product on the market (i.e. the first point at which it is made available to the market, when it is first supplied for distribution).

The ecodesign energy rating for boilers is a combination of thermal efficiency and other factors, such as electricity consumption and type of control. The figures produced are not comparable with, and should not be confused with, other efficiency measures, such as PCDB/SEDBUK for boilers (see section 1.6.1.2).

Similar energy efficiency and labelling requirements were introduced for water heaters with a rated output lower than 400 kW, and hot water storage tanks with a storage volume lower than 2000 litres. The requirements came into force in September 2017, and apply to all devices connected to the mains network and which include a heat generator, such as combustion of fossil fuels, an electric resistance heater or ambient heat recovery. Water heaters using liquid or gaseous biofuels and solid fuels are not in scope.

Lastly, regulations were also introduced in 2015 for 'local space heaters' (i.e. room heaters) with a nominal heat output of 50 kW or less for domestic products and 120 kW or less for commercial local space heaters. The requirements entered into force in 2018, and products covered include electric local space heaters (portable and fixed electric panel heaters, storage heaters and electric underfloor heating), and gaseous and liquid fuel room heaters. Air-heating products and room heat pumps are not within the scope of these regulations.

Solid fuel boilers with a rated heat output of 500 kW or less became subject to ecodesign requirements from January 2020.

1.6.1.2 The Products Characteristics Database (PCDB, formerly SEDBUK)

In the UK, a measure of the efficiency of heating systems with gas and liquid fuel boilers was developed by the government in collaboration with boiler manufacturers in 1999, and became widely used. It is known as SEDBUK, which is an acronym for Seasonal Efficiency of a Domestic Boiler in the UK. It provided a basis for fair comparison of the thermal efficiency of different boilers, which was especially important at a time when condensing boilers were not yet widely used. Since then, changes to building regulations require the use of condensing boilers in almost all circumstances, and the variations in efficiency between boilers now on sale have been greatly reduced.

SEDBUK is the average annual efficiency of a boiler under typical domestic conditions, making reasonable assumptions about the pattern of usage, climate, control and other influences. It is calculated from the results of standard laboratory tests together with other important factors such as the boiler type, ignition arrangement, internal store size, fuel used, and knowledge of the UK climate and typical domestic usage patterns.

SEDBUK is a better guide for estimating annual fuel costs than laboratory test results alone. It can easily be applied to most gas and liquid fuel domestic boilers for which data is available from tests conducted to the relevant European standards. The SEDBUK method is used in SAP, which applies to both new and existing dwellings and estimates the ongoing amount and cost of energy used for space and water heating. New boilers must now bear an energy label defined by the EU Energy Labelling Regulation, which shows an energy rating at point of sale. The rating is calculated using a different method and is not comparable with the SEDBUK efficiency.

SEDBUK has been renamed the Products Characteristics Database (PCDB, https://www.ncm-pcdb.org.uk).

1.6.2 Gas Boilers

Gas central heating boilers are an established heating technology in the UK, coming to prominence with the advent of North Sea gas being discovered in the mid-20th century, and as UK homes progressively moved from decentralised local space heating to gas-fired central heating solutions. Currently, around 85% of UK heat demand is met by gas, including mains natural gas and off-grid stored LPG.

With the UK announcing that fossil-fuel-based heat generators will be banned for new-build homes by 2025, there are some concerns about the future within the industry. In future there will be a growing demand for alternative heat generators, primarily heat pumps, with an ongoing legacy demand for replacement boilers in the next few years.

Gas boilers are combustion appliances, whereby heat from the combustion of a gaseous fuel, primarily natural gas, is captured via a heat exchanger, which transfers this heat energy to primary water circulating within the heating system. The technology has evolved considerably since its inception, not least with the move to condensing boiler technology, as mandated in the UK via amendments to Part L of the Building Regulations 2010 (or regional equivalent as per Table 1.1) in April 2005. When operating in condensing mode, condensing boilers remove the latent heat of the flue gases, bringing the flue gas temperature below their dew point, and resulting in condensation being produced, alongside greater efficiency gains.

The high temperatures produced by the combustion of natural gas mean that gas boilers have highly thermally responsive primary heat exchangers. They are typically manufactured from stainless steel or aluminium alloy, and with a correctly specified ancillary heating system they are able to provide rapid heat-up times for dwellings of varying thermal mass. This is a particular consideration where the conventional UK preference for bi-modal heating patterns is adopted.

The most common types of domestic gas boiler include:

- *Combination* – These provide central heating and also hot water on demand, by instantaneous firing when a demand for hot water is created (e.g. hot tap opened). They are invariably sealed system appliances.
- *System* – These are typically sealed system boilers that provide central heating and are able to heat separately connected hot water storage. The boiler incorporates key system components within the appliance casing/footprint (e.g. circulating pump, expansion vessel).
- *Heat only* – These are open-vented or sealed system appliances that provide central heating and are able to heat separately connected hot water storage. System circulation, and in most cases, accommodating thermal expansion of the system, is achieved via external components sited elsewhere in the dwelling.

1.6.2.1 Gas Boiler Considerations

The heat output of maximum-rated domestic gas boilers typically ranges from as low as 7–9 kW up to about 50–55 kW, but the appliances are able to modulate their output down depending on settings, temperature and external inputs (e.g. compensating controls). Several models having high turn-down ratios are available.

The highest output domestic appliances (e.g. 42–50 kW) are often combination boilers, although system and heat-only boilers with outputs in this range are available. This is to satisfy consumer demand for high flow-rate hot water draw-offs (i.e. showers), and also to meet potential simultaneous use requirements (see section 4). Appliances of this type have a lower output for space heating, which is frequently range-rateable by the installer or commissioning engineer, to match the requirements to the property's heat loss.

Depending on certain variables, such as the excess air supplied for combustion, the dew point of the flue gases is approximately 55°C. Therefore, system design and commissioning should be optimised to facilitate low primary return temperatures below 55°C, in order to maximise efficiency and the boiler time spent in condensing mode (see sections 1.6.2.3 and 5.5.2). This may require the use of return-temperature limiting valves (see section 5.11.3.1).

As mentioned earlier, compensating heating controls can further optimise the heating temperature regime. Reacting to external weather (weather compensation) or internal temperatures (load compensation) to modulate the flow temperature of the boiler, such controls ensure that the heat output is matched to demand and conditions, thus lowering return temperatures and energy consumption. Such devices, alongside 'smart heating controls', which 'learn' occupant and/or building behaviours, are widely available, although heat generator and system compatibility should be checked in advance, especially for retrofit applications (see section 5.11).

For retrofit projects where existing heat emitters are not to be replaced, a full assessment should be undertaken of the building heat loss and existing emitter size, to establish the compatibility of existing emitters for lower primary circuit temperature regimes (see section 3).

For new dwellings, the emitter sizing, and any associated building design considerations (e.g. emitter placement and dimensions), may be designed into the project at the build stage, to embrace low-temperature heating.

Other important considerations for gas boilers and connected heating systems include:

- *Availability of mains gas* – Is mains gas currently, or to be, provided to the dwelling, or is a new connection to the local gas distribution grid feasible and cost-effective? If mains gas is not an option, then stored LPG may be (see section 1.6.2.5).
- *Fuel price and energy running costs* – Natural gas is a considerably cheaper fuel than grid mains electricity (per kW h), at standard tariff prices, by approximately 3–4 times for the same energy demand/ consumption; LPG costs sit roughly in the middle.
- *Consumer acceptance/familiarity (client expectations)* – Gas boilers are generally a familiar technology. They are low noise, and most models are relatively compact and easily housed in a standard kitchen or utility room compartment, without the need for special provisions such as compartment ventilation.
- *Annual service and maintenance* – While currently in the UK a legal obligation to check gas appliances for safety (nominally every 12 months) exists only for rented dwellings, it is best practice for all gas appliances to be serviced annually, and invariably it is a condition of any manufacturer's warranty that this is adhered to.
- *Boiler chimney/flue* – As a gas boiler is a combustion technology, a flue is required to safely convey products of combustion to outside air. This is generally most easily achieved by siting the boiler on an external wall, although vertical flues are also commonly available, which allow the boiler flue to rise vertically and terminate above the roofline, should a more central siting (e.g. airing cupboard) within the dwelling be preferred.
- *Condensate* – As discussed earlier, condensing boilers will produce a waste condensate, which is mildly acidic in nature, and invariably this must be routed to a foul drain. The boiler condensate waste pipe should terminate 'internally', within the thermal envelope of the dwelling, wherever practicable, in order to avoid any external pipe runs and protect against freezing in inclement weather. Reference should be made to the manufacturer's instructions, BS 6798:2014, and the Heating and Hotwater Industry Council (HHIC) guidance.[6]
- *User hot water demands and preferences* – Multi-hot-water-outlet properties, where simultaneous use may be required (e.g. two showers being taken at one time) may often be suited to a hot water storage solution. However, there are also high-output combination boilers available (c. 35–50 kW), which are designed to service simultaneous use demands, and which meet National House Building Council (NHBC) warranty requirements for minimum hot water performance. Hot water storage will require additional space for a cylinder to be located, and for it to be accessible, which can impact on the habitable space available. See section 4 for more details.
- *Availability of adequate mains water pressure and flow rate* – This applies particularly to combination boilers, but also to thermal stores and the pairing of heat-only or system boilers with unvented hot water storage systems.
- *Electrical supply* – Gas boilers and the ancillary heating system require an electricity supply to operate correctly, but do not place an excessive load on the house supply, with the method of connection generally being via a standard 3 A fused supply.
- *Flue gas heat recovery* – Generally suitable for combination boilers only, such devices, which can be appliance-integral or 'add on', preheat the incoming cold mains water to be heated by the appliance for hot water production. This extracts further useful heat from the flue gases which have already passed the primary heat exchanger, and minimises the energy used to reach the hot water temperature set-point (see section 1.6.2.4).

---

[6] HHIC (2021) Installer Guide: Condensate Discharge Pipe Installation, issue 2.1. https://www.hhic.org.uk/uploads/6006FFA5C5C6A.pdf

1.6.2.2 Alternative Gaseous Fuels
As well as natural gas and LPG, there are two main potential less carbon intensive gaseous fuels, biomethane and hydrogen.

Biomethane
With the well-known UK agenda to decarbonise various sectors, including heating, biomethane is playing an increasingly important role in decarbonising the natural gas distributed to UK homes.

Produced from renewable sources, such as biomass, or waste streams, such as sewage or 'black bag' waste, the production of biomethane has been supported by the Renewable Heat Incentive (RHI) for some time.

Producers arrange a network entry agreement with the local gas distribution company, which details the acceptable gas quality (e.g. calorific value, Wobbe Index, maximum siloxane levels per m^3), in contractual terms, facilitating its injection for use within the gas supply grid. Here, biomethane mixes with other, more conventional, fossil-fuel-derived natural gases.

Domestic appliances designed to operate purely on biogas are unlikely, but as biomethane is supplied as a mix with natural gas, and the accepted gas supply parameters are safeguarded, there is no impact on the certification of domestic natural gas appliances.

Hydrogen
Research is underway to establish if hydrogen can be successfully supplied to homes and businesses to replace natural gas. Trials are underway to study the characteristics of hydrogen as a blend with natural gas, and others are planned to investigate nominally 'pure' hydrogen. Once the trials have been completed, and if it is considered safe for national distribution, hydrogen may be used to replace natural gas for space and water heating, and cooking.

Research has already shown that hydrogen boilers can deliver comparable levels of performance to natural gas for a similar cost, and, importantly, there is only minimal disruption to a property as changes are often likely to be limited to replacement of the boiler.

Fundamentally, the advent and installation of a hydrogen boiler would contribute to the reduction of CO_2 emissions and the government's obligation to decarbonise the UK's energy sector by 2050.

In the domestic sector, the conversion of existing, pre-installed natural gas appliances to operate on 100% hydrogen is not viable, and a replacement appliance would need to be installed. Boilers and appliances can be designed to be 'hydrogen-ready' (i.e. operating initially on natural gas with a straightforward conversion to burn hydrogen). Some boiler manufacturers are already producing a hydrogen-ready boiler that can be converted from natural gas to operate on pure hydrogen gas as and when it becomes mainstream. Similar research into and development of hydrogen-ready space heaters (fires) and cooking appliances remains ongoing.

Current UK projects looking at evidencing the safety case to distribute up to 20% hydrogen in distributed natural gas, aim to prove that existing, pre-installed natural gas appliances, as well as new ones currently marketed, can safely burn hydrogen without modification.

Fundamental design considerations for a hydrogen appliance
- The design of hydrogen appliances needs to incorporate flashback prevention, as hydrogen has a higher flame speed than natural gas. The burner design needs to provide a stable hydrogen flame against its high speed.
- The combustion of hydrogen produces more condensate.
- A hydrogen flame is near invisible and does not create an electrical signal (ionisation current), but is detectable by its ultraviolet emissions.
- Like natural gas, hydrogen has no odour; an odorant is added to hydrogen so that it can be detected, as with natural gas.
- Hydrogen is a very small molecule, and energy leakage rates are comparable to those for natural gas.
- Apart from heat, the by-products of the combustion of hydrogen are a small amount of nitrogen dioxide and water.

The gas network
The current iron gas distribution infrastructure is being upgraded for safety reasons under a replacement programme to remove old metal pipes which are nearing the end of their useful and functional mechanical life. The underground pipework is being replaced with polyethene or existing pipe is lined with a polythene liner. The pipework replacement programme has an additional benefit of allowing repurposing for the safe transmission of hydrogen.

Installation
All gas pipework entering consumer premises will require testing before hydrogen can be deployed, in order to identify the materials used and to ascertain its suitability.

Building ventilation requirements may be different for properties fed with pure hydrogen fuel, and standard carbon-based gas leak-detection equipment may need to be changed to other forms of non-carbon-based leak-detection equipment.

1.6.2.3 Gas Boiler Efficiency

Since 2005 for gas, and 2007 for liquid fuel, the building regulations have required most new and replacement boilers installed in the UK to be condensing boilers. The heat exchanger in a condensing boiler is designed to extract maximum heat from the flue gases. To do this, it reduces the temperature of the flue gases to below the dew point[7] of the flue gases, which causes water vapour to condense on the surfaces of the heat exchanger, a situation that is deliberately avoided in other boilers because it would cause corrosion. The presence of condensation in large quantities requires the heat exchanger to be made of corrosion-resistant materials, and a drain to be provided to dispose of the liquid condensate. Condensing boilers are significantly more efficient, as non-condensing boilers have to be designed to operate with flue gas temperatures that are high enough to avoid the accumulation of condensate that would cause corrosion.

It is sometimes thought that there is a sudden leap in efficiency when the temperature of the return water falls below the dew point. This is not quite true, as can be seen from the general relationship between efficiency and the return water temperature shown in Figure 1.3. Efficiency increases gradually as the water temperature is reduced, and it increases at a much faster rate below the dew point. To exploit this, heating systems can be designed so that boilers operate at low temperatures for a greater proportion of the time, and this is achieved by installing larger radiators and adjusting controls. However, even when a condensing boiler is not operating in condensing mode (below the dew point), it is still more efficient than a non-condensing boiler.

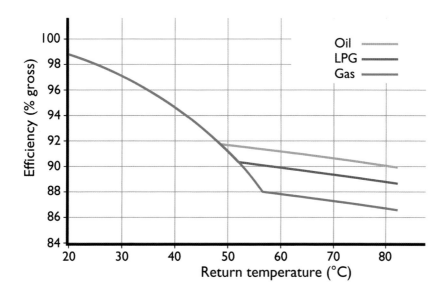

Figure 1.3 General relationship between boiler efficiency and water temperature

---

[7] The dew point is the lowest temperature to which air can be cooled without condensation occurring; below this temperature, condensation will occur.

1.6.2.4 Flue Gas Heat Recovery

One feature that is starting to be found on gas boilers is a flue gas heat recovery (FGHR) device. Such devices enable condensing boilers to reuse heat that would otherwise be wasted. They can be included in the normal footprint of a combination boiler, or as a retrofit device. They capture waste heat from the flue gases and reuse it, to improve efficiency, thus saving fuel and money. Current products are typically designed to work only with combination boilers that produce instantaneous hot water, not system or 'heat-only' boilers.

FGHR devices can broadly be divided into two types: those with additional thermal storage and those without. Those without thermal storage only provide energy savings when the boiler is operating in 'domestic hot water' mode (or 'summer' mode). Those with thermal storage typically have a 5–10 litre store, providing additional energy savings when the boiler is operating in 'space heating' mode (or 'winter' mode), as well as when operating in 'domestic hot water' mode.

FGHR technologies are recognised in the SAP for the energy rating of buildings, and are also included as a recognised way of improving the efficiency of a combination boiler in the UK government's Boiler Plus legislation, which was implemented on 6 April 2018.

Within the European Commission's current 2020 review process for ecodesign (ENER Lots 1 and 2 for space, combination and water heaters), the technology is also being considered for inclusion within the EU energy 'package' label.

1.6.2.5 LPG Storage

LPG installations are controlled by the Gas Safety (Installation and Use) Regulations 1998. LPG storage facilities, including cylinders and bulk storage tanks, should comply with the guidance set out in Liquid Gas UK's[8] Code of Practice 1 – Part 2 (Bulk LPG Storage at Fixed Installations) and Code of Practice 24 – Part 1 (Use of LPG Cylinders). BS 5482-1 also refers to this subject.

Building regulations also give guidance that, if followed, would normally ensure compliance with the Gas Safety (Installation and Use) Regulations 1998. LPG tanks should be adequately separated from buildings, the boundary of the property, any fixed sources of ignition and from one another. The guidance also specifies acceptable forms of barrier to place between tanks and the items to be separated from them, and minimum separation distances for different tank capacities with and without barriers.

Recommended LPG storage tank capacities are listed in Table 1.3. Tanks must be accessible for fuel deliveries, usually not more than 25 m from the delivery tanker position.

Table 1.3 Recommended LPG storage capacity

Boiler output (kW)	Minimum storage (litres)
Up to 15	360
15 to 25	1,200
25 to 45	1,800

1.6.3 Liquid Fuel Boilers

Liquid fuel fired appliances are available that provide solutions for both heating and hot water in homes that are not on the gas grid, with some appliances also providing cooking facilities.

---

[8] Liquid Gas UK: https://www.liquidgasuk.org

With the UK announcing that fossil-fuel-based heat generators will be banned for new-build homes by 2025, and the government's Clean Growth Strategy aiming to remove all new installations of high-carbon fossil fuel heating, there are understandably some concerns about the future within the industry. Assuming either ban goes ahead, there is expected to still be a demand for liquid fuel boilers in the retrofit market for at least the near future.

Modern condensing liquid fuel boilers offer efficiencies in excess of 90%, and they are available in a range of outputs and designs, including wall hung, floor standing and externally located. Liquid fuel is easily stored, and customers have the flexibility to shop around to purchase their fuel at the best price. Traditionally, fuel prices are lowest in July and August, and customers should be encouraged to purchase fuel in these months to cover their annual usage.

Liquid fuel boilers are suited to both open-vented and sealed primary systems. Combination boilers are also available.

Liquid fuel boilers most commonly have a fixed output, being fitted with an on/off burner, although some boilers are available with varying outputs, utilising multi-stage burners or fully modulating burners, that have connectivity with intelligent heating control systems that further increase overall system efficiency.

Liquid fuel boilers are suitable for heating systems utilising both traditional heat emitters, such as radiators, and underfloor heating.

Unless stated otherwise by manufacturers, to achieve the maximum efficiency from a boiler, radiator systems should typically be designed to the following parameters (see section 5.5.2):

- flow temperature 70°C
- return temperature 50°C
- differential 20°C.

System controls, particularly those incorporating weather compensation, should generally be designed to maintain return temperatures below 55°C, but in order to prevent possible internal corrosion of the boiler water jacket, the guidance of individual boiler manufacturers should be sought. This may require the use of a pipe thermostat or return temperature limiting valve (see section 5.11.3.1) and system layouts and controls should be designed accordingly.

Unless fitted with a multi-stage or modulating burner, combination boilers should be selected based on the space-heating demand, and *not* hot water demand, so as to avoid 'short-cycling' of the boiler. Most liquid fuel combination boilers incorporate a 'heat store' to provide instantaneous hot water, and the liquid fuel burner only fires to replenish this store. It is recommended that, to save energy, the hot water supply is timed 'off' overnight and when the home is unoccupied. The timer should be set for at least half an hour before normal hot water demand is expected, in order to reheat the heat store.

Liquid fuel boilers also lend themselves to being integrated into heating systems that employ other renewable technologies such as solar thermal and heat pumps. This can be particularly advantageous with older, poorly insulated buildings, where renewable solutions can take the lead on supplying heat for most of the year and the liquid fuel boiler can meet the higher heat demands in winter.

Further guidance on the selection of liquid fuel appliances can be found in BS 5410-1:2019 and Oil Firing Technical Association (OFTEC) Technical Book 4.

1.6.3.1 Liquid Fuel Storage and Supply Facilities

The installation of liquid fuel storage and supply facilities at domestic buildings is covered by regional control of pollution regulations and building regulations.

When specifying storage and supply facilities the following points should be considered:

- *Quantity of fuel to be stored* – A larger storage capacity reduces the number of deliveries required and the fuel cost. For domestic installations, the minimum storage capacities shown in Table 1.4 are recommended.
- *Fire protection* – If the storage tank is closer than 1.8 m to a non-fire-rated building, or an opening into a building, or 760 mm to a non-fire-rated boundary, some simple fire protection measures are required. All tanks must be installed over a fireproof base.
- *Environmental protection* – For storage tanks located in England, Scotland, Northern Ireland and the Republic of Ireland, with a capacity of 2,500 litres or less, the risk assessment in OFTEC Technical Book 3 must be completed for every new or replacement fuel storage tank installation. Unless the risk of environmental damage being caused by a potential loss of fuel from the tank is especially low, as shown on the risk assessment, the storage tank should be provided with secondary containment in the form of a bund that can contain 110% of the primary tank's contents. The bund is usually an integral part of the tank. Tanks with capacities greater than 2,500 litres must be bunded. All new and replacement storage tanks installed in Wales, the Channel Islands and the Isle of Man must be provided with secondary containment.
- *Tank construction* – Steel tanks should comply with the OFTEC Oil Firing Equipment Standard OFS T200. Plastic tanks should comply with OFS T100.
- *Tank location* – Fuel storage tanks should be located on firm foundations, with good access for delivery, inspection and maintenance.
- *Tank gauges* – Fuel storage tanks must be provided with an easily readable gauge, either mounted on the tank or remotely located in a convenient position. Gauges should comply with OFS E103.
- *Overfill protection* – Overfill protection is required if the tank cannot be seen from the delivery point. Equipment should comply with OFS E105.
- *Fuel supply pipes* – Fuel supply pipes should be installed in accordance with the requirements of BS 5410-1:2019; remote-acting fire valves to OFS E101 are required for all installations.

Further guidance on the selection of liquid fuel storage and supply facilities can be found in BS 5410-1:2019 and OFTEC Technical Book 3.

Note: Tanks with a capacity in excess of 3,500 litres installed in domestic buildings should be installed as if they were located in a non-domestic building. Further guidance in relation to such tanks can be found in BS 5410-2:2018 and OFTEC Technical Book 3.

Table 1.4   Minimum recommended liquid fuel storage capacity

Appliance rated output (kW)	Nominal tank capacity (litres)
0–15	1,000–1,500
15–25	1,500–2,000
25–35	2,000–2,500
35–45	2,500–3,500
45–70	3,500–5,000

1.6.4 Biomass Fuel

While the use of solid fuels (coal and smokeless fuel) has been steadily declining in the last decade, the use of biomass (wood fuel) has been increasing. A significant part of the take up for biomass boilers has been driven by government financial incentives. Separately, the popularity of dry space heaters is driven by other factors, such as cost and self-reliance, as well as their growing cultural popularity.

Thought of in the UK as a new type of appliance, biomass boilers are a very well-established technology. The UK has spent the past decades developing efficient solid fuel and then gas and liquid fuel appliances due to its domestic reserves. Over the same time period, significant proportions of Continental Europe have focused on developing biomass technology due to their lack of domestic fossil fuel reserves. With appliances ranging from 3 to 45 kW or more in output, biomass boilers can often be used as a less carbon intensive alternative to a fossil fuel boiler, and where a higher temperature or larger heat output is required over what a heat pump or direct electric boiler can provide.

The term 'biomass' technically covers all biological matter, but in the discussion here it is used to refer to a subset of biomass, wood. There are three main types of wood fuel:

- *Logs* are the least processed, and therefore typically the cheapest, form of wood fuel. They almost always require further processing by the customer, and typically are the least efficient type of wood fuel to burn. Because of this they are generally not suited to whole-house heating unless the customer is already processing their own timber. They are often used in dry room heating appliances, which are outside the scope of this Guide.
- *Pellets* are at the opposite end of the scale to logs, being the most processed, require the least manual intervention and are generally the most efficient type of wood fuel to burn. Because of this they are generally the most suitable form of wood fuel for domestic whole house heating. However, they are also the most expensive form of wood biomass. Pellets (in the UK) are manufactured simply by compressing waste sawdust under extreme pressure, with no extra additives, leading to a very regular, refined and dry fuel. The manufacturer's requirements should be followed, but it is recommended that only ENPlus A1 certified pellets are used.
- *Chips* sit in the middle of logs and pellets on all factors. Because of the high initial cost of chip-burning appliances, they are typically not suitable for domestic properties.

1.6.4.1 Biomass – Advantages and Disadvantages
Advantages
- *Lower carbon* – The primary advantage of biomass heating is its lower carbon intensity. Biomass combustion emits carbon dioxide (CO_2) at a similar level to other fossil fuels in its combustion, but it is considered as near carbon neutral. This is because of the relatively short period between the CO_2 being emitted and it being reabsorbed and converted into a new tree, as compared with the period between CO_2 being emitted from a fossil fuel boiler and it being reabsorbed and converted into new coal, oil or gas. While this process isn't perfectly balanced, the effective carbon emissions are significantly lower than for a fossil fuel boiler, as long as for every tree that is burnt at least one new one is planted; sustainable practices are a key part of fuel quality standards such as ENplus.
- *Lower cost* – While pellets are the most expensive form of wood fuel, they are typically lower in cost, or at least comparative in cost, to liquid fuels, and their price is equally less volatile. Therefore, for a property that is not on the mains gas grid, they make a financially viable long-term investment. On top of this there are incentives and grants that can help with the upfront as well as the ongoing running costs.
- *Self-sufficiency* – While not an option for many, for a customer who is able to supply their own wood fuel (logs and, for large-scale installations, wood chip), a biomass boiler can effectively reduce their heating fuel bills to zero.
- *Longer design life* – Biomass boilers typically have a longer design life than modern fossil fuelled equivalents. While this generally leads to a higher upfront cost, it can help to make the technology financially viable over the long term.

Disadvantages
- *Pollution* – The combustion of wood fuel is, on the chemical level, substantially more complicated than the combustion of liquid or gaseous fuels. As such, biomass appliances can be large emitters of pollutants and other dangerous emissions, including fine particulate matter (PM 2.5) and carbon monoxide (CO). These emissions are typically only associated with appliances that are not operated correctly (manually controlled appliances), appliances fuelled with poor-quality fuel (wet wood, dusty pellets or biomass such as bark and leaves with high levels of inorganic compounds) or poorly maintained appliances. Because of the potential for high levels of pollutants being emitted, certain areas of the country prevent the burning of wood under the Clean Air Act 1993, or require the appliance to have been tested and approved by the Department for Environment, Food and Rural Affairs (DEFRA).
- *High initial cost* – As discussed previously, biomass appliances tend to have a significantly higher upfront cost than an equivalent fossil fuelled boiler. While this can prevent many from accessing the technology,

grants and incentives may help, and the longer design life plus lower running costs often make the investment worthwhile.

- *Larger footprint* – Biomass boilers often need a larger footprint than an equivalent fossil fuel boiler. In addition to the boilers themselves being larger, typically a buffer tank will also be needed, and because the fuel is less energy dense than liquid fuel and gas, the volume required for fuel storage will be greater.
- *Higher maintenance* – As discussed previously, the combustion of wood is chemically complicated and, as such, emissions tend to be higher, and therefore maintenance requirements are greater. Maintenance should also only be undertaken by manufacturer-approved technicians who are aware of the specific appliance requirements.
- *Tighter design requirements* – Again because of the more complicated nature of the combustion of wood fuel, biomass boilers generally have poor turn-down efficiency and are usually not suitable for condensing operation. While condensing biomass boilers are now available, due to the highly corrosive nature of biomass condensate these tend to be more complicated and expensive appliances, requiring even higher levels of maintenance. The manufacturer's advice should be followed, but, to avoid corrosion, return temperatures should typically be greater than 55°C and combustion cycles should be long in duration. To compensate for the poor turn-down efficiency, the higher thermal mass typically involved in a biomass boiler and the requirement for long-period combustion cycles, a buffer store will almost always be required. While a buffer store takes up more space and adds cost to the installation, it does allow for the design temperature of the heating system to be separated from the design temperature of the heat generator. Therefore, low-temperature heat distribution may be used while maintaining the high return temperatures required by a biomass boiler.

Note: The design and specification of buffer tanks and accumulators is intended to be covered by the forthcoming companion to this Guide, the Integration Guide, which will also be published by the Domestic Building Service Panel (https://www.dbsp.co.uk).

For more information about the design and installation of biomass heating systems, see CIBSE Applications Manual 15 (*AM15: Biomass Heating*), or contact the Heating Equipment Testing and Approval Scheme (HETAS).

1.6.4.2 Wood Pellet Storage

When specifying storage facilities, the following points should be considered:

- *Quantity of fuel to be stored* – As for stored liquid and gaseous fuels, a larger storage capacity reduces the number of deliveries required and the fuel cost. For small biomass systems, pellets may be purchased in sealed bags by the pallet, to be manually loaded into the appliance as required. In this case a 1 m^2 covered area, such as in a garage, may be sufficient. For bulk storage, a purpose-built external store is often required. The footprint of this will vary, but at least a month's worth of onsite store capacity is recommended; local fuel suppliers should be consulted to discuss delivery capacities.
- *Fire protection* – This is typically dependent on the manufacturer and local building control guidance, but it is recommended that there is a fireproof separation between the boiler and the fuel store. All stores must be installed on a structurally sound and fireproof base.
- *Store location* – Fuel storage tanks should be located on firm foundations, with good access for delivery, inspection and maintenance. Bulk deliveries will require access for a large vehicle, as close as possible to the store, as well as space for the vehicle to turn around and leave; local fuel suppliers should be consulted regarding their access requirements. Bulk pellets are blown into the store, which damages the pellets; the distance they are blown over should therefore be minimised.

All biomass fuel emits carbon monoxide (CO) as part of its natural degradation. Because pellets are compressed, and therefore heated, during their manufacture they emit significantly higher levels of CO; this is particularly the case for the initial period after their manufacturer. As such, the storage of wood pellets can lead to the build-up of fatally high levels of CO. CO is a colourless, odourless and tasteless gas that is highly toxic.

The Health and Safety Authority (HSA) issued the following safety alert on 5 November 2012 on CO in pellet fuel stores. Operators, maintenance personnel and members of the public were warned about the dangers associated with bulk feed hopper tanks normally used with wood pellet boilers. The alert followed a fatal accident where a home owner entered a bulk wood pellet storage hopper/tank and was overcome by CO gas.

Wood pellets are normally stored in a large sealed hopper/tank that is fitted with a screw feed (auger) connected to the boiler, or alternatively the hopper/tank is mounted over the boiler for gravity feeding. Due to the enclosed nature of these hopper/tanks, the atmosphere inside can become oxygen depleted and a toxic atmosphere can accumulate. The HSE is asking all operators, maintenance personnel and users of this equipment to do the following:

- *Do not enter* or place your head into the wood pellet hopper under any circumstances. The unit can contain toxic gases.
- Ensure that your wood pellet hopper storage tank and the boiler has been installed and commissioned by a competent person. If in doubt, contact the supplier and/or manufacturer and request assistance.
- Ensure the boiler is cleaned and serviced by a competent person at the frequency required by the manufacturer's instructions.
- If any problems are encountered with the unit, such as the system not heating correctly or flue gas is flowing into the boiler room, turn the unit off and seek assistance immediately.
- No personnel should enter the hopper/tank unless they are fully trained and competent in confined spaces and entry procedures. The hopper/tank should be fully ventilated and controls put in place to ensure safe entry as per the HSA Code of Practice for Working in Confined Spaces.
- Ensure the boiler room is well ventilated at all times to ensure that there is no inadvertent build-up of toxic gases.
- Notices must be affixed to pellet storage access points and a full note included in the operating and owner's manuals.

1.6.5 Heat Pumps

With the UK government announcing the phasing out of fossil fuel boilers in new build property, more attention is being focused on the use of heat pumps as a potentially less carbon intensive way to heat our homes.

A heat pump operates in a similar way to a refrigerator, which extracts heat from inside the refrigerator and delivers it to the surrounding room from the coil at the back. For the purpose of providing heat for comfort, and occasionally hot water, a heat pump is used to upgrade heat energy from a low temperature level to a higher temperature level – hence the term 'heat pump'. This it achieved by mechanical compression, which 'forces' the heat to change levels. It uses the principle of Boyle's Law, which states that the boiling point and condensing temperature of a fluid will vary in accordance with its absolute vapour pressure at constant volume. For example, water boils at 100°C at sea level but at about 66°C at the top of Mount Everest due to the reduced atmospheric pressure.

By forcing a refrigerant to condense and evaporate at different temperatures (by varying the pressure), relatively large quantities of heat energy can then be transferred from one side of the refrigerant-containing system (evaporator) to the other side (condenser).

Most of the heat that is 'pumped' is energy absorbed for evaporation, known as the latent heat of vaporisation. The air or liquid surrounding the evaporator first raises the refrigerant to its boiling point (due to its low pressure), after which any extra heat changes its state from liquid to gas (latent heat); this is equal to the heat energy released during condensing after the compressor. To illustrate this process, consider how much heat is required to raise water from, say, 0°C to 100°C, and then compare the considerable extra (latent) heat required to boil the water off completely (i.e. change its state from liquid to gas, although its temperature never rises above 100°C).

Heat pump performance depends on the temperature rise required. Clearly, the closer the two conditions are (source temperature and delivery temperature) the less work the system has to do in pumping the heat, thus increasing both capacity and efficiency. Therefore, in heating mode, higher source temperatures and lower delivery (flow) temperatures result in higher capacity and greater operating efficiency. Hence, when expressing the capacity and efficiency of a heat pump, the relevant conditions must also be defined to make the statement in any way meaningful.

1.6.5.1 Types of Heat Pump
Heat pump systems for domestic application generally use either air or water as the heat source medium and also either air or water for the delivery – hence giving the multiple options of:

- air to air
- air to water
- water to air
- water to water
- ground to water
- ground to air.

In air-sourced systems, heat in the outside air is absorbed by the refrigerant, causing it to change from liquid to vapour in the evaporator. The vapour is then compressed, raising its temperature. The higher temperature vapour passes through the condenser, where it changes back to liquid, which releases the extra heat produced during compression.

In ground-sourced systems, it is heat from the ground that is absorbed by the refrigerant. The process of producing heat is then the same as for air-sourced systems. Ground source heat pump systems in domestic applications usually refer to 'closed-loop' pipework buried in the ground in horizontal trenches or in vertical boreholes. The pipework forms a closed circuit in the ground, through which thermal transfer fluid (usually water mixed with antifreeze and a biocide) passes to extract heat energy from the ground via conduction through the pipe wall. (See section 5.6.3.2 for the flow rate performance of pipework containing glycol.)

Open-loop heat pump systems utilise water taken directly from an underground aquifer, before extracting the heat and then returning the water to a distant borehole or leach field. There is also the possibility of using open water sources such as rivers, lakes, canals and even the sea, but these are rare in domestic situations because of the complexity and the resulting expense.

1.6.5.2 Types of Heat Pump Units
There are various different naming terminologies used when describing heat pump units.

Separate or packaged units
Some heat pump appliances are made up of individual components similar to 'traditional' gas boiler/radiator systems for site assembly and installation; the key element is a separate domestic hot water cylinder.

Other systems are manufactured as packaged systems, whereby the complete system (controls, domestic hot water cylinder, circulation pumps, etc.) comes from one manufacturer or pre-selected supply partners, and generally comes packaged as one unit.

Split or monobloc systems
Often associated with air-source heat pumps, a split system consists of separate units outside (typically containing just the evaporator and a fan) and inside (typically containing the condenser/heat exchanger and the rest of the components) the dwelling.

A monobloc system will have all of its components in one unit; in the case of air-source heat pumps, this will usually be located outside the dwelling.

Exhaust air heat pump
A subset of air-source heat pumps, exhaust-air heat pumps are typically combined with mechanical ventilation (see section 3.5.4.3) to extract and reuse heat from the exhaust air.

1.6.5.3 High Temperature Heat Pumps

Much development work has been carried out to produce high temperature heat pumps (producing water flow temperatures in the range 55–80°C, but with relatively good efficiencies of >2.6), which can provide energy and carbon savings at or below 'average' outdoor source temperatures.

High temperature heat pumps are intended to be used primarily with existing installations where conventional boilers are being replaced, and/or where heat emitters have been sized using temperatures in excess of those normally found with heat pump systems, and for sanitary hot water generation to 60°C.

1.6.5.4 Heat Pump Efficiency

Heat pumps transfer heat from a plentiful 'source' to a 'sink' at higher temperature. Doing so requires input of power (usually electricity) to drive the heat pump. In a domestic heating system, nearly always the source will be the outside air or ground, the sink will be the inside air or water circulating through the heat emitters, and the power input will be electricity. The energy performance is measured by the amount of useful heat output divided by the electricity input needed to drive the heat pump. This figure is not strictly an 'efficiency', because the energy input does not include the 'free' energy coming from the source. Instead, the term used for the basic measure is the 'coefficient of performance' (CoP), and it is typically 2.5 or higher for an air-source heat pump. A CoP of 2.5 means that 2.5 units of heat are produced for every unit of electricity supplied to drive the heat pump. This is very much better than electrical 'resistance' heating, such as traditional convectors and fan heaters, where only one unit of heat output is produced from one unit of electricity.

However, the CoP of a heat pump varies considerably according to the operating conditions. The difference between source and sink temperatures has a strong effect, and the CoP reduces as this temperature difference becomes greater. Also, the maximum available heat output falls as the temperature difference becomes greater. For these reasons, it is important that heating systems with heat pumps are designed carefully to match the heating needs of the building. If it would be uneconomic to provide a heat pump large enough to meet the maximum heating needs (usually only for a few days in the winter), then provision must be made for top-up from an auxiliary heat source.

Measurements of the CoP cannot be compared with one another unless the test conditions are the same, and these should always be quoted. To allow for the changes in the CoP that can be expected over varying operating conditions throughout the year, there is an alternative measure, the 'seasonal coefficient of performance' (SCoP). This can be calculated from a combination of multiple test results, and there are standards[9] to specify how the calculation can be done. The SCoP is intended to provide a better estimate of the annual average performance of a heat pump.

While the CoP and SCoP are measures of performance of a heat pump regarded as an isolated product, the wider concern is the performance of the heating system as a whole. This should take into account the other components of the system, such as circulators, auxiliary heaters and water heating. Numerous features of design, configuration and operation contribute to overall system performance (e.g. radiators or underfloor heat emitters, water circulation temperature, hot water service, 'top-up' or auxiliary heating, de-frost cycles and control methods). Consequently the performance of complete systems is complicated to analyse, and simplifying assumptions may have to be made.

The 'seasonal performance factor' (SPF) is estimated using a specified method that may include some or all of these other components and features. A European research project on heat pump system performance, known as SEPEMO,[10] has stressed the importance of defining the system boundaries so that it is clear what has been included in or excluded from the test measurements and modelling. SEPEMO has defined at least seven different ways in which system boundaries can be drawn.

---

[9] See BS EN 14825:2018 (Air conditioners, liquid chilling packages and heat pumps, with electrically driven compressors, for space heating and cooling. Testing and rating at part load conditions and calculation of seasonal performance).

[10] 'SEasonal PErformance factor and MOnitoring for heat pump systems in the building sector': https://ec.europa.eu/energy/intelligent/projects/en/projects/sepemo-build

1.6.5.5 Sizing Heat Pump Systems – The '100%' Rule

Sizing of any heat generator is outside the scope of this Guide, and, as such, manufacturer and specialist guidance should be sought. The following high-level sizing guidance is provided for information only.

As the output and efficiency of a heat pump are primarily dependent on the variable source and fixed delivery temperatures, the heat pump shall generally be selected to provide not less than 100% of the calculated design space heating power requirement at the winter design condition,[11] which is not the same as the standard test performance conditions.

The selection must take into consideration the space heating design flow temperature required for the heat emitter circuit and any variation in heat pump performance that may result. For example BS EN 14511 provides a standard for published data for air-to-water heat pumps using an external temperature of 7°C and a system water flow temperature of 35°C (described as A7/W35). The capacity of any heat pump will be much reduced though when the source (ambient) temperature is lower or the system water flow temperature is higher than these conditions. The Microgeneration Installation Standards (MIS) as outlined for Microgeneration Certification provide essential advice and examples on this and should be consulted (e.g. MIS 3005).

1.6.5.6 Heat Emitters

From the above it is clear that with heat pumps, whether air, ground or water source, both the source and system water flow temperature are very important for the correct selection and application of a heat pump.

Moreover, the choice and correct selection of heat emitters is significant, and retrospective installation brings its own challenges. In order to assist the domestic market, the *Heat Emitter Guide for Domestic Heat Pumps*[12] has been produced by cooperation between a number of British trade associations, professional bodies, and government departments and agencies for new and existing buildings.

When sizing heat emitters for systems served by heat pumps, it is best practise to use primary system flow temperatures that are as low as possible, typically between 35°C and 55°C (unless a high temperature heat pump is being used), together with a circulating water temperature differential in accordance with the manufacturer's instructions. The actual water flow temperature will be dictated by the choice of a high or a low temperature heat pump, or, in many cases, the reuse of existing heat emitters, which can considerably influence a design.

Note: As discussed in sections 5.5.4 and 5.5.5, existing radiators will not deliver the same level of heating if the flow and return temperature are different from those initially used to specify them. Typically, either new larger surface area radiators or additional radiators will be required if converting an existing high flow temperature system to work with a low flow temperature heat pump; reducing the heat loss from the building will also help, and in general this should be the first consideration.

Underfloor heating is particularly suited to the optimum operating temperature range for heat pumps. These systems should preferably be designed to make use of the lowest possible water flow temperatures (35–45°C), as this produces the best performance and results in greater perception of comfort at lower actual air temperatures, leading to reduced heat loss and increased energy conservation.

Note: For further information on underfloor heating, see the companion publication to this Guide, the *Underfloor Heating Design & Installation Guide*, also published by the Domestic Building Service Panel (https://www.dbsp.co.uk).

1.6.5.7 Water Circulators

Heat pumps require more accurate water flow rates than conventional boilers due to the presence of the vapour compression cycle and resulting protective devices. This demands greater attention to water circulator flow rates and sizing relative to the system requirements. It is likely that in existing properties a

---

[11] For design conditions see Table 2 of MIS 3005, based on data supplied by CIBSE, which provides figures that cover either 99% or 99.6% of the year.

[12] The *Heat Emitter Guide for Domestic Heat Pumps* can be found on the Heat Pump Association (HPA) and MCS websites.

new replacement water pump will be required to cope with new demands. Thus, minimum water flow rates should be based on the manufacturer's recommendations.

For existing systems with differential temperatures in the range 10–20°C or fitted with speed-controlled pumps, the inclusion of a buffer tank will most likely be necessary.

1.6.5.8 Buffer Tanks for Heat Pumps

Note: The design and specification of buffer tanks and accumulators are intended to be covered by the forthcoming companion to this Guide, the Integration Guide, also to be published by the Domestic Building Service Panel (https://www.dbsp.co.uk). However, when used specifically with heat pumps, different criteria are necessary.

While buffer tanks increase the system water volume, which extends the return water temperature controller reaction time, the system type must be properly identified in order to select the appropriate buffer vessel that should occupy the minimum amount of floor space for the largest user benefit.

Note: Different areas of the industry use the words buffer, volumiser, accumulator and thermal store interchangeably. It is important to understand the purpose of the vessel you are describing.

Advice on buffer requirements for air-source heat pumps with inverter-controlled variable-speed compressors should be sought from the manufacturers.

Ground-source heat pumps with single-speed compressors (without speed control) will require a buffer tank to provide greater run hours and fewer stops and starts. The number of compressor starts per hour varies from manufacturer to manufacturer, but is normally in the range 3–10 starts/h. This range produces a run-time interval of between 20 and 6 minutes, depending on the manufacturer. The buffer is then designed to these requirements to ensure the energy is stored in the buffer rather overheating the system/heat pump.

Inverter-driven compressors have the advantage that they can regulate their output. However, this does not mean that no buffer is required for these systems. It is still recommended to fit a buffer, albeit a smaller one, to ensure that the minimum output does not cause any problems.

When connected to existing emitter systems designed for a 20°C temperature drop, the heat pump will not be able to operate efficiently with a 5 K differential unless a buffer tank is provided to separate the two very different temperature regimes.

It is important to note that compressor cycling becomes more noticeable above the mean winter temperature (7°C) and increases towards room temperature.

Series-type buffer vessels (BS EN 15450:2007, Figure B4) connected to simple systems require the entire system water content to flow simultaneously through all open and bypassed circuits.

Note: Continuity of the fluid volume available must be guaranteed.

Parallel-type buffer vessels (BS EN 15450:2007, Figure B6) connected to more complex systems provide much greater scope for multiple, partially open subsystems, using an optimised system volume. Although larger by default, they serve a greater purpose.

When sizing a buffer vessel for heat pump (only) use, the buffer capacity requires prior knowledge of the actual system water content (litres) and the design water flow/return temperature drop (°C), plus the heat pump control thermostat differential.

1.6.5.9 Domestic Hot Water Sources

Heat pumps can be used as a heat source for domestic hot water, although efficiencies may be lower than for space heating due to the increased water flow temperatures required (up to or more than 60°C) with standard units. High temperature heat pump units are available using suitable refrigerants, and/or tandem compressors or just purpose-designed high temperature compressors to significantly improve efficiencies.

There are also heat pump systems that may be assembled from separate components or from packaged proprietary systems. These usually provide both space heating and hot water, with complementary purpose-designed ancillaries such as hot water cylinders and controls.

1.6.5.10 Ventilation and Heat Pump Refrigerant Safety

Heat pumps systems contain refrigeration and phase change fluids. The most commonly used are known as F-gases, which are fluorinated gases that include HCFCs, HFCs and CFCs. Some systems use alternatives such as hydrocarbons (R290 (propane), R600a (isobutane) and R1270 (propylene)), ammonia or carbon dioxide. All of these fluids when used as refrigerants have specific regulatory safety, handling and operating requirements which must be followed, and careful attention to the manufacturer's guidance is needed.

F-gases have been proven to deplete the ozone layer, whilst others directly contribute to greenhouse gases associated with global warming. EU and UK legislation limits the use of these gases, and heat pump installations that contain more than specified limits of an F-gas refrigerant should be leak checked and tested on installation and at least once a year (bi-annually or quarterly if a system meets certain thresholds). These checks and tests must by law be done by a contractor certified to work with F-gases – accredited by agencies including the Department for Environment, Food and Rural Affairs (DEFRA) and REFCOM (Register of Companies Competent to Manage Refrigerants). For more information about F-gas regulations, see UK government guidance.[13]

Heat pumps installed inside very confined spaces (below stairs, in cupboards, or equal) within which maintenance engineers must work will require ventilation of that space to prevent asphyxiation in the event of a high-pressure refrigerant gas leak, which can occur if the room volume is less than the minimum volume required to accept the fully expanded refrigerant gas contents into the atmosphere.

The minimum room volume (m^3) can be calculated using the formula:

   V = refrigerant charge (kg)/refrigerant practical limit (kg/m^3)

The refrigerant type will be found on the heat pump manufacturer's information data plate. Practical concentration limits for refrigerants can be found in BS EN 378.

For example, 1 kg of refrigerant R407C with a practical concentration limit of 0.30 kg/m^3 will require a volume of not less than 3.33 m^3 into which it can expand.

This volume must also allow for room contents (sealed boxes, etc.) plus fixtures and fittings, which would otherwise effectively reduce the true volume available.

Thus, a safe volume will always be appreciably larger than the calculated result. Seek the manufacturer's advice if the proposed position of the indoor unit gives rise to concern.

For more information on ventilation, see section 1.7.

1.6.6 Electric Heating

Fossil fuels (gas, oil, LPG and coal) have traditionally been used for the heating of our buildings, but the use of electricity in now beginning to displace these for some use cases. In addition to driving heat pumps (see section 1.6.5), electricity can be used directly for heating, and this is briefly discussed in this section.

---

[13] Guidance: managing fluorinated gases and ozone-depleting substances. https://www.gov.uk/government/collections/fluorinated-gas-f-gas-guidance-for-users-producers-and-traders

1.6.6.1 Electric Heating – Advantages and Disadvantages

There can be a number of benefits to the electrification of heating:

- Ease of installation – where direct electric heating delivery systems (panel heating, etc.) are used, there is no need to run 'wet' heating systems.
- There is close to 100% energy efficiency conversion, and systems can be used with local electricity generating technologies such as solar PV to lower carbon intensity.
- Systems can be included in load control systems to assisting the smart electricity grid.
- There is no need for the boiler to be sited by an external wall as no flue is required.

The major disadvantage of electric heating is its running costs. In general, electricity has a higher cost per kW h of electricity than that of gas, liquid fuels or biomass. This can be partially mitigated through:

- The omission of a mains gas connection and the relevant pipework within a new build.
- The use of electric heating in buildings with very low levels of heat loss, such as those that exceed minimum building regulation levels and those that meet the Passivhaus[14] standards.
- The use of dual-rate electricity tariffs such as Economy 7, where energy used during a set off-peak period is significantly discounted (devices using this tariff typically require a dual electrical connection). These systems must store the heat generated during the discounted period through to the period when it is needed.
- The use of 'time-of-use' (ToU) tariffs if offered by energy suppliers. In this case dual connections are then not required, as the electrical loads of the entire buildings can benefit from varying tariffs. These systems must store the heat generated during the discounted period through to the period when it is needed. They also need to be able to communicate with the energy supplier, as well as being under the control of the occupier, to ensure they generate heat only when appropriate.
- The use of on-site renewable energy generation. This can be a significant factor, especially when integrated with electrical storage (battery) or thermal storage systems.

Note: The introduction of LOT20 (on 1 January 2018) ensured that all electricity-consuming devices must now meet minimum energy-efficiency measures, including all local space heaters for sale in the EU.

1.6.6.2 Design Considerations

The following should be considered when designing for an electric heat generator:

- A suitably qualified, trained and experienced electrical contractor should always be used for the installation of electrical equipment.
- When designing for the electrification of heat, the requirements of BS 7671:2018 (Requirements for electrical installations) shall be followed.
- Manufacturers' instructions shall be taken into account in addition to the requirements of BS 7671:2018.
- The installation of electric heating in a dwelling will most likely fall under Approved Document P (Electrical safety – dwellings) (or the regional equivalent as per Table 1.1). Therefore, it is key that the requirements therein are followed.
- With regard to fixed electric local space heaters, suitable consideration must be given to the prevention of overheating of surrounding areas. Examples include the siting of electrical heat emitters beneath or behind full-length curtains, which may create a fire hazard. The electrical loading of the building needs to be considered. This is particularly important when retrofitting electric heating into a building to ensure that the additional loading does not exceed the rated current of the building's supply, or the rating of circuits and cabling within the building.

Diversity may be taken into account as shown in Table 1.5.

---

[14] The Passivhaus standards are developed by the Passivhaus Institute in Germany and aim to dramatically reduce the requirement for space heating and cooling, while also creating excellent indoor comfort levels. This is primarily achieved by adopting a 'fabric first' approach to building design, by specifying high levels of insulation to the thermal envelope with exceptional levels of airtightness and the use of whole-house mechanical ventilation. See: https://passivhaustrust.org.uk

Table 1.5 Allowances for diversity between final circuits for the sizing of a distribution circuit (extract from the IET Electrical Installation Design Guide)

Purpose of final circuit fed from conductors or switchgear to which diversity applies	Type of premises		
	Individual household installations including individual dwellings of a block	Small shop, stores, offices and business premises	Small hotels, boarding houses, guest houses, etc.
Heating and power (caveated by the conditions below)	100% of total current demand up to 10 A + 50% of any current demand in excess of 10 A	100% f.l. of largest appliance + 75% f.l. of remaining appliances	100% f.l. of largest appliance + 80% f.l. of second largest appliance + 60% f.l. of remaining appliances
Water heaters (instantaneous type)	100% f.l. of largest appliance + 100% f.l. of second largest appliance + 25% f.l. of remaining appliances		
Water heaters (thermostatically controlled)	No diversity allowed		
Floor-warming installations	No diversity allowed		
Thermal storage space-heating installations	No diversity allowed		

Note: f.l. = full load

1.6.6.3 Fixed Electric Local Space Heaters

Fixed electric local space heaters are outside the scope of this Guide but are included here for information. It is important to remember when discussing the client's needs (see section 2) that a full wet heating system may be unnecessary or unaffordable. While a direct electric heating system may often be more expensive to run, it is likely to be cheaper to install, and for a well-insulated space the running costs will still be low.

Electric storage heaters

Electric storage heaters can offer a cost-effective heating solution by utilising lower-cost off-peak electricity rates (e.g. Economy 7). The electricity is used to heat thermal bricks that are designed to have high heat-retention properties. The storage heaters are well insulated to prevent undue thermal losses, thereby storing the heat for release during the day or when required. Historically, electrical storage heaters were far from perfect in operation and function, but recent technological developments and the requirements from LOT20 have paved the way for an efficient generation of modern storage heaters.

Traditionally, electric storage heaters were connected to the end-user's installation through a dual electrical connection. Modern, smart meter enabled, time-of-use tariffs have enabled manufacturers to offer single-connection electric storage heaters, which are now available to the installer.

The compliance guides indicate that the following requirements should be met for electric storage heaters:

- automatic control of the input charge based on measurement of the internal temperature
- temperature control by adjustment of heat release using a damper or other thermostatically controlled means
- the frame and enclosure of space heating appliances should be of non-combustible material.

Electric convection heaters

Electric convection heaters operate by warming the air, and fall into the following categories:

- *Electric panel heaters* – Electric panel heaters work by convection. The electricity is directly converted to heat through the internal elements, heating the surface panels. These panels then transfer the heat into the room through the same convection process as traditional radiators, sometimes with the assistance of an inbuilt fan.

- *Electric radiators* – Electric radiators are an enhanced version of the electric panel heater, radiating the heat in addition to heating via convection. While more expensive than standard convection heaters, they are more efficient and lend themselves to providing a more comfortable heating experience for the end user.

Electric radiant heaters Electric radiant heaters operate by warming the surfaces and the occupant of a room directly and fall into the following categories:

- *Electric Infrared heaters* – Infrared (or far infrared) heating differs from convection heaters by heating the surface area of solid objects or people, which then radiate the heat back into the room, as opposed to heating the air, which is very poor at heat retention. As the air isn't being heated, rooms and buildings are less prone to heat loss when opening external doors.

This method works by emitting electromagnetic radiation with longer wavelengths than those of visible light. Far infrared heaters tend to be of a lower wattage than electric heaters, as there is no fan and no visible 'wasted' light. Often the surfaces of these devices can reach above 90°C, so consideration of their location is important in areas where there may be children, animals or vulnerable people in proximity. As such, it is common to see these heaters positioned on ceilings and high on walls, angled downwards to allow more energy to be absorbed by objects and people. As these heaters are slim and flat, they can also be disguised as wall art, mirrors, etc.

- *Embedded floor, wall and ceiling heating* – Electric underfloor heating systems are not uncommon in the UK, and this technology is now also being used in wall and ceiling heating systems. The advantage of these systems is that they are hidden from view. While surface temperatures are significantly lower than the electric infrared heaters discussed above (in floor areas where contact with skin or footwear is possible, the surface temperature of the floor must be limited to no more than 35°C), they cover a significantly larger area and are more vulnerable to damage. As such, the requirements of section 753 of BS 7671:2018 must be adhered to.

Note: Specialist advice should be sought on the installation requirements for embedded floor, wall and ceiling heating.

1.6.6.4 Electric Boilers
Electric boilers may provide a solution for smaller properties and in locations where a gas connection or flue access is not possible, and allow for the heating of a typical 'wet' central heating system and for hot water.

The advantages of these boilers are that they:

- do not need to be placed on an outside wall as there is no flue or gas pipe
- can be straightforward and cost-effective to install
- are quiet in operation
- carry no risk of CO poisoning
- have lower maintenance costs
- have a low to no carbon footprint when coupled with on-site renewable energy generation.

The disadvantage of these boilers is that they potentially have higher running costs.

There are a number of variations of electric boilers available, and careful selection is required to match the boiler to the user's requirements. Requirements can include the need to making use of off-peak or time-of-use energy tariffs, when the kW h cost is much lower. These systems would then require storage capability.

Direct-acting electric boiler
Sometimes known as flow boilers, these are the simplest type of electric boiler and are the least expensive to install. They work by heating the water using an electrical resistance element (similar to a kettle or an electric shower), and can be used for central heating or for hot water.

Note: As the water is heated on demand, time-of-use and dual tariffs are not applicable.

Note: The flow temperatures achievable will depend on the rated power of the selected boiler, which will in turn be influenced by the electrical supply available. Expert advice should be sought on this.

Storage electric boiler
Storage electric boilers have either a separate hot water cylinder (see section 4.4.1) or a built-in storage unit. This gives versatility over direct-acting electric boilers by enabling time-of-use tariffs to be used. They are, however, physically larger due to their storage capabilities, and are more expensive.

Electric combined primary storage unit
A combined primary storage unit (CPSU) has the ability to store a large volume of water. In addition to this they can also rapidly heat a large amount of water. The higher volumes and pressures make CPSUs well suited for commercial applications and large dwellings.

1.6.7 Solar Heating

The implication and requirements for the design of a solar heating system are covered in the companion publication to this, the *Solar Heating Design & Installation Guide*, also published by the Domestic Building Service Panel (https://www.dbsp.co.uk/). This includes the use of electric immersion hot water heating supplemented by PV generation.

1.6.8 Heat Networks and Heat Interface Units

The design of domestic heating and hot water systems for connection to heat networks is outside the scope of this Guide, and therefore specialist advice should be sought. In general, particular attention needs to be given to design return temperatures, as this will affect the efficiency of the heat network itself. For guidance on how to design suitable radiator and underfloor heating systems, reference should be made to CIBSE Code of Practice 1 (*CP1: Heat Networks: Code of Practice for the UK*).

1.7 Ventilation

Ventilation is in general outside the scope of this Guide, but this section gives a brief overview of the subject with regard to its effects on heating system design.

1.7.1 Ventilation in Living Space

Ventilation is needed to provide enough fresh air to living spaces to restrict the build-up of moisture, pollutants and odours. Building regulations set requirements for ventilation in dwellings, which are usually met by the installation of extractor fans in kitchens and bathrooms, and by openable windows and trickle ventilators in other rooms. The heat loss arising from ventilation has already been discussed in section 1.5, and it is clearly preferable to minimise ventilation when considering heating requirements. However, ventilation must not be reduced to the extent that it harms indoor air quality, and the task of the heating system designer is to provide a system that is capable of coping with the total expected heat load.

1.7.1.1 Minimum Requirements for Ventilation

The building regulations (Approved Document F for England, Building Regulations Guidance: Part F (Ventilation) for Wales, Section 3 for Scotland, and Building Regulations Part K: Technical Booklet for Northern Ireland) contain the requirements and guidance on how adequate extract ventilation may be provided in dwellings. They aim to achieve on-demand rapid extraction of moisture from kitchens, bathrooms and sanitary accommodation, while at the same time providing background ventilation in other rooms, independently of natural infiltration. Typical requirements are summarised in Table 1.6. Refer to the relevant part of the current building regulations applying where the dwelling is located.

Table 1.6 Extract ventilation rates

Room	Minimum intermittent extract rate (l/s)	Continuous extract (l/s)	
		Minimum – high rate	Minimum – low rate
Kitchen	30 (adjacent to hob) 60 (elsewhere)	13	Total extract rate must be at least the whole building rate in Table 1.7
Utility room	30	8	
Bathroom	15	8	
Sanitary accommodation	6		

Note: 10 l/s = 36 m^3/h

Note: Sanitary accommodation in Scotland uses a different standard of either:

- a ventilator with an opening area of at least 1/30 of the floor area it serves, or
- mechanical extraction capable of at least three air changes per hour.

Table 1.7 Whole-building ventilation rates

	Number of bedrooms in dwelling				
	1	2	3	4	5
Whole-building ventilation rate (l/s)	13	17	21	25	29

Note: In addition, the minimum ventilation rate would not be less than 0.3 l/s per m^2 of internal floor area (this includes each floor).

Note: Tables 1.6 and 1.7 apply to England and Wales only.

Note: Table 1.7 is based on two occupants in the main bedroom and a single occupant in all other bedrooms. This should be used as the default value. If a greater level of occupancy is expected, then add 4 l/s per occupant.

> **Example**: A two-storey building, with four bedrooms and 80 m^2 of floor area per floor, would have a minimum whole-building ventilation rate of 48 l/s; four bedrooms would require a 25 l/s minimum whole-building ventilation rate, but this is not enough to satisfy the minimum of 0.3 l/s per m^2 of floor area (80 × 2 × 0.3 = 48 l/s).

Passive stack ventilation may be used as an alternative to mechanical extract ventilation, provided it is designed in accordance with BRE Information Paper 13/94 (*Passive Stack Ventilation Systems: Design and Installation*) or with appropriate third-party certification.

Further guidance on ventilation may be found in BS 5250:2011 (Code of practice for control of Condensation in buildings.

1.7.1.2 Fan-Duty Selection

The possibility exists for the performance of any fan or cooker hood, even when used intermittently, to exceed the design air-change rate of the room and thereby increase the amount of heat required to meet the design temperature. This, however, can usually be disregarded, as the temperature gains from the cooking appliances or bathing water will offset the problem. Careful consideration should, however, be given to the selection of fan duties to ensure larger volumes of air than necessary are not extracted.

1.7.1.3 Whole-House Mechanical Ventilation

The ventilation requirements given in the Building Regulations 2010 may also be met through the provision of whole-house mechanical ventilation; often known as either mechanical ventilation and heat recovery (MVHR) or mechanical extract ventilation (MEV). This type of ventilation is typically only used in buildings with very low ventilation heat losses due to improved levels of airtightness (see section 3.4.1); most UK properties are not currently constructed to a sufficiently high airtightness level to require this, although its use will still deliver some of the benefits. Whole-house mechanical ventilation typically involves the recovery of heat from stale and damp air extracted from the property, which is then supplied back into the property via the fresh air drawn in from outside; this can reduce the ventilation heat load. Ducts and fans should be sized to ensure that the cost of electricity consumption of the intake and exhaust fans is much less than the cost of recovered heat.

Specialist advice should be sought on the design, specification and installation of such systems.

1.7.1.4 Combustion Air and Ventilation Requirements for Heating Appliances

Building regulations set requirements for ventilation relating to heating appliances; this subject is dealt with below in section 1.7.2.

1.7.2 Combustion Air and Safe Operation of Flues

The design of and specification for combustion air ventilation and flues are outside the scope of this Guide, but are relevant to the combustion heat generators discussed in section 1.6, and so a summary is included here. Specialist advice should be sought on all aspects of this section.

1.7.2.1 Air Supply Requirement

Heating appliances require a supply of air for combustion and for cooling. Specific requirements for air supply relating to heating appliances aim to ensure that:

- there is sufficient air for proper combustion, flue operation and cooling
- no hazards to health arise from combustion products
- no damage occurs to the fabric of the building through heat or fire.

For all non-room-sealed combustion appliances, permanent air vents are required. These should be sized according to the type of appliance. In addition, for all types of appliance, it is necessary to comply with any special requirements stated by the manufacturer.

A space containing a non-room-sealed appliance must have purpose-designed vents at low and high level. The vents must be non-closable and at least large enough to admit all of the air required by the appliance for combustion and ventilation, whether the space draws its air from a room or directly from outside.

For room-sealed appliances, ventilation is still required, but the air is drawn directly from the outdoors. The installation of a room-sealed appliance is subject to:

* the appliance being stated as suitable by the manufacturer
* the appliance being installed as per the manufacturer's requirements
* a risk assessment having being completed regarding the appliance being room sealed.

It has been common to find room-sealed gas and liquid fuel boilers, but only recently has it been possible to install room-sealed solid- and wood-fuel appliances; for more details on this, see HETAS Technical Note HETAS_TN_0020 (*General Guidance for the Installation, Risk Assessment & Commissioning of Solid Fuel Batch Fed Appliances Fitted with a Dedicated External Air Supply*). Appliances in spaces also need cooling ventilation air to circulate around them, whether they are room sealed or not.

Guidance for the installation of solid fuel appliances is given in the Building Regulations 2010, Approved Document J (or the regional equivalent as per Table 1.1) and BS 8303-1:1994.

It should be noted that it is often the case that solid-fuel and wood-burning appliances may be found in a room in which no combustion-air inlet has been installed. This is due to the common belief that a 5 kW or below appliance does not require one. In fact, this is only true when the building fabric's air permeability is greater than 5 m^3/h m^2. This may be shown via testing, or assumed if the building was built before 2008, but only if it has had no improvement works which will reduce the air permeability (double glazing, rendering, etc.).

As for open appliances, the absence of air infiltration due to a lack of permeability or fresh-air inlet grills can have significant health implications. While outside the scope of this Guide, if a lack of combustion air for the appliance is identified, the client should be made aware of the situation and be provided with suitable recommendations (e.g. to seek the advice of a HETAS-approved installer).

Requirements for gas appliances are given in the relevant parts of the Gas Safety (Installation and Use) Regulations 1998 and BS 5440-2:2009.

Requirements for the installation of liquid fuel appliances in domestic buildings are given in the Building Regulations 2010, Approved Document J (or the regional equivalent as per Table 1.1) and BS 5410-1:2019.

In all cases, refer to the manufacturer's instructions for additional requirements applying to particular equipment.

1.7.2.2 Interaction of Extract Ventilation and Open-Flued Appliances

If a room containing an open flue appliance is depressurised by mechanical extract ventilation, flue gases may be drawn into the room from the appliance. This can happen even when the extraction is not from the same room that contains the appliance, and may be aggravated by fans in equipment such as tumble driers. Flue gases can cause hazardous levels of CO. Where open-flue appliances are to be installed in areas affected by mechanical extractor fans, the following precautions should be observed.

* For gas appliances, where the appliance and the extract fan are located in a kitchen, follow the spillage test procedure set out in the relevant appendix to BS 5440-1:2008.
* For liquid fuel appliances, comply with the recommendations in OFTEC Technical Book 4.
* For solid fuel wood and biomass appliances, follow the recommendations in accordance with: the Building Regulations 2010, Approved Document J, Appendix E (or the regional equivalent as per

Table 1.1); smoke test II and a draught test in accordance with the HETAS *Technical Handbook*; as well as the requirements of HETAS Technical Note HETAS_TN_0020 for room-sealed appliances. More information can also be found in section 1.7.2.1

- Extract ventilation should not be installed in the same room as a solid fuel appliance, in accordance with BS 6173:2020.

Further guidance may be obtained from BRE Information Paper IP 7/94 (*Spillage of Flue Gases from Solid-Fuel Combustion Appliances*).

1.7.2.3 Non-shared Flue Systems

All combustion appliances must:

- have adequate provision for the discharge of the products of combustion to the outside air without creating a nuisance
- be so installed, with fireplaces, flues and chimneys so constructed, as to minimise the risk of the building catching fire as a result of their use.

For gas-fired appliances, guidance is given in the Gas Safety (Installation and Use) Regulations 1998. Some important general points include:

- Any appliance in a bath or shower room must be of the room-sealed type.
- A gas fire or other gas space heater of more than 14 kW must not be installed in a room intended for sleeping accommodation, unless the appliance is room sealed.
- LPG-fired appliances should not be installed in basements.

The same regulations also cover:

- the positioning of flues in relation to boundaries and openings
- protection from heat for people likely to come into contact with flues
- the diameter of flues required for different types of appliances
- materials from which flue chimneys may be constructed and how chimneys may be lined to serve gas-fired appliances.

Flues for liquid fuel fired appliances should meet the requirements of BS 5410-1:2019:

- Masonry chimneys must be lined. Liners should not be oversized.
- Any appliance in a bath or shower room, bedroom or garage must be a room-sealed type.

1.7.2.4 Shared-Flue Systems

Shared-flue systems in multi-occupancy dwellings have historically often been of the SE- or U-duct varieties. These systems allow a number of room-sealed appliances (type C2) on different storeys to receive their air supply from, and discharge their combustion products to, a common duct.

Shunt duct systems have also been utilised in some cases, for open-flued appliances only, providing a shared-flue outlet duct for the individual appliances to discharge their products of combustion into, with combustion air for each appliance drawn from the room or space it is situated within.

In more recent times, modern communal flue systems (CFS) have become the preferred shared-flue system, and these are invariably designed for use with modern, room-sealed boilers only (typically types C4, C8, C10 and C12). As with all shared-flue systems, they require careful design and sizing, with prior knowledge of all dwellings and appliance heat loads to be connected, to ensure that the final system operates safely and effectively.

The evolution of BS EN 1749:2020 (Classification of gas appliances according to the method of supplying combustion air and of evacuation of the combustion products (types)) has seen the number of CFS appliance and system 'types' grow considerably in recent years, including 'renovation' options which can facilitate the replacement of older SE- and U-duct types of shared flue with modern CFS (e.g. by housing the new duct(s) within the redundant SE- or U-duct.

IGEM/UP/17 (*Shared Chimney and Flue Systems for Domestic Gas Appliances*) from the Institution of Gas Engineers and Managers provides indispensable general information on the characteristics and key considerations where shared flues are concerned, but is itself not focused on the installation of new systems, in which event specialist design and installation advice should be sought.

2 Customer Liaison

2.1 Contents

2.1   Contents   2-2

2.2   Version Control   2-3

2.3   Introduction   2-4

2.4   Pre-installation Documentation   2-5

    2.4.1   The Specification   2-5

    2.4.2   The Quotation   2-7

2.5   Post-installation Documentation 2-11

    2.5.1   Commissioning 2-11

    2.5.2   Handover 2-14

    2.5.3   Maintenance 2-15

2.6   Appendix 2-16

    2.6.1   Sample Survey Checklist – Blank 2-16

    2.6.2   Sample Quotation Sheet – Blank 2-18

2.2 Version Control

Version number	Changes	Date
10.01	Initial version	10-Nov-2020

The Domestic Building Service Panel Guide reporting tool can be used to notify the panel of any suggested corrections, or comments. These will be collated and used as the basis for review of forthcoming updates. Please feel free to use the tool, which is located at https://www.dbsp.co.uk/reporting-tool

2.3 Introduction

There are several areas of the process of designing, installing and maintaining a heating system that will require liaising with the customer. While the core scope of this Guide relates to the design section of the process, considerations of the design will affect these other stages. As such, this section discusses the requirements of the survey, specification, quotation, commissioning and handover processes, with a specific focus on the following:

- the collection of all the necessary information to design the heating system is an essential part of the survey
- the requirements of commissioning and maintenance of the system will affect the design and specification of the heating system.

2.4 Pre-installation Documentation

Two import documents are needed prior to the installation of a heating system. Firstly, the specification, which collects all the details from which the heating system will be designed. Secondly, the quotation, which is where the details of what will be installed and at what cost is presented back to the client.

2.4.1 The Specification

Prior to developing a specification for the installation of a heating system, the requirements and expectations of the client should be discussed and understood. Consideration should be given to the following points to try to achieve a specification and installation which meets the client's needs and the relevant requirements of current legislation. The following text should assist in the completion of the sample client requirement survey checklist in section 2.6.1. In addition to this, the heat loss worksheet A discussed in section 3 should be completed for each heated space in the building.

2.4.1.1 Specification Parts
The following parts should, as minimum, make up the specification.

Fuel selection
If natural gas or electricity is preferred, does the site have a supply and the correct sized meter currently installed? If alternative fuels are being considered, does the fuel need a storage facility and is there sufficient space for this? Can the fuel supply be routed to the boiler or heat source location? Is access required for delivery of the fuel? For more information, see section 1.6.

General client requirements
The system design should be appropriate for the current and future building occupancy levels, as well as the occupancy patterns. How the building is to be used can play a part in the decision regarding which system to install. Special requirements for clients such as the frail or elderly can also be identified. For more information on design temperatures and considerations for intermittent heating, see sections 3.5.3 and 3.5.5.

Existing systems
If any parts of the existing system are to be reused, it should be ensured that they are correctly sized and suitable for the new system. Any part of the existing system which is being reused should be flushed and cleaned in accordance with BS 7593:2019 (Code of practice for the preparation, commissioning and maintenance of domestic central heating and cooling water systems). This can be either chemical or power flushed, depending on requirements. A system filter will then be required on the installation, and this again can be discussed with the client to ensure they are aware of the requirements to clean the system and the implications if this is not carried out (see section 5.13.1). Not only will a dirty system block heat exchangers and heat emitters, and reduce the efficiency and the lifespan of appliances and components, it can also invalidate the warranty on some appliances if not completed. For more information on the requirements for system care and water treatment, see sections 2.5.3 and 5.13.

Services
What are the current supplies to the property with regard to water, gas and electricity, and what sort of systems will they be suitable for? Do they meet current regulations, such as adequate backflow protection on the mains cold water supply? This may involve taking various readings for pressures and flow rates (both static and dynamic) at this early stage.

Heat generator
Alternatives to a traditional boiler should be discussed, and the advantages, disadvantages and potential cost implications put forward to the client. Alternatives may include renewable energy sources such as a biomass boiler, heat pumps and solar thermal installations. The location of the heat generator and any other appliances such as fuel stores, cylinders and cisterns should also be decided, considering size, weight, flueing and condensate discharge requirements, aesthetics and any ventilation requirements. Access for future maintenance of all appliances and controls must always be considered. For ventilation, combustion

air and flueing requirements, see section 1.7. Further information on the following heat generators and their fuel requirements can be found in:

- gas – section 1.6.2
- liquid fuel – section 1.6.3, or contact the Oil Firing Technical Association (OFTEC)
- biomass – section 1.6.4, or contact the Heating Equipment Testing and Approval Scheme (HETAS)
- solar thermal installations – see the companion publication to this Guide, *The Solar Heating Design & Installation Guide*, also published by the Domestic Building Service Panel (https://www.dbsp.co.uk)
- heat pumps – section 1.6.5, or contact the Heat Pump Association (HPA)
- direct electric – section 1.6.6, or contact the Electrical Contractors' Association (ECA).

Note: Organisation contact details are available in section 0.3.

Energy efficiency opportunities
There should be a discussion around the general building fabric and how the heat loss and efficiency could be improved. This could be through improving insulation of the building fabric and reducing heat loss through windows, doors, etc. It should be emphasised to the client that the financial savings from energy-saving measures will usually be greater in the long term than those from upgrading the heating system, and that afterwards a smaller and cheaper system will be needed. For more information on energy efficiency, see section 1.5.

System type
The system should work for the property as well as meeting the legislative requirements. Properties with multiple bathrooms will be better served with a store of hot water (perhaps an unvented cylinder) and combination boilers will not perhaps be suitable. Also, if alternative heating sources such as biomass boilers or heat pumps are selected, an additional large volume of buffer storage is likely to be needed to ensure their efficient operation. This can all be decided when discussing the occupancy and use of the building, as this may have an impact on system selection. It should be noted that large vessels such as hot water cylinders may have access and structural implications for the building. These should be discussed with the client at this stage. For further information on hot water storage, see section 4.

Pipework
Different materials should be discussed along with the costs and implications of the various alternatives. Plastic pipework is cheaper and quicker to install, but copper pipework is more robust. Pipework runs and locations should also be discussed in order to avoid any surprises at the time of installation. Future maintenance should also be considered, as should any access requirements. For further information on pipework layouts, see section 5.4.

Heat emitter choice and location
Where existing heat emitters are to be reused, their condition and suitability should be checked – particularly if a different flow and return temperature are to be used to that for which the system was previously designed.

Alternatives to radiators, such as underfloor heating, should be considered, as they can deliver greater comfort and can avoid complications over siting, albeit generally at a greater financial cost. Discussions with the client around requirements for the position of the heat emitter and wall space requirements are important initial design considerations.

For further information on radiator selection, see section 5.5. For further information on underfloor heating, see the companion publication to this, *The Underfloor Heating Design and Installation Guide*, which is also published by the Domestic Building Service Panel (https://www.dbsp.co.uk).

Controls
The function and benefit of heating and hot water system controls should be explained to the client, including their effect on comfort and running costs. Any requirements to heat specific parts of the property individually or to higher temperatures should be identified. Opportunities to improve energy efficiency should also be considered. These discussions may impact on the selection of the controls, and benefit the client by making the system work better for them. For further information on system controls, see section 5.11.

Safety and protecting the client's property
Specific requirements for personal protective equipment and safety requirements should be discussed. Specifically, any requirements for working at heights or in confined spaces should be discussed, along with the level of qualifications required and the extra costs for any hazard mitigations that might be needed. Covering of carpets and furniture can be discussed, as can the removal of any equipment that could be potentially damaged in certain areas. Any pre-existing damage to any items or the property should be identified and recorded before the job starts, to ensure that no blame is referred back to the company for such damage. Strategies for bacteria (*Legionella*) protection should also be discussed. For further information on bacteria protection, see section 4.5.1.

Resources required
Materials lists are generally not provided to the client (although they may be), but they are a key part of pricing the job effectively and ensuring that the installation runs smoothly without any delay in identifying key resources. Things to consider include the amount of labour, timeframes and any specialist equipment and resources required.

Handover
Allocating time to properly commission the system and then hand it over to the client is essential to ensure that the client can operate the system effectively and efficiently. Poorly operated controls and incorrectly set up appliances are ineffective and inefficient, so this is a key aspect of the installation. Discussing this handover period with the potential client can give them confidence they will have time allocated to ensure they know how to operate the system correctly. For more details on the handover requirements, see section 2.5.2.

2.4.1.2 Survey Checklist

Details and outcomes of the various discussions with the client should be recorded; a sample client requirement survey checklist is provided in the appendix to this section (see section 2.6.1). This can then form the technical detail behind a quotation and the design work, and forms a record of the scope of work.

2.4.2 The Quotation

The quotation is the second important document required prior to installation. Whether for a new heating installation, an extension to an existing system or a replacement system, the quotation should give information about the design and the materials to be used, and should be fully detailed so that the customer has no doubt about the work included. The price and conditions of trading should be stated, together with a full description of the work to be undertaken, and a full breakdown of the costs. Any additional work necessary to enable the installation to be carried out or the system to operate, but which has not been included in the quotation, should also be clearly stated.

The following provides a guide to the technical information that could be included in a specification if one is required for the proposed installation. A sample quotation sheet is given in section 2.6.2.

2.4.2.1 Quotation Parts

Design conditions and temperatures
A schedule should be provided showing, for each heated area:

- the list of rooms to be heated
- the temperatures to be achieved in every room (in °C) (see section 3.5.3)
- the type and size of the heat emitter (see section 5.5).

Additionally, it should be stated what assumptions have been made for the following:

- the number of air changes per hour in every room (see section 3.5.4)
- the external temperature (in °C) (see section 3.5.3.3)

- the heating flow temperature (in °C) (see section 5.5.2)
- the assumed usage patterns of the building (i.e. the number of people, hot water draw-off times, heating schedule).

Incoming and existing services

Comment on the adequacy of existing services, or any improvements required to make them adequate.

Heat generators

- Location of the boiler, etc.
- Make and type of boiler.
- Heat output (in kW).
- If a combination boiler, state the hot water flow rate in litres/minute and the temperature rise in °C.

For more information on various heat generators, see section 1.6.

Boiler flue and chimney

- Type of flue – conventional or room sealed.
- Terminal position and type.
- Terminal guard flue liner if required, and size.

For more information on flues, see section 1.7.2 and seek manufacturers' advice.

Condensate drain provision

- Drain termination pipe route.
- Anti-freezing precautions.
- Pipe sizes and materials.

Seek manufacturers' advice, as well as guidance from the Heating & Hotwater Industry Council (HHIC), Oil Firing Technical Association (OFTEC) guidance and BS 6798:2014.

For more information on protecting condensate pipework from freezing, see section 5.12.4.

Fuel storage

- Liquid fuel, biomass, solid fuel or LPG installations – the size of the storage tank and its construction, location and filling position.
- Access information and insurance details.

For more information on various heat generator fuel storage requirements, see section 1.6.

Ventilation

- Type and location of air vents for combustion air and ventilation.

For more information on combustion air and ventilation requirements, see section 1.7.

Heat emitters

- Make and type.
- Any special paint finish.
- Location and control.

For more information on heat emitters, see section 5.5.

Hot water cylinder

- Location, type and storage capacity.
- Reheat times, if appropriate.
- Heat source, and any back-up or alternative heat source details.

For more information on hot water storage, see section 4.

Circulators
- Make and type.
- Locations, if external to the appliance.

For more information on circulators, see section 5.8.

Sealed system equipment
- Expansion vessel size.
- Location, if external to the appliance.
- Safety valve discharge location.

For more information on sealed systems, see section 5.9.1.

Open-vented system equipment
- Size, location and insulation requirements.
- Feed and expansion cistern and pipework.

For more information on open-vented systems, see section 5.9.2.

Programmers and controls
- Make, type and location.
- Programming facilities.
- Location of the room and cylinder thermostats.
- Location of sensors.

For more information on control systems, see section 5.11.

Electric wiring
- Specification of work included.
- Fused spur requirement and location.
- Size of fuse.

Pipework
- Material, and fittings type.
- Location of pipe runs – surface or concealed routing.
- Commissioning of cleansing procedure and inhibitor to be used.

For more information on pipework, see section 5.4. For information on pipework commissioning, see section 2.5.1. For information on water treatment, see section 5.13.

Insulation
- Material.
- Parts to be insulated.
- Thickness specification.
- Type of jointing.

For more information on pipe insulation, see section 5.12.

Programme of work
- Who will be attending the site and when.
- Timeframes for completion of the job.
- As-required dates agreed.

Tools and specialist plant requirements
- Any specialist equipment for activities such as core drilling, working at height or lifting.

Health, safety and access requirements
- Specific safety requirements that the client needs to be aware of, and which areas will need to be accessed and when.
- Refer to any risk assessments, method statements and permits to work, as required.

Flushing and water treatment
- All new equipment and pipework are to be chemically flushed and identified as 'clean' by recorded test results.
- Any system which has been extended or to which replacement parts have been added should be flushed as above.
- If one is not already present, an in-line system filter should be installed (see section 5.13.1).

For information on pipework commissioning, see section 2.5.1. For information on water treatment, see section 5.13.

Building work
- Description of work included or excluded, and work required to be done by others.
- Level of making good.

Waste and scrap
- Disposal of waste and scrap materials.

Variations to contract
- State how variations will be handled.

Commissioning and handover procedure
- State the procedures.
- Use the Benchmark scheme.

For more information on commissioning, see section 2.5.1. For more information on handover, see section 2.5.2.

Guarantees
- Enclose a copy of the terms of relevant guarantee schemes.

For more information on handover, see section 2.5.2.

Extended warranty and breakdown insurance
- State that a Benchmark scheme may be applicable.
- Offer relevant extended warranties, if applicable.
- Offer service.

For more information on handover, see section 2.5.2.

2.4.2.2 Quotation sheet
The customer should be provided with all the details discussed above, along with a price for the work. A sample quotation is provided in the appendix to this section (see section 2.6.2).

2.5 Post-installation Documentation

2.5.1 Commissioning

Commissioning a system is an important part of the installation (whether it be a new installation, a repair, a replacement or an upgrade) as it can often make a significant difference to a system's operating efficiency and longevity. Without commissioning, the manufacturer's warranty or guarantees will be voided.

Various installer membership schemes will have their own requirements for commissioning of heating systems, and these should be followed where applicable (see section 2.5.1.1).

On top of the requirements of the schemes, major components of the system will usually have a commissioning checklist provided by the manufacturer. These should always be used if available. Often, such a checklist will need to be returned to the manufacturer for the customer to receive a warranty.

Finally, section 2.5.1.2 provides a list of the minimum technical information that should be checked and recorded as part of the commissioning of the heating system.

2.5.1.1 Scheme Requirements

Benchmark

The Benchmark scheme, developed and managed by the Heating and Hot Water Industry Council (HHIC), is aimed at raising standards of installation, commissioning and servicing of central heating systems in the UK. It provides a readily available means to demonstrate compliance with the requirements of Part L of the Building Regulations 2010, or the regional equivalent (see Table 1.1) for fixed building services.

A commissioning checklist and service history log are provided as part of the appliance installation manual, and these are also available digitally via the Benchmark app, for the installer to complete and sign, to confirm that the heat generator has been installed and commissioned following the manufacturer's instructions.

The consumer can also access this information in either format, as a dedicated secure consumer app is also available.

The installer should make the consumer aware of the Benchmark scheme as part of the required handover of the heating system. At handover, the correct use of the appliance and all associated controls should be fully explained, to ensure that the system is operated and maintained efficiently, delivering comfort while minimising the carbon footprint.

Other heating system appliances/components, such as heat pumps and hot water cylinders, may also be supplied with Benchmark documentation for completion in a similar manner.

Householders are encouraged to keep access to these electronic and/or paper documents safe, and to ensure they are updated whenever the heat generator or system is serviced. The documents can then be passed on to the new owner if the property changes hands.

Competent Person Schemes

Competent Person Schemes (CPS), approved by the Ministry of Housing, Communities and Local Government (MHCLG), allow individuals and enterprises to self-certify that their work in new and existing dwellings complies with the Building Regulations in England and in Wales. The schemes permit these works to be undertaken by persons classed as being competent, without the need to involve the building control body. The work must be covered by approved documentation.

Details of the various schemes available can be found at https://www.gov.uk/building-regulations-competent-person-schemes.

In Scotland, the Scottish Government Building Standards division allows self-certification through Certification of Construction Schemes. The Scottish and Northern Ireland Plumbing Employers' Federation (SNIPEF) provides a scheme for drainage, heating and plumbing.

2.5.1.2 Commissioning Minimum Checks
The following is a list of minimum checks that should be done during commissioning, and data that should be recorded and provided to the customer. These checks do not replace those stipulated by any manufacturer or scheme.

Circulator settings
Has the circulator been set-up as required for the system as designed? See section 5.8.

The following should be recorded:

- the design system flow rate
- the design system head.

If a constant-speed pump is used:

- the pump speed setting.

If a variable-speed pump is used:

- the pump's operating mode (i.e. constant pressure or proportional pressure)
- the control set point (i.e. target pressure)
- any other control parameters used (e.g. minimum flow rate).

Valve positions and settings
The default position of all valves in the system should be recorded and checked. This includes all required safety valves. See section 5.4; see also section 5.9.1 for sealed systems and section 5.9.2 for open-vented systems.

Water treatment
Has the water treatment for the system been done as designed? See section 5.13.

The following should be recorded:

- Was the system flushed and cleaned in accordance with BS 7593:2019 and the heat generator manufacturer's instructions?
- What system cleaner was used?
- What inhibitor was used and at what concentration?
- What antifreeze was used (if applicable)?
- What biocide was used (if applicable)?
- Has an in-line filter been installed?

Insulation
Has the pipework insulation for the system been done as designed? See section 5.12.

System pressure
For sealed systems, have the system pressure and expansion vessel pre-charge been set correctly? Has the correct safety pressure relief valve installed, as specified in section 5.9.1.4, and in accordance with the heat generator manufacturer's instructions?

The following should be recorded:

- the design and actual system pressure
- the design and actual expansion vessel pre-charge
- the safety pressure relief valve setting.

System balancing
It is important to ensure that the required flow rate (as calculated in section 5.6.3.2) is getting to each heat emitter in the property. If the heating system is a manifold design (see section 5.10), this is a simple case of adjusting the flow for the circuit to the setting calculated or supplied by the manufacturer. For more traditional layouts, a description of the process is given below, but advice should be sought from manufacturers and industry bodies such as the HHIC.

The basic steps in balancing a heat emitter are as follows:

1. The building should be cold, and all radiator valves (lockshield valves, thermostatic radiator valves and manual valves) should be fully open.
2. The heating should then be set to come on, with the circulator set to its normal operating settings.
3. A differential temperature thermometer, with two clamp-on temperature sensors, should be attached to the furthest heat emitter from the heat generator. One sensor should be on the flow pipe, and the other on the return pipework.
4. The lockshield valve of the radiator being measured should be adjusted until the design temperature differential as used in section 5.5 is achieved across the heat emitter
5. Steps 3 and 4 should then be repeated for all heat emitters, in order from the furthest from the heat generator to the nearest, for each circuit.
6. Step 5 should then be repeated until one complete cycle through steps 3 and 4 can be achieved with no adjustments needing to be made. This may require the adjustment of each heat emitter several times.

Once complete, the temperature differentials, the system flow and return temperatures, and the valve settings should be recorded.

Domestic hot water performance
For systems with hot water storage, has the system been installed and set up as designed, including the required two levels of over-temperature protection? Has this been all done in accordance with the requirements of manufacturers and Part G3 of the Building Regulations 2010? See section 4.4.1. or the regional equivalent as per Table 1.1.

The following should be recorded (for all sources of hot water):

- the cold water inlet temperature
- the water temperature and flow rate at all outlets
- the settings of all safety valves.

Controls settings
Have the system controls been installed and set up as designed? See section 5.11.

The following should be recorded:

- the room thermostat time and temperature settings (for all zones)
- the hot water thermostat time and temperature settings
- the thermostatic radiator valve settings (for all valves)
- the weather compensation settings (if appropriate)
- the optimum start/stop settings (if appropriate)
- the smart/remote operation functionality settings (if appropriate)
- the automatic bypass settings (if appropriate)
- the interlock setting (if appropriate).

2.5.2 Handover

The system should be commissioned, fully operated and shown to work satisfactorily before handover. Once this is the case, the following actions should be taken:

- The winter and summer operation of the system and the controls should be clearly explained to the client, with particular attention given to demonstrating the operation of the controls and how they are adjusted.
- The client should be instructed on how to fill and repressurise the system (sealed systems).
- The client should also be shown the location of all shut-off valves and electrical fuses.
- Instructions should be given to the client on the correct maintenance procedure for the system (see section 2.5.3).

2.5.2.1 Handover documentation

The following documents should be shown to, explained to and left with the client once the installation is complete.

Safety instructions

It must be explained that air supply and flueing equipment must not be interfered with. Also, it should be explained that limit thermostats, bypass valves, safety valves and any other similar controls must not be tampered with.

Written instructions

For all except the simplest control systems, a written explanation of the operation should be given to the client. This may be best in the form of a diagrammatic layout.

A full set of manufacturer's installation and operating instructions for all the equipment and a schedule of the equipment should be left on site for future reference.

A complete list of the settings used and the procedures followed during commissioning (for all equipment) should be left on site. This is important in case the equipment needs to be recommissioned at any point in the future.

Guarantees

Manufacturers' registration cards should be completed on behalf of the client and returned without delay, or completed online.

Guarantees applicable to the system and its component parts should be explained so that the customer is aware of the comprehensive guarantees that will be in force, and covering workmanship, materials and performance, providing the conditions of the guarantee are met.

Any extended warranties to be offered should also be explained.

Equipment record

The Schedule of Installed Equipment should list all items of equipment, together with the operational settings of the controls, valves and other equipment.

Drawings

Full and detailed electrical and mechanical drawings of the works undertaken should be left with the system.

Emergency contacts

The contact telephone number and the installer's name and address label should be fixed in a suitable position for easy reference.

2.5.2.2 Special Tools
At least two air-vent keys and any operating tools and spares that were supplied with the installed equipment should be handed to the client.

2.5.3 Maintenance

The client should be advised of the importance of entering into a regular service contract, which will include visits by a competent service engineer. To work on a gas appliance it is a legal requirement to be registered with the Gas Safe Register. For other appliances, installers and technicians should be members of appropriate schemes such as HETAS or OFTEC. Installers of heat pumps or other renewable energy heating systems should be registered with the Microgeneration Certification Scheme for the appropriate technology.

For heat pump installations, the client should be also advised on the importance of having the F-gas refrigerant checked and tested at least once a year. These checks and tests must by law be done by a contractor certified to work with F-gases – accredited by agencies include the Department for Environment, Food and Rural Affairs (DEFRA) and REFCOM (Register of Companies Competent to Manage Refrigerants); see section 1.6.5.10 for more information.

Information on recommended energy-efficiency monitoring in use by the clients should be given, such as regularly:

• monitoring fuel and electricity consumption to identify increases that could be linked to a failure
• checking equipment for signs of wear (e.g. leaks, new noises, excess or different ash (for biomass boilers), corrosion)
• reassessing heating and hot water schedules compared with the lifestyle of the occupants at that time.

All of the above require the client's understanding of the system and its requirements.

It is strongly recommended that unvented hot water storage systems (UHWSS) are similarly checked on an ongoing basis by a competent service engineer. This can also be a condition of the UHWSS manufacturer's warranty provision.

Any heating appliance or heating system breakdown insurance which is available should then be explained. The terms of the heat generator manufacturer's warranty may require that system water checks are carried out. See BS 7593:2019.

The heating system should also be checked annually. In particular, the cleanliness of the system water should be checked.

It is recommended to advise clients to arrange a check of the appliance and key system components before the onset of winter, due to the increased load conditions they will likely be subject to at this time, and as parts of the system (e.g. heating zone valves) may have been idle over the warmer summer period.

2.6 Appendix

2.6.1 Sample Survey Checklist – Blank

See next page.

Client Requirement Survey Checklist

Stage 1 - Job information

Job [   ]   Page [   ]   of   [   ]

Address and location description

[   ]

Stage 2 - General requirements   See section 2.4.1.1

Fuel choice

What fuel is suitable? Where will it be stored? How will it be accessed?

General client requirements

What does the customer want/need?

Existing systems

What is already present? What condition is it in? Is it suitable for flushing requirements?

Plumbing services

Available water quality/water pressure/gas pressures?

Stage 3 - Heating appliances   See section 2.4.1.1

Heat generator selection

What technologies are and are not suitable?

Energy-efficiency opportunities

What is and is not suitable? Insulation/windows/doors/draught-proofing?

System type

Type of system, hot water and heating requirements to work for the client?

Pipework

Type of material, general routing requirements and location?

Stage 4 - Heating delivery   See section 2.4.1.1

Heat emitters selection and location

Type, temperatures and location?

Controls

Type and functionality?

Stage 5 - Health and safety   See section 2.4.1.1

Access

Any working at heights, confined spaces, or other access considerations?

Bacteria (*Legionella*) and scalding protection

Bacteria protection? Scalding prevention strategy?

Stage 6 - Client confirmation

I, the client named below confirm that the requirements above have all been discussed in detail with myself, and I am happy for a quote and specification to be produced on their basis

Client name

[   ]

Client signature

[   ]

Date signed

[   ]

DBSP - DHDG -V2020.0

2.6.2 Sample Quotation Sheet – Blank

See next page.

Installation Specification Quotation - page 1

Stage 1 - Job information

Job [   ]   Page [   ]   of   [   ]

Quote valid till [   ]

Address and location description

Company providing quotation

Stage 2 - Quote details   See section 2.4.2.1

Client brief / job description

Details of work programme including labour requirements, dates, timings and areas of work

Tools and plant requirements

Health, safety and access requirements

Details of fuel and system selection

Details of components to be installed including manufacturers or model details

Property protection requirements

Preparatory work required to building fabric

Details of component locations and pipe runs

Additional comments or requirements

DBSP - DHDG -V2020.0

Installation Specification Quotation - page 2

Stage 1 (continued) - Job information

Job [   ]   Page [   ]   of   [   ]

Stage 2 (continued) - Quote details   See section 2.4.2.1

Breakdown of costs

Stage 3 - Quote acceptance

I, the system designer named below confirm that the above quotation meets the stated client requirements, and I am happy to install the specified system for the specified price

System designer name

System designer signature

Date signed

I, the client named below am legally empowered and happy to accept the above quotation and for work to proceed as specified

Client name

Client signature

Date signed

DBSP - DHDG -V2020

3 System Design (Heat Loss)

3.1 Contents

3.1   Contents 3-2

3.2   Version Control 3-3

3.3   System Design (Heat Loss) – Introduction 3-4

3.4   Heat Loss Calculation – Principles 3-5

    3.4.1   Ventilation and Natural Infiltration Heat Loss 3-5

    3.4.2   Calculation of Fabric Heat Loss 3-5

3.5   Heat Loss Calculation – Considerations 3-7

    3.5.1   Surface Area of a Building 3-7

    3.5.2   U-values 3-8

    3.5.3   Design Temperatures 3-14

    3.5.4   Ventilation 3-20

    3.5.5   Intermittent Heating 3-22

3.6   Annual Energy Estimation 3-25

3.7   Heat Loss Procedures 3-26

3.8   System Design (Heat Loss) – Appendix 3-27

    3.8.1   Thermal Conductivity Table 3-27

    3.8.2   U-value Tables 3-29

    3.8.3   Worksheet A – Heat Losses – Blank 3-42

    3.8.4   Worksheet A – Heat Losses – Instructions 3-44

3.2 Version Control

Version number	Changes	Date
10.01	Initial version	10-Nov-2020

The Domestic Building Service Panel Guide reporting tool can be used to notify the panel of any suggested corrections, or comments. These will be collated and used as the basis for review of forthcoming updates. Please feel free to use the tool, which is located at https://www.dbsp.co.uk/reporting-tool

3.3 System Design (Heat Loss) – Introduction

Before a heating system can be designed correctly, an assessment must be made as to how much heat will need to be supplied. To do this, a full heat loss assessment must be undertaken. The heat loss assessment will consider what level of heat is required to provide thermal comfort to the occupants of each room.

The driving principle of heat loss is that heat will flow from a warmer area to a cooler area. The rate at which the heat flows is governed by the temperature differential between the two areas – the greater the differential, the greater the heat loss.

Note: Insulation does not prevent heat loss, it just slows it down.

Given that heat flows by conduction through materials, or by convection in fluids such as air, and by radiation between opposing surfaces, all three mechanisms are relevant to domestic heating system design. The designer's primary task is to estimate the amount of heat the system must provide to maintain the dwelling at the required indoor temperature under the most demanding conditions specified. Calculations are undertaken on a room-by-room basis to allow the required heat output for each room to be assessed and heat emitters to be sized. The overall heat load to be provided by the heat generator can then be calculated and the heat generator sized accordingly.

The calculation of heat loss from a building is complex. This section introduces the principles of calculating heat loss, and details the considerations that need to be made when undertaking the calculation, before finally introducing a procedure that can be used to calculate the total heat loss for a house on a room-by-room basis.

Most of the information in the following sections is given in CIBSE's *Guide A: Environmental Design*.

3.4 Heat Loss Calculation – Principles

There are two significant mechanisms to consider when calculating the heat lost from a house:

* Heat is lost when warm air leaves the house, and cold incoming air must be warmed to replace that heat. This may be through open doors, windows and ventilation, but will also be through gaps and cracks in the building structure. This is generally known as 'ventilation' heat loss.
* Heat is conducted through the fabric of the building – its walls, roof, ground floor, windows and doors. This is generally referred to as 'fabric' heat loss.

Both types of heat loss need to be calculated and considered in the design of the heating system.

3.4.1 Ventilation and Natural Infiltration Heat Loss

Ventilation heat loss depends on the rate at which air enters and leaves the building, the heat capacity of the air itself, and the temperature difference between indoors and outdoors. The heat capacity of air is approximately constant under the conditions encountered in a house, so the other two factors determine the overall result. The quantity of air passing through the building depends on the volume of the building and the air-change rate, which is usually expressed in air changes per hour (ACH). The ventilation heat loss (in W) of a room or building may be calculated using the formula:

$$Q_V = 0.33 \times V \times N \times (T_{in} - T_{out}) \qquad \text{(Equation 1)}$$

where

Q_V is the ventilation heat loss rate in W
V is the volume of the room in m^3 (see the considerations discussed in section 3.5.1.2)
N is the number of air changes per hour (see the considerations discussed in section 3.5.4)
T_{in} is the indoor temperature in °C (see the considerations discussed in section 3.5.3.2)
T_{out} is the outdoor temperature in °C (see the considerations discussed in section 3.5.3.3)

The factor 0.33 is the product of the specific heat and density of air under standard conditions.

> **Example**: A room with a volume of 60 m^3, a target of 1.5 ACH (no fans, whole-house mechanical ventilation, chimneys or flues; see section 3.5.4), and an indoor design temperature of 21°C and an outdoor design temperature of −3°C would have a ventilation heat loss rate of:
>
> $0.33 \times 60 \times 1.5 \times [21 - (-3)] = 0.33 \times 60 \times 1.5 \times 24 = 712.8$ W

Note: Due to changes in building regulations, the airtightness of new buildings is now a fraction of what it was previously; in some cases, less than 0.5 ACH. With very high levels of airtightness, mechanical ventilation heat recovery (MVHR) systems may need to be installed, which will in themselves affect the building heat loss (for more detail see section 1.7.1.3).

3.4.2 Calculation of Fabric Heat Loss

The rate at which heat is lost by conduction through a building element depends on the temperature difference across the element, its area and its propensity to conduct heat. The last of these factors depends on the thermal conductivity of the materials from which the element is constructed and the thickness of the layers of those materials. For example, a solid brick wall conducts heat faster than a wall of the same thickness made of insulating concrete blocks, while a thin wall conducts heat faster than a thick one.

The rate at which a building element conducts heat is given by its U-value, which is the number of watts of heat that will flow through an area of 1 m² when subjected to a temperature difference of 1 kelvin (K).

Note: 1 K = 1°C differential.

> **Example**: A standard cavity wall (brick, open cavity, brick) with no insulation has a U-value of about 1.7 W/m² K. Therefore, 1.7 W of heat will flow from the inside surface to the outside of each square metre of the area of the element, for every degree the indoor temperature is above the outdoor temperature.

Note: The direction of the heat flow may be reversed if the outdoor or adjacent room temperature is higher than the indoor temperature.

The fabric heat loss (*Q*) of a surface may be calculated using the formula:

$$Q_F = A \times U \times (T_{in} - T_{out})$$ (Equation 2)

where

Q_F is the fabric heat loss rate in W
A is the area of the building element in m² (see the considerations discussed in section 3.5.1.2)
U is the U-value in W/m² K (see the considerations discussed in section 3.5.2)
T_{in} is the indoor temperature in °C (see the considerations discussed in section 3.5.3.2)
T_{out} is the outdoor temperature in °C (see the considerations discussed in section 3.5.3.3)

Note: T_{in} and T_{out} refer also to the temperature difference across internal partitions (see the considerations discussed in section 3.5.3.3 on adjoining properties and unheated spaces, and adjoining rooms).

Therefore, to calculate the rate at which heat is lost through a section of wall per degree of temperature difference:

- multiply the wall area *A* by the U-value, giving a result in W/K
- then multiply the result by the temperature difference across the section to give the heat loss rate in W/m² K.

> **Example**: A section of wall with an area of 20 m² has a U-value of 0.38 W/m² K, an indoor design temperature of 21°C and an outdoor design temperature of −3°C would have a fabric heat loss rate of:
>
> 20 × 0.38 × [21 − (−3)] = 20 × 0.38 × 24 = 182.4 W

This must be done for each surface of the room through which heat is lost, with the results summed to obtain the total heat loss for the room. The same process must then be followed for each room in the building to obtain the total building heat loss. This process is discussed in more detail in section 3.7.

3.5 Heat Loss Calculation – Considerations

As discussed above, there are several considerations regarding the variables used in Equation 1 and Equation 2 to calculate the heat loss from a building. These have been broken down into the subsections below.

3.5.1 Surface Area of a Building

Which surfaces and elements of a building should be included in a heat loss calculation (Equation 1 (section 3.4.1) and Equation 2 (section 3.4.2)), and, when measuring the building, where should the dimensions be taken from and to?

3.5.1.1 Elements to Include
In simple terms:

- any heated volume within the building should be included in the ventilation heat loss calculation; Equation 2 (section 3.4.2)
- any surface and element through which heat will flow (given the definition above that heat will flow from any area or space that is warmer to any area or space that is cooler) should be included in the fabric heat loss calculation; Equation 1 (section 3.4.1). For example, roof, ground floor, doors, windows, external walls, and internal walls where there is a temperature differential between the sides (see Figure 1.1).

3.5.1.2 Measuring the Building
When assessing the dimensions of a room, measurements should be taken as the internal dimensions of the room, as shown in Figure 3.1. This includes walls, floors and ceilings.

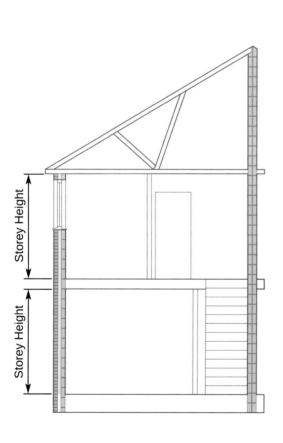
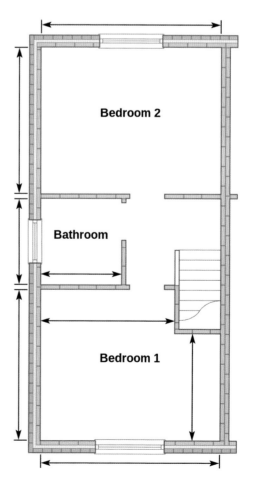

Figure 3.1 Measuring the dimensions of structural elements

For windows, doors and roof lights, U-values (preferably supplied by the manufacturer, or as given in Table 3.20) are usually calculated for the frame and glazing combined. Therefore, measurements should include the frame (see Figure 3.2).

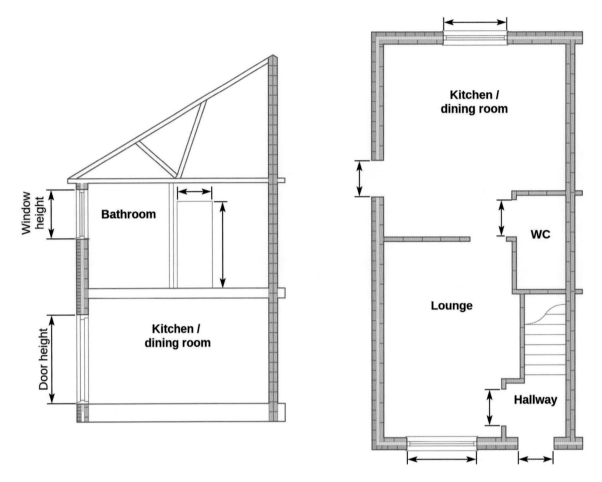

Figure 3.2 Measuring the dimensions of windows and doors

3.5.2 U-values

As discussed above, U-values are a measure of the rate at which a building element conducts heat, and are used in Equation 2 (section 3.4.2). U-values for common construction methods can be obtained from the tables given in the appendix to this section (see section 3.8.2). Unfortunately, real-world construction often does not match up with the methods provided, and corrections need to be made. This section discusses a few of the common corrections that often need to be made:

- calculation of U-values from scratch for methods that are not in the tables (section 3.5.2.1)
- modification of U-values, for example if extra insulation needs to be added (section 3.5.2.2)
- calculation of U-values for floors of complex shapes (section 3.5.2.4)
- modification of U-values for windows to allow for sloped roof windows (section 3.5.2.5)
- modification of U-values to allow for thermal bridging (section 3.5.2.6).

3.5.2.1 U-value Calculation
When the U-value for a construction element is not available, it can be calculated. This is done by using the thickness and thermal conductivity of every layer in the construction to create a summary of all the thermal resistance values before inverting the total resistance to obtain the U-value.

For each separate layer, the thermal resistance (R in m² K/W) can be calculated by dividing its thickness (L in m) by its thermal conductivity (k-factor in W/m K; or its scientific term the lambda value (λ-value)) using the standard equation $R = L/k$. The thermal conductivity of the building material can be obtained from the manufacturer, from CIBSE's *Guide A: Environmental Design*, from approved documents, or from tables such as Table 3.12 given in the appendix to this section (see section 3.8.1).

The thermal resistance of air gaps and surface films should also be considered using the values given in Table 3.1.

The total thermal resistance of the element is calculated by adding up the thermal resistances of its layers:

$$R = R_{si} + R_1 + R_2 \ldots + R_a + R_{so} \qquad \text{(Equation 3)}$$

where

R	is the total thermal resistance of the element
R_{si}	is the internal surface resistance
$R_1, R_2, \ldots$	is the thermal resistances of the layers
R_a	is the resistance of the airspace
R_{so}	is the outside surface resistance

The U-value is simply the reciprocal of thermal resistance:

$$U = 1/R \qquad \text{(Equation 4)}$$

Table 3.1 Standard surface film thermal resistance coefficients

Type of surface/air gap	Thermal resistance (m² K/W)
Outside surface of exterior wall	$R_{so} = 0.06$
Inside surface of wall	$R_{si} = 0.12$
Air gap (cavity)	$R_a = 0.18$

Example: The following shows a U-value calculation for the external wall construction shown in Figure 3.3. The outside surface is **a** on the left of the figure. The thermal resistance of the wall used in the calculation is obtained as shown in Table 3.2.

U-value of construction (using Equation 4) = 1/1.776 = 0.56 W/m² K

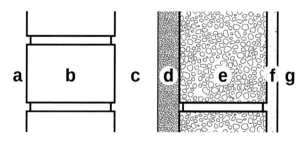

Figure 3.3 Typical outside wall

Table 3.2 Properties of the layers contributing to the thermal resistance of the outside wall in Figure 3.3

Layer		Thickness (m)	Thermal conductivity, λ (W/m K)	Calculation: thickness/λ = R	Thermal resistance, R (m² K/W)
a	External surface resistance	n/a	From Table 3.1		0.060
b	Facing brick (102.5 mm)	0.1025	0.84 (from Table 3.12)	0.1025/0.84	0.122
c	Airspace (50 mm)	0.05	From Table 3.1		0.180
d	Insulation (25 mm)	0.025	0.04 (from Table 3.12)	0.025/0.04	0.625
e	Thermal block (100 mm)	0.1	0.17 (from Table 3.12)	0.1/0.17	0.588
f	Plaster (13 mm)	0.013	0.16 (from Table 3.12)	0.013/0.16	0.081
g	Inside surface resistance	n/a	From Table 3.1		0.120
Total thermal resistance (m² K/W) – using equation 3					1.776

3.5.2.2 U-value Modifications

Tables such as those in the appendix to this section (see section 3.8.2) list the U-values of typical forms of construction. However, it is possible to calculate how a U-value will change if additional insulation is introduced.

Example 1: An external cavity wall is constructed with a 102 mm brick outer layer, a 50 mm (2 in.) open ventilated cavity, a 100 mm breeze block inner layer and 13 mm of dense plaster.

The closest match to that configuration in Table 3.14 is the third item, which gives a U-value of 0.87 W/m² K and includes a k-factor for the inner layer of 0.17 W/m K.

The k-factor supplied by the manufacturer of the breeze blocks is 1.28 W/m K, so we must adjust the U-value accordingly. How? We saw above (section 3.5.2) that a U-value is built from the sum of the thermal resistances of the various layers of a construction, and that the resistance of an individual layer is found by dividing its thickness in metres by its thermal conductivity (k-factor).

So, if the thermal resistance of the inner layer as shown is 0.588 m² K/W (= 0.100/0.17), this is replaced by the thermal resistance of the breeze block, i.e. 0.078 m² K/W (= 0.100/1.28).

The total thermal resistance of a 0.87 W/m² K U-value is 1.149 m² K/W (= 1/0.87), from which 0.588 m² K/W is deducted and to which 0.078 m² K/W is added, giving 0.639 m² K/W (= 1.149 − 0.588 + 0.078).

Therefore, the corrected U-value of the brick–cavity–breeze–plaster wall is 1.56 W/m² K (1/0.639).

Example 2: Cavity insulation is added to the wall in Example 1 at a later date. If the cavity is filled with urea formaldehyde foam (k-factor 0.040 W/m.K), what is the U-value of the wall now?

Deduct the thermal resistance of the cavity air gap to be filled (0.18 W/m² K) and add the thermal resistance of the foam fill, which is 1.25 W/m² K (= 0.050/0.040).

Calculation: 0.639 − 0.18 + 1.25 = 1.709 W/m² K, which equates to a U-value of 0.59 W/m² K.

This process may be used for any building element to establish the benefit of added insulation. For example, where 150 mm of loft insulation is added to a previously uninsulated loft, add the thermal resistance of the insulation to the existing thermal resistance, and convert back to the new U-value.

3.5.2.3 U-values – Complex Structures

The calculation of U-values for complicated structures, including composite structures made of multiple materials in parallel, is beyond the scope of this Guide. If needed, reference should be made to Section A3 of CIBSE's *Guide A: Environmental Design*, where the subject is fully covered. The 'proportional area method' is currently required by Approved Document L (or the regional equivalent, see Table 1.1) for dealing with certain types of constructions. Proposals for amending the energy-efficiency provisions in Approved Document L, which are currently under consultation, recommend the 'combined method' specified in the current editions of BS EN ISO 13370:2017 and Section A3 of CIBSE's *Guide A*.

3.5.2.4 Ground Floor U-values

The calculation of U-values for ground floors is complex and cannot be achieved in the same way as for other structural components (see BS EN ISO 13370:2017), as the thermal transmission varies according with the shape of the room and the proportion of exposed edge to the total floor area. For regular shaped floors, see Tables 3.21 to 3.26 in section 3.8.2. For irregular shaped floors, either the formula provided in Section A3 of CIBSE's *Guide A: Environmental Design* or the following simplified version from the Building Research Establishment (BRE) Information Paper IP 3/90 (*U-value of Ground Floors: Application to Building Regulations*) can be used:

$$U = 0.05 + [1.65 \times (P/A)] - [0.6 \times (P/A)^2] \qquad \text{(Equation 5)}$$

where

    U is the uninsulated irregular floor U-value in W/m² K
    P is the length of the exposed perimeter in m
    A is the area of the floor in m².

Note: Calculate the numbers inside the brackets first, starting with those inside the innermost brackets, then work outwards.

Note: Equation 5 applies to all types of floor construction, including slab-on-ground and suspended floors. Unheated spaces outside the insulated fabric, such as attached garages or porches, should be treated as if they are not present when determining P and A.

Note: The U-value calculated using Equation 5 is for an uninsulated floor. If insulation is present, the calculated U-value should be converted to a resistance and treated as an element in a composite construction; as described in section 3.5.2.2.

> **Example**: Figure 3.4 shows the floor plan of a room with an irregular shape. It has an exposed perimeter (P) of 10.5 m (9 m external, 1.5 m internal, unheated garage). It has an area (A) of 15.5 m² (dividing the floor area into two smaller rectangles, rectangle one is 2 m × 4 m = 8 m², rectangle two is 5 m × 1.5 m = 7.5 m²; therefore the total floor area is 8 + 7.5 = 15.5 m²). The U-value of the uninsulated floor is therefore:
>
> $U = 0.05 + [1.65 \times (10.5/15.5)] - [0.6 \times (10.5/15.5)^2]$
> $= 0.05 + [1.65 \times 0.7] - [0.6 \times 0.7^2]$
> $= 0.05 + [1.65 \times 0.68] - [0.6 \times 0.45]$
> $= 0.05 + 1.12 - 0.27$
> $= 0.9$ W/m² K

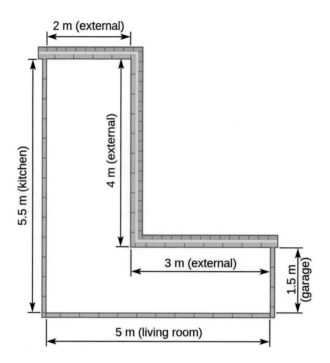

Figure 3.4 Floor plan of an irregular shape room

Example: If the floor in the above example has 50 mm of expanded polystyrene beneath its concrete slab (λ = 0.035 W/m K, from Table 3.12), the U-value will change from 0.9 to 0.39 W/m² K.

Uninsulated floor resistance = 1/0.9 = 1.11 m² K/W

Layer	Calculation	Resistance, R (m² K/W)
Complex shaped floor slab (concrete)		1.11
Insulation (expanded polystyrene)	0.05/0.035	1.43
	Total resistance (R)	2.54

The insulated U-value of construction = 1/2.54 = 0.39 W/m² K

3.5.2.5 Sloped Roof Windows

Unless specified, the U-values such as those for windows given in Table 3.20 (see section 3.8.2) are for situations when the glass is vertical. If the glass is to be installed in a roof, a correction needs to be made to compensate for the extra heat that will be conducted through it. Table 3.3 shows suggested corrections for double-glazed windows angled from horizontal to vertical; if available, the manufacturer's data should be used in preference.

Example: A double-glazed roof window with a wooden frame, low-E glass and argon fill is installed at an angle of 52°. If vertical it would have a U-value of 2.1 W/m² K (from Table 3.20). The U-value correction for the actual angle is +0.3 W/m² K (from Table 3.3). Therefore, the U-value for the window as installed is 2.4 W/m² K (= 2.1 + 0.3)

Table 3.3 U-value adjustments for windows (twin skin or double glazed) on a slope

Slope of roof window	U-value adjustment (W/m²K)
70° or more (treat as vertical)	0.0
<70° and >60°	+0.2
<60° and >40°	+0.3
<40° and >20°	+0.4
<20° (treat as horizontal)	+0.5

3.5.2.6 Thermal Bridging

A thermal bridge (sometimes called a 'cold bridge') is a detail of a building's construction that allows heat to pass through significantly more easily than through the surrounding materials. This is typically where there is either a break in the insulation, less insulation or the insulation is penetrated by an element with a higher thermal conductivity, such as wall ties, junctions in materials, or lintels. This can lead to a higher heat loss at this point than the calculated value.

Global warming and evolutionary technological progress are the primary driving forces behind progressive design changes in buildings, and have added unavoidable complexity to existing and long-established design processes. The estimation of thermal bridges is one such area that has been affected.

The current edition of BS EN 12831, which gives the method for designing the heat load, together with its UK National Annex, provides extensive information for determining the heat loss in both residential and commercial buildings. Information is also given in CIBSE's *Guide A: Environmental Design* and publications such as BRE's publication BR 497 (*Conventions for Calculating Linear Thermal Transmittance and Temperature Factors*).

There are a few main complications with thermal bridging:

- The level of impact of thermal bridges depends strongly on the quality and attention to detail of the building construction.
- The level of impact of thermal bridges is often proportional to the building's insulation levels. Therefore, where fabric heat losses are reduced, such as in new builds and ultra-low-energy buildings, the previously insignificant losses via thermal bridges become very important.
- Thermal bridges are usually hidden within the construction and cannot be identified post-construction without the aid of tools such as a thermal imaging camera.

As such, it is recognised that thermal bridges should only be determined by the architect, whose detailing must be provided before design work continues.

For existing buildings where this is not possible, the following simplified standard method from BS EN 12831 can be used to allow for thermal bridging. Table 3.4 shows additional thermal transmittance values for various types of building. The closest type of building to that being considered should be chosen, and the additional thermal transmittance value should then be added to all the U-values used in the calculation of fabric heat loss (see sections 3.4.2 and 3.5.2).

Table 3.4 Thermal bridging additions

Type of construction	Additional thermal transmittance (W/m² K)
Buildings built with a high level of heat insulation (over and above current national standards) and which implement minimisation of thermal bridging practices that exceed generally recognised rules of practice	0.02
Buildings built to current national standards and in compliance with generally recognised rules of practice regarding the minimisation of thermal bridges	0.05
Buildings with exterior wall insulation broken by solid ceilings (e.g. reinforced concrete)	0.15
All other buildings	0.1

Example: A building built in 2003 to the building regulations in force at the time has a filled twin-brick skin external cavity wall, with an internal skin of 12 mm plasterboard on dot and dab. The U-value for this wall given in Table 3.14 is 0.53 W/m² K. Allowing for thermal bridging, the U-value used in the calculation of the fabric heat loss for this wall would therefore be:

0.53 + 0.1 = 0.63 W/m² K

3.5.3 Design Temperatures

As discussed above, the rate at which heat is lost via both the fabric and ventilation is driven by the temperature differential between the inside of the room under consideration and the space where the heat is escaping to. Correct selection of design temperatures is key to the accuracy of the calculation of ventilation heat loss using Equation 1 (section 3.4.1) and fabric heat loss using Equation 2 (section 3.4.2). Consideration therefore needs to be given to:

- the temperature the heating system is designed to heat the space under consideration up to
- how high ceilings will affect the indoor design temperature
- the worst-case outdoor temperature that the system will need to achieve the design indoor temperature
- the temperature of the ground, adjoining rooms (those in the same as well as in adjoining properties), and how exposed the building is will all affect the outdoor design temperature used

What temperature we heat an indoor space to will depend on the thermal comfort requirements of the occupants of that space. Therefore, we will first discuss the definition of thermal comfort.

3.5.3.1 Thermal Comfort

Thermal comfort requirements are very individual to a person. In simple terms, it is a balance between the heat our bodies naturally produce through processes such as metabolising food and movement, and the heat received from or lost to the space around us. If our bodies are not required to take actions to preserve or lose heat (sweating, diverting blood to or from our extremities, shivering, etc.), they feel thermally comfortable, or are in a state of thermal neutrality. If this is not the case, and the hypothalamus in our brains is required to actively maintain our body's core temperature, the level of action required is proportional to the level of uncomfortableness that we feel.

Many factors affect thermal comfort, but the main six are:

- Air temperature – How much heat our body can gain from, or how fast we lose heat to, the air that surrounds us.
- Radiant temperature – How much heat we gain from the radiant energy within the space we are occupying (i.e. long wave solar infrared, as well as the shorter wave radiation emitted from all surfaces).
- Humidity – How much moisture there is in the air, and how much that contributes to speeding up heat gains from the air, or detracts from our ability to lose heat by mechanisms like sweating.
- Air speed – How fast the air is moving around us and thus removing the insulating boundary layer of air that surrounds us.
- Clothing level – How insulating the clothes we are wearing are.
- Metabolic rate – How much heat our body is naturally producing that is not under the control of the hypothalamus. This is heat produced by activities such as digesting food and muscle repair after exercise, along with the general background exothermic chemical reactions within our body's cells (e.g. due to movement and maintaining our body's stasis). The level of heat produced will differ between individuals due to age, gender, whether menstruating, body composition, etc.

The first four of these parameters can be measured and controlled to a certain extent, but the last two are the most important when it comes to an individual's specific thermal comfort requirements, and are also the hardest to measure. Providing a level of comfort that is acceptable to everybody is therefore near impossible, but we can take steps to maximise the number of people who will be comfortable and minimise the discomfort to others.

It should be noted that providing zoning and localised occupant-controlled controls is important, and this is discussed further in section 5.11.5.

Two approaches to tackling this complex situation are provided in BS EN 16798–1:2019:

- The constant comfort approach (BS EN ISO 7730: 2005), which is specified for mechanically heated and ventilated buildings, and will therefore be the method used here.
- The adaptive thermal comfort approach, which is currently only specified for naturally ventilated buildings, and is therefore outside the scope of this Guide. Some of the principles of this approach, such as empowering building occupants to take more ownership of their thermal comfort and drifting indoor temperatures in line with outdoor temperatures, should be encouraged for their contribution to energy-use reduction and potential health benefits.

BS EN ISO 7730:2005 uses an index called the 'operative temperature' as a measure of thermal comfort. The operative temperature is assumed to be made up of a ratio of 50% indoor air temperature plus 50% indoor radiant temperature. Target ranges of the operative temperature can be calculated using assumed values for the thermal comfort components occupant metabolic rate (MET), clothing level (Clo), air humidity (RH) and air speed (Va). Typical ranges for the operative temperature and component values are listed in Table 3.5. Given the assumptions in the footnote to the table, and for a standard domestic property, an appropriate level of thermal comfort can be provided by maintaining the air temperature within the ranges of the operative temperature given in the table. However, it should be remembered that these assumptions are correct only for a specific situation. Also, it is acknowledged that the majority of domestic heating control systems are only able to sense air temperature, but for situations where the above ratio is not likely to be correct (spaces with highly intermittent heating, large amounts of solar gain or a primarily radiant heat source), you may want to consider having a more specialist control system that allows the sensing of radiant temperature instead or as well as air temperature.

Table 3.5 Comfort criteria range (adapted from Table 1.5 in CIBSE's *Guide A: Environmental Design*)

Dwellings	Operative temperature (°C)	Occupant metabolic rate (MET)	Clothing level (Clo)	Air supply ventilation (l/s)
Bathrooms	20–22	1.2	0.25	15
Bedrooms	17–19	0.9	2.5	>0.4
Halls and Landings	19–24	1.8	0.75	N/A
Kitchens	17–19	1.6	1.0	60
Living rooms	21–23	1.1	1.0	>0.4
Sanitary accommodation	19–21	1.4	1.0	6

Note: 1.0 MET corresponds to sedentary; relative humidity 40–60%; air speed <0.15 m/s, clothing (1 Clo) includes a jumper, shirt, vest, underwear, trousers, socks and shoes (bedroom MET and Clo values are sleep settings).

3.5.3.2 Indoor Design Temperatures

There are two indoor temperatures that need to be considered as part of a heating system: the design temperature and the operational temperature. As this Guide focuses on the design of the heating system, the design indoor temperature will be the main point of discussion.

The operational temperature should not be overlooked though, as it is critical to achieving comfortable and energy-efficient operation of the heating system. It is used for the purposes of the setting of controls, and the day to day operation of the system. Consideration needs to be given to the thermal comfort considerations as well as the operative temperature ranges discussed above, in addition to the preferences of the household.

When designing a heating system, we need to allow for a realistic worst-case scenario to ensure the heating system is sufficiently sized to maintain a comfortable indoor temperature. We also need to ensure that the system is not significantly oversized, as this would also lead to inefficient operation. BS EN 12831 and its UK National Annex contain a range of design temperatures for different rooms.

For a common perspective, all new (post-2006), well-insulated buildings should use a design temperature of 21°C throughout, except for 22°C in bathrooms.

For existing buildings that are not well insulated, the room design temperatures in Table 3.6 should be used, to offset any economic disadvantage of using higher values.

Where higher room temperatures are required, for example for the elderly or infirm, a design temperature of 23°C is recommended for those rooms.

Example: The calculation of the heat loss for a study should use 21°C as the indoor design temperature.

Table 3.6 Indoor design temperatures

Room	Temperature (°C)	Room	Temperature (°C)	Room	Temperature (°C)
Lounge/sitting room	21	Cloakroom/WC	18	Internal room or corridor	18
Living room	21	Toilet	18	Bedroom/study	21
Breakfast room	21	Utility room	18	Landing	18
Dining room	21	Study	21	Bathroom	22
Kitchen	18	Games room	21	Shower room	22
Family/breakfast room	21	Bedroom	18	Dressing room	18
Hall	18	Bedroom, including en suite bathroom	21	Store room	18

High ceilings

Rooms with unusually high ceilings often need additional heat to compensate for the stratification of warmer air at the higher level. Figure 3.5 shows the recommended high ceiling factors that should be added to the basic heat losses (fabric and ventilation) for rooms heated by panel radiators (those heated with underfloor heating systems should not use this correction).

Example: A double-height room (floor-to-ceiling height 5.5 m) with a calculated basic heat loss of 2,300 W will have a high ceiling factor of 1.05. Allowing for the extra height, the room heat loss will therefore be 2300 × 1.05 = 2,415 W, a 5% increase.

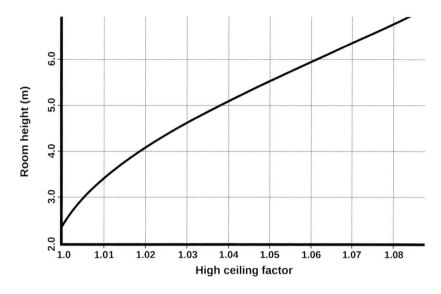

Figure 3.5 Addition to room heat loss to compensate for high ceilings

3.5.3.3 Outdoor Design Temperatures – UK

As for indoor temperature, it is important to select a design outdoor temperature that will ensure the system is able to provide a reasonable level of comfort in any realistic worst-case conditions, while not oversizing the system to the point of inefficiency.

Outdoor design temperatures for the latitude of the property's location should be used from Table 3.7, unless otherwise known. Figure 3.6 can be used to identify the latitude of the property.

Table 3.7 Typical winter external design temperatures for sites in the British Isles up to 50 m above sea level

Region	Latitude (see Figure 3.6)	Outdoor design temperature (winter minimum) (°C)	Ground reference temperature (winter mean) (°C)
Scotland and Islands	56–60°N	−5	+5.5
Northern England, Northern Ireland	54–56°N	−4	+6.0
Midlands, Wales, Republic of Ireland	52–54°N	−3	+6.5
London, south-west England	51–52°N	−2	+7.0
Southern England	50–51°N	−1	+7.5

Note: Specific locations can be found in Section 2 of CIBSE's *Guide A: Environmental Design*, and in the UK National Annex of BS EN 12831.

Note: Consideration should also be given to the client's requirements and any building warranty provisions (e.g. National House Building Council (NHBC)), as these may conflict with the figures given in the Table 3.7.

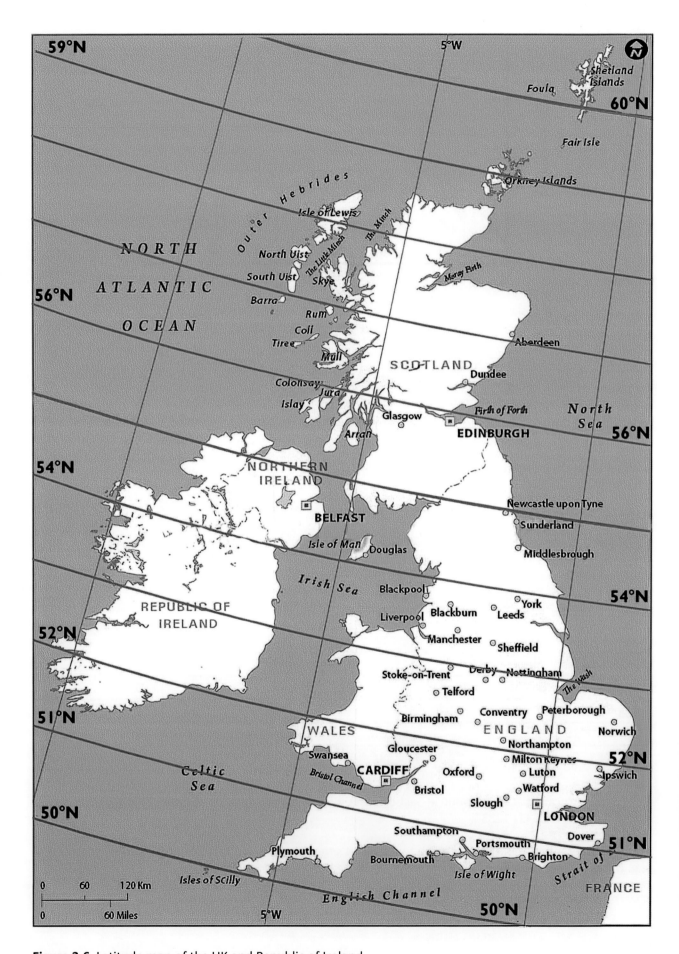

Figure 3.6 Latitude map of the UK and Republic of Ireland

In addition, with regard to the location of the property, it is recommended that account is taken of altitude, proximity to water and whether the location is susceptible to increased wind speed conditions, such as those found in rural and coastal parts of the British Isles. To account for altitude, the outdoor design temperature used should be lowered by 0.3°C for every additional 50 m, above sea level. For sites that are severely exposed to adverse weather conditions (e.g. located in reasonable proximity to the coast, a river or a steep cliff), a further 1°C lowering of the external design temperature is recommended.

> **Example**: A dwelling is located in Wales, in an exposed location near the coast, and is 125 m above sea level. The outdoor design temperature is −4.6°C and is compiled as follows:
>
> - Step 1 – From Table 3.7 (Midlands, Wales, Republic of Ireland), which gives values for locations up to 50 m above sea level, the outdoor design temperature is −3°C.
> - Step 2 – For an additional 50 m over what was allowed for in step 1 (bringing the altitude up to 100 m), the outdoor design temperature is lowered by a further 0.3°C, to give −3.3°C.
> - Step 3 – For an additional 50 m over what was allowed for in step 2 (bringing the altitude up to 150 m), the outdoor design temperature is lowered by a further 0.3°C, to give −3.6°C.
> - Step 4 – The location is exposed, therefore the outdoor design temperature is lowered by a further 1.0°C, to give −4.6°C.

Ground temperature

Ground temperature has an effect on the amount of heat lost from the ground floor to the earth the building is built upon, rather than the air surrounding it. The temperature of the earth under the ground floor and its surroundings, and basements, may be assumed to be equal to the ground reference temperature for the latitude of the property. Values of the ground reference temperature are given in Table 3.7, and should be used instead of the outdoor design temperature for heat loss calculations for elements in a floor or basement.

> **Example**: For a dwelling in Bristol, +7.0°C should be used as the outdoor temperature for ground floor heat loss calculations.

Adjoining properties and unheated spaces

The heat loss calculations for rooms in flats, semi-detached and terraced houses should assume that the adjoining property is unheated, even when it is known that a heating system is installed. This will then ensure that the design temperatures will be achieved when the adjoining building is unoccupied.

Under normal conditions, unheated adjoining properties will be at a temperature considerably above the outside design temperature. In the absence of specific information, the temperature in an adjoining property can be taken to be about the same as the mean UK average temperature of 10°C.

The same principle should be applied if adjoining room is an unheated space, such as a utility room or store cupboard.

> **Example**: A living room heated to 21°C would have a temperature difference of 11°C (= 21 − 10°C) across the party wall to an adjoining unheated property.

> The U-value of the party wall should be used as given in the tables in section 3.8.2 or as calculated.

Adjoining rooms

Heat transfer between rooms should be disregarded if the same indoor design temperature is used for all rooms.

For adjoining rooms where the indoor design temperature is different, T_{in} and T_{out} in Equation 2 (see section 3.4.2) will take the following form: T_{in} will be the indoor design temperature of the room being analysed, and T_{out} will be the indoor design temperature of the room that is adjoining.

> **Example 1**: For a wall adjoining a living room and a dining room for a property where the same indoor design temperature is used for all rooms, the heat loss through the wall would be 0 W, as both sides will have the same indoor design temperature (21°C).

> **Example 2**: For a wall adjoining a living room with an indoor design temperature of 21°C and a bathroom with an indoor design temperature of 22°C, the heat loss through the wall would be negative, as the temperature difference ($T_{in} - T_{out}$) is −1°C, i.e. heat is flowing into the living room.

3.5.4 Ventilation

In addition to the temperature differential, another key parameter in ventilation heat loss (Equation 1 in section 3.4.1) is the number of air changes per hour for the room. Ventilation may be unwanted infiltration via gaps and cracks in the structure, or by controlled mechanical ventilation; both types will result in heat loss. Depending on the age, level of construction, airtightness and ventilation strategy of the building, the ventilation heat loss may be 50% or more of the total heat loss, particularly in older more draughty buildings. As discussed in section 1.7, there are a number of elements to building ventilation that need to be considered when calculating the ventilation heat loss. The principal considerations are:

- air changes per hour due the airtightness of the structure
- fan duty selection
- whole-house mechanical ventilation
- open and closed appliances, chimneys and flues.

These principles are discussed further below.

3.5.4.1 Air Changes per Hour
Table 3.8 shows recommended air change rates for use in calculating design heat loads.

All values, except category C (New Buildings – restricted infiltration), are chosen to reflect reasonable worst-case conditions where extract fans may be in use, or windows are open, rather than long term averages. Category C is based on the SAP 2012 prescription where the 'whole building' infiltration description is applied to individual rooms.

Additional allowances for extract fan operation may be included at the designer's discretion and preferably with the user's agreement if possible.

Note: Consideration should also be given to the client's requirements and any building warranty provisions (e.g. NHBC), as these may conflict with the figures given in Table 3.8.

Note: For buildings where extra attention has been given to reducing ventilation losses, the values given in Table 3.8 may result to an oversized heating system. In these situations, it is recommended to seek specialist advice.

> **Example**: A study in a building built in 2002 to the minimum regulations at the time but no greater (double glazing and regulatory minimum insulation), and with no additional mechanical extraction, would have an expected 1.5 ACH.

Table 3.8 Recommended room design number of air changes per hour

Room	Category			Room	Category		
	A	B	C		A	B	C
Lounge/sitting room	1.5[†]	1.0[†]	0.5	Games room	1.5	1.0	0.5
Living room	1.5[†]	1.0[†]	0.5	Bedroom	1.0	1.0	0.5
Breakfast room	1.5	1.0	0.5	Bedsitting room	1.5	1.0	0.5
Dining room	1.5	1.0	0.5	Bedroom, including en suite bathroom	2.0	1.5	1.0
Kitchen	2.0*	1.5*	0.5*	Internal room or corridor	0.0	0.0	0.0
Family/breakfast room	2.0*	1.5*	0.5*	Bedroom/study	1.5	1.5	0.5
Hall	2.0	1.0	0.5	Landing	2.0	1.0	0.5
Cloakroom/WC	2.0*	1.5*	1.5*	Bathroom	3.0*	1.5*	0.5*
Toilet	3.0*	1.5*	1.5*	Shower room	3.0*	1.5*	0.5*
Utility room	3.0*	2.0*	0.5*	Dressing room	1.5	1.0	0.5
Study	1.5	1.5	0.5	Store room	1.0	0.5	0.5

Note:

Category A: Air change rates for older existing buildings (pre-2000). Those with several chimneys and/or subject to preservation orders may require greater infiltration allowance than shown above.

Category B: Air change rates for modern buildings (2000 or later) with double glazing and regulatory minimum insulation.

Category C: New (or existing) buildings constructed after 2006 and complying with all current building regulations.

*Where mechanical extract ventilation is to be installed in a room and the extract volume exceeds the natural infiltration, it is advisable to make due allowance for the air extracted from any connecting room or corridor.

[†]Where a room contains an open fire or chimney, due ventilation allowance must be made. See section 3.5.4.4.

3.5.4.2 Fan Duty Selection

The possibility exists for the performance of any fan or cooker hood, even when used intermittently, to exceed the design air change rate of the room, and thereby increase the amount of heat required to meet the design temperature. This, however, can usually be disregarded, as the temperature gains from the cooking appliances or bathing water will offset the problem. Careful consideration should, however, be given to the selection of fan duties, to ensure that larger volumes of air than necessary are not extracted.

3.5.4.3 Whole-House Mechanical Ventilation

The ventilation requirements laid out in the Building Regulations 2010 may also be met through the provision of whole-house mechanical ventilation (see section 1.7.1.3). This type of ventilation may include heat recovery, which typically reduces the ventilation heat load by at least 50%. Ducts and fans should be sized to ensure that the cost of the electricity consumption of the intake and exhaust fans is much less than the cost for recovered heat. This is beyond the scope of this Guide, and further advice should be sought from a specialist.

3.5.4.4 Open and closed appliances, chimneys and flues

Open appliances

Where appliances with open flues are installed in a room (e.g. an open fire) the air change rate should be increased to allow for the movement of air into the chimney. Table 3.9 shows the rates for rooms with open-fire flues up to 40,000 mm² (= 200 × 200 mm). Air change rates will approximately double when the open fire is in use. Very tall chimneys, such as found in a multi-storey house, produce a very strong draught, and a correspondingly high ventilation rate.

While outside the scope of this Guide, the absence of air infiltration due to a lack of permeability or a combustion-air inlet will require the designer to make the client aware of the potential risk of incomplete combustion in the appliance, poor indoor air quality and health factors. These risks should be made clear to the client, along with suitable recommendations (e.g. to seek the advice of a HETAS-approved installer).

Table 3.9 Ventilation arising from open chimneys and flues

Room volume (m³)	Throat restrictor fitted to flue	Air changes per hour
Up to 40	No	5
Up to 40	Yes	3
Up to 70	No	4
Up to 70	Yes	2

Very old buildings with numerous chimneys and open fires have experienced excessive and often uncomfortable infiltration in the past, but this is unlikely to continue if energy is to be conserved. Consequently, a strategy is required to reduce excessive ventilation and the resulting heat loss; in such cases, designers will need to be more diligent.

> **Example**: The heat loss calculation for a 42 m² living room with an throat restrictor equipped open fire, in a property built in 1963, would use an air change rate of 3.5 ACH (1.5 ACH for a Category A living room (Table 3.8), and 2 ACH for an open chimney with a throat restrictor in a room between 40 and 70 m³ in volume (Table 3.9)) for its ventilation heat loss.

Closed appliances

For closed appliances (e.g. a wood-burning stove that only operates with the door closed), no additional allowance needs to be made for heat loss through the flue. The additional heat lost via the appliance's combustion-air inlet when the appliance is not alight is insignificant, and the heat gain when it is alight will more than compensate.

HETAS and section 1.7.1.4 give further information on combustion air recommendations.

It should be noted that it is often the case that solid-fuel and wood-burning appliances may be found in a room in which no combustion-air inlet has been installed. This is due to the common belief that a 5 kW or below appliance does not require one. In fact, this is only true when the building fabrics air permeability is greater than 5 m³/h m². This may be shown via testing, or assumed if the building was built before 2008, but only if it has had no improvement works which will reduce the air permeability (double glazing, rendering, etc.).

As for open appliances, the absence of air infiltration due to a lack of permeability or fresh-air inlet grills can have significant health implications. While outside the scope of this Guide, if a lack of combustion air for the appliance is identified, the client should be made aware of the situation and be provided with suitable recommendations (e.g. to seek the advice of a HETAS-approved installer).

3.5.5 Intermittent Heating

Where spaces are heated intermittently, the heating power required to get the space up to the desired temperature from the setback temperature in an acceptable time may be significantly greater than the calculated peak heat loss of the space. While slightly oversizing a heating system is usually not a problem, significantly oversizing it to achieve a rapid reheat time may lead to significantly higher energy consumption overall. This is dependent on the heat source, but most combustion appliances will be run inefficiently once the target temperature is reached due to low load.

It is therefore recommended that the approximate reheat time of the space is calculated using the factors given in Table 3.10. This can then be compared to the ventilation and fabric heat loss for the room calculated using Equation 1 (section 3.4.1) and Equation 2 (section 3.4.2) to help decide if the system needs to be oversized for that space to achieve a satisfactory reheat time. Heating-up power depends on several factors, such as the construction of the building and the climatic conditions, but the approximations presented in Table 3.10 assume:

- a high standard of thermal insulation (near to current or building regulation requirements or above)
- a small room height (average ceiling height ≤3.5 m)
- a temperature drop not greater than 5°C (the difference between the desired temperature and the setback temperature)
- a period of disuse less than 11 hours.

Situations beyond these assumptions are outside the scope of this Guide. For such cases, BS EN 12831 contains further details of this calculation, and expert advice should be sought.

The values in Table 3.10 should be used to calculate the expected reheat time for the space. If the expected reheat time is unacceptable to the client, then consideration should be given to the level of insulation in the space, or the system may be slightly oversized. In the latter case, it is recommended that the system is only oversized by 10–15% (intermittent heating factor 1.1–1.15), and as a maximum by 20% (intermittent heating factor 1.2).

Note: Specialist advice should be sought before oversizing heat pumps using this method.

Table 3.10 Reheat factors for intermittent heating (based on BS EN 12831)

		Reheat factor (W/m² of floor area)							
Period of disuse*		Up to 8 hours				Up to 11 hours			
Building air permeability†		Low		High		Low		High	
Building mass‡		Low	High	Low	High	Low	High	Low	High
Reheat time (h)§	0.5	63	16	74	26	76	27	83	41
	1	34	10	43	16	42	20	47	30
	2	14	3	21	8	21	11	25	19
	3	5	–¶	10	2	11	6	14	12
	4	–¶	–¶	3	–¶	6	4	8	8
	6	–¶	–¶	–¶	–¶	2	1	3	3
	12	–¶	–¶	–¶	–¶	–¶	–¶	–¶	–¶

Note:

*The time for which the desired internal space temperature will be the setback temperature. This period includes the time when the building is cooling down at the start and heating back up at the end. This is typically 8 hours for overnight only or 11 hours for a workday. Shorter periods of disuse will result in shorter reheat times.

†Category C building, Low; and Category A or B building, High (see section 3.5.4.1).

‡This is found by measurement or calculation. If the walls are mainly bare or plastered brick, or stone, a high mass should be assumed. If the walls are internally insulated or plaster boarded, a low mass should be assumed.

§The approximate time for the space to go from the setback temperature to the desired internal temperature.

¶ The reheat factor is low enough not to be a concern.

Example: A living room has a floor area of 13 m², a ceiling height of 2.4 m, primarily brick walls with internal dot-and-dab insulated plaster board (low mass), and is in a building built before 2000 (Category A). The house is unoccupied during the day while the occupants are at work, and the thermostat is set to the setback temperature during this period (period of disuse up to 11 hours). The heat loss calculation for the space shows a total heat loss of 526 W. Table 3.11 shows the expected reheat times for the space.

A heating system sized to the calculated total heat loss will therefore be sufficient to reheat the space in 1–2 hours. Therefore, the room heating controller should be set to raise the internal temperature to the desired temperature 1–2 hours before occupancy. If this is not acceptable to the client, a heating system oversized by 20% (design total heat loss 631 W) should reheat the space in less than 1 hour. However, the client should be advised that doing this will result in a more expensive heating system, may lower its efficiency during normal operation, and the reheat time for shorter periods of disuse will be less than that calculated here.

Table 3.11 Reheat times for the space in the worked example

Reheat time (h)	Reheat factor	Heat-up power (W)
0.5	83	1079
1	47	611
2	25	325
3	14	182
4	8	104
6	3	39

3.6 Annual Energy Estimation

Customers may enquire about the annual running cost for the heating and hot water system, and it is possible to calculate this by making reasonable assumptions about hours of use, internal and external temperatures, heat generator efficiency, heating controls, fuel prices and other factors. This is not a simple calculation though, and the methods are not explained here. In principle, the heating requirement can be estimated from degree-day records for the area in which the dwelling is located, but the calculation is vulnerable to large errors. For more information about using degree-day data, see CIBSE TM41 (*Degree Days: Theory and Application*).

The UK government's Standard Assessment Procedure for Energy Rating of Dwellings (SAP) calculates the annual energy consumption and costs and carbon dioxide (CO_2) emissions. It is described briefly in section 1.5.5. Some Energy Performance Certificates show the annual heat demand for heating and hot water in kW h per year, under the heading 'Your home's heat demand'. The figures for space and water heating can be added, then divided by an approximate system efficiency (say 90% for systems with new gas boilers) to give the delivered energy in kW h per year. This value is multiplied by the price of the heating fuel to give an estimate of annual running costs. As always, the estimate should be treated with caution, as it is affected by the behaviour of the occupants with regard to the hours of heating, the internal and external temperatures, the amount of hot water used and other factors.

3.7 Heat Loss Procedures

Heat losses are calculated on a room-by-room basis so that the heat output required in each room can be estimated in order for the radiators to be sized accordingly. Heat loss is calculated according to the principles set out above. This may be conveniently done using worksheets, which provide a framework for ensuring that all heat losses are treated systematically.

Worksheet A – Heat Losses, which can be found in section 3.8.3, may be used to make the necessary calculations for a room. Step by step instructions for filling in Worksheet A can be found in section 3.8.4.

3.8 System Design (Heat Loss) – Appendix

3.8.1 Thermal Conductivity Table

Table 3.12 Thermal conductivity (k-factor) for common building materials

Element	Material	Density (kg/m³)	k-factor (W/m K)
Walls	Asbestos cement sheet	700	0.360
	Autoclaved aerated concrete block	600	0.180
	Brickwork (inner leaf)	1,700	0.620
	Brickwork (outer leaf)	1,700	0.840
	Concrete (lightweight)	1,200	0.380
	Concrete (medium density)	1,800	1.130
	Concrete (dense)	2,100	1.400
	Concrete (high density)	2,400	1.930
	Concrete block (heavyweight)	2,300	1.630
	Concrete block (lightweight)	600	0.190
	Concrete block (medium weight)	1,400	0.510
	Fibreboard	300	0.060
	Gypsum	600	0.180
	Lightweight aggregate concrete block	1,400	0.570
	Limestone (soft)	1,800	1.100
	Limestone (hard)	2,200	1.700
	Mortar (exposed)	1,750	0.940
	Mortar (protected)	1,750	0.880
	Reinforced concrete (1% steel)	2,300	2.300
	Reinforced concrete (2% steel)	2,400	2.500
	Sandstone	2,600	2.300
	Stone (artificial)	1,750	1.300
	Stone (granite)	2,640	2.930
	Tile hanging	1,900	0.840
	Timber (hardwood)	700	0.180
	Timber (softwood, plywood, chipboard)	500	0.130

Contd

Table 3.12 contd Thermal conductivity (k-factor) for common building materials

Element	Material	Density (kg/m³)	k-factor (W/m K)
Surface finishes	External rendering	1,300	0.570
	Fibreboard	400	0.100
	Plaster (dense)	1,300	0.570
	Plaster (lightweight)	600	0.180
	Plasterboard	900	0.250
	Tiles (ceramic)	2,300	1.300
Roofs	Aerated concrete slab	500	0.160
	Asphalt	1,700	0.500
	Asphalt	2,100	0.700
	Felt/bitumen layers	1,100	0.230
	Felt/bitumen layers	1,700	0.500
	Screed (lightweight)	1,200	0.410
	Stone chippings	1,800	0.960
	Tiles (clay)	2,000	1.000
	Tiles (concrete)	2,100	1.500
	Wood wool slab	500	0.100
Floors	Cast concrete	2,000	1.350
	Metal tray (steel)	7,800	50.000
	Screed (concrete)	1,950	1.200
	Timber (softwood, plywood, chipboard)	500	0.130
	Timber (hardwood)	700	0.180
	Timber flooring	650	0.140
	Wood blocks	650	0.140
Insulation	Expanded polystyrene slab	15	0.040
	Expanded polystyrene slab	25	0.035
	Glass fibre quilt	12	0.040
	Glass fibre slab	25	0.035
	Mineral fibre slab	30	0.035
	Mineral wool batt	25	0.038
	Mineral wool quilt	12	0.042
	Phenolic foam	30	0.040
	Phenolic foam board	30	0.025
	Polyurethane board	30	0.025
	Urea formaldehyde foam	10	0.040

Note:

If available, certified test values from manufacturer's data should be used in preference to those in the table.

k-factor = λ value.

3.8.2 U-value Tables

Table 3.13 External walls – solid

		U-value (W/m² K)
Solid brick wall, dense plaster		
	102 mm brick, plaster	3.10
	228 mm brick, plaster	2.11
	343 mm brick, plaster	1.64
Solid brick wall, insulated externally		
	19 mm render, 75 mm foam board, 102 mm brick, plaster	0.26
	19 mm render, 75 mm foam board, 228 mm brick, plaster	0.25
	19 mm render, 75 mm foam board, 343 mm brick, plaster	0.24
Solid brick wall, insulated internally		
	102 mm brick, 75 mm foam board, 12.5 mm plasterboard	0.30
	228 mm brick, 75 mm foam board, 12.5 mm plasterboard	0.29
	343 mm brick, 75 mm foam board, 12.5 mm plasterboard	0.28
Solid stone wall, unplastered		
	305 mm (12 in.) stone	2.41
	457 mm (18 in.) stone	1.89
	610 mm (24 in.) stone	1.54
Solid stone wall, insulated internally		
	305 mm stone, 100 mm mineral wool, plasterboard on battens	0.30
	457 mm stone, 100 mm mineral wool, plasterboard on battens	0.31
	610 mm stone, 100 mm mineral wool, plasterboard on battens	0.30
Solid concrete wall, dense plaster		
	102 mm concrete, plaster	3.51
	152 mm concrete, plaster	3.12
	204 mm concrete, plaster	2.80
	254 mm concrete, plaster	2.54
Solid concrete wall insulated externally, dense plaster		
	19 mm render, 75 mm foam board, 102 mm concrete, plaster	0.31
	19 mm render, 75 mm foam board, 152 mm concrete, plaster	0.30
	19 mm render, 75 mm foam board, 204 mm concrete, plaster	0.30
	19 mm render, 75 mm foam board, 254 mm concrete, plaster	0.30

Table 3.14 External walls – cavity

		U-value (W/m² K)	
Cavity wall (open cavity or mineral wool slab), lightweight plaster		Open cavity	Mineral wool slab 50 mm
	102 mm brick, 102 mm brick, 13 mm plaster and skim	1.37	0.56
	102 mm brick, 102 mm brick, 12 mm plaster on dabs	1.21	0.53
Cavity wall, aerated block inner leaf, lightweight plaster		Inner-leaf thickness	
		100 mm	125 mm
	102 mm brick, open cavity, standard aerated block (k = 0.17), 13 mm plaster	0.87	0.77
	102 mm brick, open cavity, standard aerated block (k = 0.17), 12.5 mm plasterboard on dabs	0.80	0.72
	102 mm brick, mineral wool slab in cavity 50 mm, standard aerated block (k = 0.17), 13 mm plaster	0.45	0.42
	102 mm brick, mineral wool slab in cavity 50 mm, standard aerated block (k = 0.17), 12.5 mm plasterboard on dabs	0.43	0.41
	102 mm brick, 50 mm cavity wall bead insulation, standard aerated block (k = 0.17), 13 mm plaster	0.39	0.37
	102 mm brick, 50 mm cavity wall bead insulation, standard aerated block (k = 0.17), 12.5 mm plasterboard on dabs	0.38	0.36
Cavity wall, high-performance aerated block inner leaf, lightweight plaster or plasterboard		Inner-leaf thickness	
		100 mm	125 mm
	102 mm brick, cavity, high-performance aerated block (k = 0.11), 13 mm plaster	0.80	0.79
	102 mm brick, cavity, high-performance aerated block (k = 0.11), 12.5 mm plasterboard on dabs	0.64	0.56
	102 mm, 50 mm mineral wool slab in cavity, high-performance aerated block (k = 0.11), 13 mm plaster	0.39	0.36
	102 mm brick, 50 mm mineral wool slab in cavity, high-performance aerated block (k = 0.11), 12.5 mm plasterboard on dabs	0.38	0.35

Table 3.15 External walls – rendered externally

		U-value (W/m² K)	
Cavity wall (open cavity or mineral wool slab), lightweight plaster		Open cavity	Mineral
	19 mm render, 102 mm brick, 102 mm brick, 13 mm plaster	1.25	0.54
	19 mm render, 102 mm brick, 102 mm brick, 12.5 mm plasterboard on dabs	1.11	0.51
Cavity wall, aerated block inner leaf, lightweight plaster or plasterboard		Inner-leaf thickness	
		100 mm	125 mm
	19 mm render, 102 mm brick, cavity, standard aerated block, 13 mm plaster	0.82	0.73
	19 mm render, 102.5 mm brick, 50 mm mineral wool slab in cavity, standard aerated block, 13 mm plaster	0.44	0.41
	19 mm render, 100 mm standard aerated block, cavity, standard aerated block, 13 mm plaster	0.61	0.56
Cavity blockwork wall, inner aerated block, lightweight plaster		Inner-leaf thickness	
		100 mm	125 mm
	19 mm render, 100 mm standard aerated block, 50 mm mineral wool slab in cavity, standard aerated block, 13 mm plaster	0.37	0.35
Cavity wall, rendered, aerated block inner, lightweight plaster		Inner-leaf thickness	
		100 mm	125 mm
	19 mm render, 100 mm standard aerated block, cavity, high-performance aerated block (k = 0.11), 13 mm plaster	0.51	0.45
	19 mm render, 100 mm standard aerated block, 50 mm mineral wool slab in cavity, high-performance aerated block (k = 0.11), 13 mm plaster	0.33	0.31
Solid wall, rendered outside, plaster inside			
	19 mm render, 215 mm high-performance aerated block (k = 0.11), 13 mm plaster	0.44	

Table 3.16 External walls – clad externally

	U-value (W/m² K)	
Cavity wall, tile clad (open cavity or mineral wool slab), lightweight plaster	Inner-leaf thickness	
	100 mm	125 mm
Tiles, airspace, 100 mm standard aerated block, cavity, standard aerated block, 13 mm plaster	0.58	0.53
Tiles, airspace, 100 mm standard aerated block, 50 mm mineral wool slab in cavity, standard aerated block, 13 mm plaster	0.36	0.34
Tiles, airspace, 100 mm standard aerated block, cavity, high-performance aerated block (k = 0.11), 13 mm plaster	0.49	0.44
Cavity wall, tile clad (open cavity or mineral wool slab), lightweight plaster	Inner-leaf thickness	
	100 mm	125 mm
Tiles, airspace, 100 mm standard aerated block, 50 mm mineral wool slab in cavity, high-performance aerated block (k = 0.11), 13 mm plaster	0.32	0.30
Solid wall, tile clad externally		
Tiles, airspace, 215 mm high-performance aerated block, 13 mm plaster	0.43	
Cavity wall, timber clad		
Shiplap boards, airspace, 100 mm standard aerated block, cavity, standard aerated block, 13 mm plaster	0.56	0.52
Shiplap boards, airspace, 100 mm standard aerated block, 50 mm mineral wool slab in cavity, standard aerated block, 13 mm plaster	0.34	0.32
Shiplap boards, airspace, 100 mm standard aerated block, cavity, high-performance aerated block, 13 mm plaster	0.45	0.41
Shiplap boards, 100 mm airspace, standard aerated block, 50 mm mineral wool slab in cavity, high-performance block, 13 mm plaster	0.31	0.29

Table 3.17 External walls – other

Brick outer timber frame wall, damp-proof membrane, plywood sheathing, studding, vapour membrane, plasterboard		U-value (W/m² K)		
		Insulation thickness		
		60 mm	80 mm	100 mm
	102.5 mm brick, cavity, membrane, 10 mm plywood, 100 mm studding with infill insulation, vapour membrane, 12.5 mm plasterboard	0.43	0.36	0.32
	Tiles, airspace, membrane, 10 mm plywood, 100 mm studding with infill insulation, vapour membrane, 12.5 mm plasterboard	0.47	0.38	0.34
	Shiplap boards, airspace, membrane, 10 mm plywood, 100 mm studding with infill insulation, vapour membrane, 12.5 mm plasterboard	0.44	0.36	0.32

Table 3.18 Internal walls – no insulation

		U-value (W/m² K)
	12.5 mm plasterboard, 75 mm studding, 12.5 mm plasterboard	1.92
	13 mm plaster, 100 mm block, cavity, 100 mm block, 13 mm plaster	1.02
	13 mm plaster, 102.5 mm brick, 13 mm plaster	1.82
	13 mm plaster, 215 mm brick, 13 mm plaster	1.37
	13 mm plaster, 100 mm breeze block, 13 mm plaster	1.43
	13 mm plaster, 100 mm standard aerated block, 13 mm plaster	1.06
	13 mm plaster, 125 mm standard aerated block, 13 mm plaster	0.93

Table 3.19 Roofs

		U-value (W/m² K)				
Flat roof, timber construction, insulation and plasterboard		Insulation thickness (mm)				
		Nil	50	100	200	300
	Chippings, 3 layers of felt, boarding, air space, insulation, 9.5 mm plasterboard	1.69	0.53	0.32	0.17	0.12
30° pitched roof with tiles						
	Slates or tiles, Sarking felt, ventilated air space, insulation between joists, 9.5 mm plasterboard	2.51	0.60	0.34	0.18	0.12
	Slates or tiles, ventilated air space, insulation between joists, 9.5 mm plasterboard	3.13	0.62	0.35	0.18	0.12
	Slates or tiles, Sarking felt, air space, insulation between rafters, 9.5 mm plasterboard	2.51	0.60	0.34	0.18	0.12

Table 3.20 Windows and doors

The U-values listed below apply to the whole window, including the frame, and assume a standard gap between panes of 12 mm

	U-value (W/m² K)
Windows with wood or PVC-U frames	
Single	4.8
Double	2.8
Double, low-E glass	2.3
Double, low-E glass, argon filled	2.1
Triple	2.1
Triple, low-E glass	1.7
Triple, low-E glass, argon filled	1.6
Windows with metal frames	
Single	5.7
Double	3.4
Double, low-E glass	2.8
Double, low-E glass, argon filled	2.6
Triple	2.6
Triple, low-E glass	2.1
Triple, low-E glass, argon filled	2.0
Doors	
Solid wooden door	3.0
Wooden door with 25% single glazing	3.7
Wooden door with 50% single glazing	4.4
Wooden door with 25% double glazing	2.9
Wooden door with 50% double glazing	2.8

Note: U-values for doors and windows are regularly available from manufacturers, and should be used over those given here when available.

Table 3.21 Solid ground floors in contact with earth – three edges exposed

Solid ground floor with *three edges exposed*, the shortest being the single exposed edge. (Use this table for square rooms.) Insulation slabs laid below screed with 25 mm edge insulation. Floor finish as above. Thermal conductivity of insulation = 0.04 W/m K.						

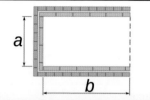

Short – length a (m)	Long – length b (m)	U-values (W/m² K) for insulation thickness (mm)				
		Nil	25	50	75	100
3	3–4	1.15	0.62	0.43	0.32	0.26
3	4–6	1.03	0.58	0.41	0.31	0.26
3	6–8	1.00	0.57	0.40	0.31	0.25
3	8–10	0.96	0.56	0.40	0.31	0.25
4	4–6	0.95	0.56	0.40	0.31	0.25
4	6–10	0.85	0.52	0.38	0.29	0.24
5	5–7	0.81	0.51	0.37	0.29	0.24
5	7–10	0.74	0.48	0.35	0.28	0.23
6	6–8	0.71	0.46	0.35	0.28	0.23
6	8–10	0.65	0.44	0.33	0.27	0.22

Example: Room = 5.0 m × 6.5 m, U-value with 50 mm insulation = 0.37 W/m² K

Solid ground floor with *three edges exposed*, the longest being the single exposed edge. Insulation as previously specified.						

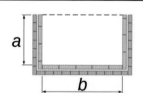

Short – length a (m)	Long – length b (m)	U-values (W/m² K) for insulation thickness (mm)				
		Nil	25	50	75	100
3	3–5	1.05	0.59	0.41	0.32	0.26
3	5–7	0.90	0.54	0.39	0.30	0.25
3	7–9	0.85	0.52	0.38	0.29	0.24
3	9–10	0.77	0.49	0.36	0.28	0.24
4	4–6	0.95	0.56	0.40	0.31	0.25
4	6–8	0.87	0.53	0.38	0.30	0.24
4	8–10	0.76	0.49	0.36	0.28	0.24
5	5–7	0.83	0.51	0.37	0.29	0.24
5	7–9	0.77	0.49	0.36	0.28	0.24
5	9–10	0.68	0.45	0.34	0.27	0.23
6	6–8	0.75	0.48	0.36	0.28	0.23
6	6–10	0.70	0.46	0.34	0.27	0.23

Example: Room = 5.0 m × 6.5 m, U-value with 50 mm insulation = 0.37 W/m² K

Table 3.22 Solid ground floors in contact with earth – two edges exposed

Solid ground floor with *two adjacent edges exposed*, insulation slabs laid below screed with 25 mm thick edge insulation. Floor finished with thermoplastic tiles or similar. Thermal conductivity of insulation = 0.04 W/m K.					

Length of exposed wall, $a + b$ (m)	U-values (W/m² K) for insulation thickness (mm)				
	Nil	25	50	75	100
5	1.02	0.58	0.41	0.31	0.26
6	0.90	0.54	0.39	0.30	0.25
7	0.82	0.51	0.37	0.29	0.24
8	0.76	0.49	0.36	0.28	0.23
9–10	0.70	0.46	0.34	0.27	0.23
10–12	0.60	0.41	0.32	0.26	0.22
12–14	0.52	0.38	0.29	0.24	0.21
14–17	0.45	0.34	0.27	0.23	0.19
17–20	0.39	0.30	0.25	0.21	0.18

Example: Room size = 6.5 × 5.0 = 11.5 m2 exposed wall, U-value with 50 mm insulation = 0.32 W/m² K

Solid ground floor with *two opposite edges exposed*. Insulation as previously specified.					

Distance between edges, a (m)	U-values (W/m² K) for insulation thickness (mm)				
	Nil	25	50	75	100
2	1.15	0.62	0.43	0.32	0.26
3	0.90	0.54	0.39	0.30	0.25
4	0.73	0.47	0.35	0.28	0.23
4–6	0.62	0.43	0.32	0.26	0.22
6–8	0.55	0.39	0.30	0.25	0.21
8–10	0.44	0.33	0.27	0.22	0.19

Example: Room width = 6.5 m, U-value with 50 mm insulation = 0.30 W/m² K

Table 3.23 Solid ground floors in contact with earth – one edge exposed

Solid ground floor with *one edge exposed*. Insulation as previously specified.					
Depth of room, *a* (m)	U-values (W/m² K) for insulation thickness (mm)				
	Nil	25	50	75	100
1.5	0.90	0.54	0.39	0.30	0.25
2	0.73	0.47	0.35	0.28	0.23
3	0.55	0.39	0.30	0.25	0.21
3–5	0.45	0.34	0.27	0.23	0.19
5–7	0.38	0.30	0.24	0.21	0.18
7–10	0.28	0.23	0.20	0.17	0.15
Example: Room width = 6.5 m, U-value with 50 mm insulation = 0.24 W/m² K					

Table 3.24 Suspended ground floors – three edges exposed

Suspended ground floor with *three edges exposed*, the shortest being the single exposed edge. (Use this table for square rooms.) Insulation slabs laid between joists on polypropylene net and covered with timber boarding. Thermal conductivity of insulation = 0.04 W/m K.						

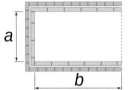

Short – length a (m)	Long – length b (m)	U-values (W/m² K) for insulation thickness (mm)				
		Nil	25	50	75	100
3	3–4	1.15	0.62	0.43	0.32	0.26
3	4–6	1.03	0.58	0.41	0.31	0.26
3	6–8	1.00	0.57	0.40	0.31	0.25
3	8–10	0.99	0.56	0.40	0.31	0.25
4	4–6	0.95	0.56	0.40	0.31	0.25
4	6–10	0.87	0.53	0.38	0.30	0.24
5	5–7	0.83	0.51	0.37	0.29	0.24
5	7–10	0.80	0.50	0.37	0.29	0.24
6	6–8	0.75	0.48	0.36	0.28	0.23
6	8–10	0.72	0.47	0.35	0.28	0.23

Example: Room size = 5.0 m × 6.5 m, U-value with 50 mm insulation = 0.37 W/m² K

Suspended ground floor with three edges exposed, the longest being the single exposed edge. (Use this table for square rooms.) Insulation as previously specified.						

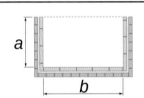

Short – length a (m)	Long – length b (m)	U-values (W/m² K) for insulation thickness (mm)				
		Nil	25	50	75	100
3	3–5	1.00	0.57	0.40	0.31	0.25
3	5–7	0.85	0.52	0.38	0.29	0.24
3	7–9	0.80	0.50	0.37	0.29	0.24
3	9–10	0.77	0.49	0.36	0.28	0.24
4	4–6	0.85	0.52	0.38	0.29	0.24
4	6–8	0.79	0.50	0.37	0.29	0.24
4	8–10	0.73	0.47	0.35	0.28	0.23
5	5–7	0.77	0.49	0.36	0.28	0.24
5	7–9	0.72	0.47	0.35	0.28	0.23
5	9–10	0.66	0.44	0.33	0.27	0.23
6	6–8	0.69	0.46	0.34	0.27	0.23
6	6–10	0.67	0.45	0.34	0.27	0.23

Example: Room size = 5.0 × 6.5 m, U-value with 50 mm insulation = 0.37 W/m² K

Table 3.25 Suspended ground floors – two edges exposed

Suspended ground floor with *two adjacent edges exposed*. Insulation slabs laid between joists on polypropylene net and covered with timber boarding. Thermal conductivity of insulation = 0.04 W/m K.					

Length of exposed wall, $a + b$ (m)	U-values (W/m² K) for insulation thickness (mm)				
	Nil	25	50	75	100
5	1.05	0.59	0.41	0.32	0.26
6	0.93	0.55	0.39	0.30	0.25
7	0.86	0.53	0.38	0.30	0.24
8	0.79	0.50	0.37	0.29	0.24
9–10	0.75	0.48	0.36	0.28	0.23
10–12	0.65	0.44	0.33	0.27	0.22
12–14	0.58	0.41	0.31	0.25	0.21
14–17	0.71	0.37	0.29	0.24	0.20
17–20	0.43	0.33	0.26	0.22	0.19

Example: Room size = 6.5 × 5.0 m = 11.5 m exposed wall, U-value with 50 mm insulation = 0.33 W/m² K

Suspended ground floor with *two opposite edges exposed*. Insulation as previously specified.					

Distance between edges, a (m)	U-values (W/m² K) for insulation thickness (mm)				
	Nil	25	50	75	100
2	1.10	0.61	0.42	0.32	0.26
3	0.95	0.56	0.40	0.31	0.25
4	0.83	0.51	0.37	0.29	0.23
4–6	0.74	0.48	0.35	0.26	0.23
6–8	0.67	0.45	0.34	0.27	0.23
8–10	0.55	0.39	0.30	0.25	0.21

Example: Room width = 6.5 m, U-value with 50 mm insulation = 0.34 W/m² K

Table 3.26 Suspended ground floors – one edge exposed

Suspended ground floor with *one edge exposed*. Insulation as previously specified.					

Depth of room, *a* (m)	U-values (W/m² K) for insulation thickness (mm)				
	Nil	**25**	**50**	**75**	**100**
1.5	1.10	0.61	0.42	0.32	0.26
2	0.83	0.51	0.37	0.29	0.24
3	0.67	0.45	0.34	0.27	0.23
3–5	0.56	0.40	0.31	0.25	0.21
5–7	0.48	0.35	0.28	0.23	0.20
7–10	0.38	0.30	0.24	0.21	0.19
Example: Room width = 6.5 m, U-value with 50 mm insulation = 0.28 W/m² K					

Table 3.27 Internal floors

		U-values (W/m² K) for insulation thickness (mm)		
		Nil	**100 mm**	**150 mm**
Timber floor with underside exposed to outside or unheated area (heat flow-down)				
	19 mm boarding, airspace between joists, insulation, 6 mm sheeting	1.75	0.33	0.23
Concrete slab with underside exposed to outside or unheated area. (heat flow-down)				
	50 mm screed, 150 mm concrete slab, insulation between battens, 6 mm sheeting	1.82	0.57	
Intermediate floors, boarding 19 mm, airspace between joists, 9.5 mm plasterboard				
	Heat flow – upwards	1.73	0.32	
	Heat flow – downwards	1.41	0.31	

Table 3.28 Air heat capacity

	U-value (W/m² K)
The heat capacity by volume of air at 20°C, use to calculate heat loss due to air changes	0.33

3.8.3 Worksheet A – Heat Losses – Blank

See next page.

Worksheet A – Heat Losses

Stage 1 - Job information

Room	1.1	Job	1.2	Page	1.3	of	1.4

Stage 2 - Design temperatures

Design room temp.	2.1
Outside design temp.	2.2
Design temp. difference	2.3
Ground reference temp.	2.4

Stage 3 - Ventilation heat loss

	No. of air changes per hour — ac/h	Length (m) —	Room volume Width (m) —	Height (m) —	Amount of air heated per hour — m³/h	W/m³k - Air change factor	°C - Design temp. difference	A Watts - Heat loss
	3.1	3.2	3.3	3.4	3.5	3.6	3.7	3.8
No. of open flues and chimneys	3.9				3.10	3.11	3.12	3.13

Stage 4

Fabric heat loss

Thermal bridging addition | 4.1

	Length (m)	Width (m)	Height (m)	Area (m²)	U-value (W/m²/k)		A
External wall (gross area) (length outside × height)	4.2		4.3	4.4			
Glazing		4.5	4.6	4.7	4.8	4.9	4.10
External doors		4.11	4.12	4.13	4.14	4.15	4.16
Net area of external wall (glazing and door areas subtracted)				4.17	4.18	4.19	4.20
Ceiling or roof (gross area)	4.21	4.22		4.23			
Roof glazing	4.24	4.25		4.26	4.27	4.28	4.29
Net area of ceiling or roof (glazing area subtracted)				4.30	4.31	4.32	4.33
Internal wall 1	4.x1		4.x2	4.x3	4.x4	4.x5	4.x6
Internal wall 2	4.x1		4.x2	4.x3	4.x4	4.x5	4.x6
Party wall	4.x1		4.x2	4.x3	4.x4	4.x5	4.x6
Other 1	4.x1		4.x2	4.x3	4.x4	4.x5	4.x6
Other 2	4.x1		4.x2	4.x3	4.x4	4.x5	4.x6
Other 3	4.x1		4.x2	4.x3	4.x4	4.x5	4.x6
Floor (gross area)	4.34	4.35		4.36	4.37	4.38	4.39

Stage 5

Design heat loss & estimated annual energy usage for room

5.1

Reheat factor

			Factors if YES		
Period of disuse	5.4		High ceiling?	5.2	5.3
Building air permeability	5.5		Intermittent heating?	5.7	5.8
Building mass	5.6				

Reheat time	Reheat factor	Heat-up power
0.5 hour	5.x1	5.x2
1 hour	5.x1	5.x2
2 hour	5.x1	5.x2
3 hour	5.x1	5.x2
4 hour	5.x1	5.x2
5 hour	5.x1	5.x2

TOTAL FOR ROOM | 5.9

Heat emission (W/m²) (total loss per unit floor area) including down loss | 5.10

DBSP - DHDG -V2020.0

3.8.4 Worksheet A – Heat Losses – Instructions

Work through the following steps, calculating or entering data as required

Stage 1 – Job information

1.1	Name of the room the worksheet is for
1.2	Job name that the worksheet is part of
1.3	Page number of the worksheet
1.4	Total number of pages of worksheets for the job

Stage 2 – Design temperatures (see section 3.5.3)

2.1	Temperature that the room is being designed to be heated to (see section 3.5.3.2)
2.2	Outdoor temperature to which the room is being designed (see section 3.5.3.3)
2.3	Subtract the value in cell 2.2 from the value in cell 2.1
2.4	Ground reference temperature to which the room is being designed (see 'ground temperature' in section 3.5.3.3)

Stage 3 – Ventilation heat loss (see section 3.4.1)

3.1	Number of air changes per hour for the room (see section 3.5.4.1)
3.2, 3.3, 3.4	Room internal dimensions (see section 3.5.1.2)
3.5	Multiply values from cells 3.1, 3.2, 3.3 and 3.4
3.6	Typically 0.33 (see section 3.4.1)
3.7	Value from cell 2.3
3.8	Multiply values from cells 3.5, 3.6 and 3.7
3.9	Number of additional air changes associated with open chimneys or flues (see section 3.5.4.4)
3.10	Multiply values from cells 3.9, 3.2, 3.3 and 3.4
3.11	Typically 0.33 (see section 3.4.1)
3.12	Value from cell 2.3
3.13	Multiply values from cells 3.10, 3.11 and 3.12

Stage 4 – Fabric heat loss (see section 3.4.2)

Thermal bridging

4.1	If being used, the appropriate thermal bridging addition to be added to all U-values below (see section 3.5.2.6)

External walls

4.2, 4.3	Dimensions of external walls (see section 3.5.1.2)
4.4	Multiply values from cells 4.2 and 4.3
4.5, 4.6	Dimensions of windows (see section 3.5.1.2)
4.7	Multiply values from cells 4.5 and 4.6
4.8	U-value for windows (see section 3.5.2 and Table 3.20; and section 3.5.2.6 if allowing for thermal bridging)
4.9	Value from cell 2.3

4.10	Multiply values from cells 4.7, 4.8 and 4.9
4.11, 4.12	Dimensions of external doors (see section 3.5.1.2)
4.13	Multiply values from cells 4.11 and 4.12
4.14	U-value for doors (see section 3.5.2 and Table 3.20; and section 3.5.2.6 if allowing for thermal bridging)
4.15	Value from cell 2.3
4.16	Multiply values from cells 4.13, 4.14 and 4.15
4.17	Subtract values from cells 4.7 and 4.13 from cell 4.4
4.18	U-value for external wall (see section 3.5.2 and Tables 3.13 to 3.17; and section 3.5.2.6 if allowing for thermal bridging)
4.19	Value from cell 2.3
4.20	Multiply values from cells 4.17, 4.18 and 4.19

Ceilings or roofs

4.21, 4.22	Dimensions of ceiling or roof (see section 3.5.1.2)
4.23	Multiply values from cells 4.21 and 4.22
4.24 – 4.29	If no roof glazing is present, enter 0 for all cells
4.24, 4.25	Dimensions of roof glazing (see section 3.5.1.2)
4.26	Multiply values from cells 4.24 and 4.25
4.27	U-value for roof windows (see section 3.5.2, Table 3.20 and section 3.5.2.5; and section 3.5.2.6 if allowing for thermal bridging)
4.28	Value from cell 2.3
4.29	Multiply values from cells 4.26, 4.27 and 4.28
4.30	Subtract values in cell 4.26 from cell 4.23
4.31	U-value for roof and internal floors (see section 3.5.2, Table 3.19 and Table 3.27; and section 3.5.2.6 if allowing for thermal bridging)
4.32	Value from cell 2.3 if roof. If connected to an adjoining room, subtract the value in cell 2.1 in the worksheet for the adjoining room from the value in cell 2.1 in this worksheet (see 'Adjoining rooms' within section 3.5.3.3)
4.33	Multiply values from cells 4.30, 4.31 and 4.32

Internal wall 1 and 2; party wall; other 1, 2 and 3

The procedures for the following six elements are similar. Therefore, the steps have been combined.

4.x1–4.x6	If the element is not required, enter 0 for all cells
4.x1, 4.x2	Dimensions of the element (see section 3.5.1.2)
4.x3	Multiply values from cells 4.x1 and 4.x2
4.x4	U-value for appropriate structure (see section 3.5.2 and Table 3.18; and section 3.5.2.6 if allowing for thermal bridging)
4.x5	For internal walls, subtract the value in cell 2.1 in the worksheet for the adjoining room from the value in cell 2.1 in this worksheet (see 'Adjoining rooms' in section 3.5.3.3)
	For party walls, subtract 10 from value in cell 2.1 (see 'Adjoining properties and unheated spaces' in section 3.5.3.3)
	For 'other', follow the instructions for similar structures and conditions
4.x6	multiply values from cells 4.x3, 4.x4 and 4.x5

Note: Internal walls are walls adjoining other rooms. Internal walls 1 and 2 may be used separately if two adjoining rooms have two different indoor design temperatures.

Note: 'Other' may be used for any other surface with a different construction or temperature difference, (e.g. internal doors, additional internal walls, and ceilings or floors spanning multiple adjoining rooms).

Floors

4.34, 4.35	Dimensions of the floor (see section 3.5.1.2)
4.36	Multiply the values in cells 4.34 and 4.35
4.37	U-value for appropriate floor type (see Tables 3.21 to 3.27, or section 3.5.2.4 for complex ground-floor structures; and section 3.5.2.6 if allowing for thermal bridging)
4.38	Temperature difference relative to the ground reference temperature (subtract value in cell 2.4 from value in cell 2.1) (see 'Ground temperature' in section 3.5.3.3)
4.39	Multiply values from cells 4.36, 4.37 and 4.38

Stage 5 – Design heat loss

5.1	Sum of all the values in column A
5.2	High-ceiling factor (see 'High ceiling' in section 3.5.3.2 and Figure 3.5)
5.3	If high ceilings are considered, multiply the values in cells 5.1 and 5.2
	If high ceilings are not considered, the value is the value in cell 5.1

Intermittent heating (see section 3.5.5)

If intermittent heating not considered:

5.4–5.7	Not required, enter 0 for all cells
5.8	The value in cell 5.3

If intermittent heating is considered:

5.4–5.7, 5.x1–5.x2	See section 3.5.5
5.4	Period of disuse for room
5.5	Building air permeability
5.6	Building mass
5.x1	Selected reheat factors from Table 3.10
5.x2	Multiply the relative value in 5.x1 by the value in cell 4.36
5.7	Selected intermittent heating factor given the heat-up power in cells 5.x2
5.8	Multiply values in cells 5.3 and 5.7
5.9	Value in cell 5.8
5.10	Divide the value in cell 5.9 by the value in cell 4.36 (see the *Underfloor Heating Design & Installation Guide*; also published by the Domestic Building Service Panel (https://www.dbsp.co.uk)

4 System Design (Domestic Hot Water)

4.1 Contents

4.1   Contents. 4-2

4.2   Version Control 4-3

4.3   System Design (Domestic Hot Water) – Introduction 4-4

4.4   Hot Water Sources 4-6

    4.4.1   Hot Water Storage Cylinders 4-6

    4.4.2   Combination Boilers 4-12

    4.4.3   Thermal Stores 4-14

4.5   Other Hot Water Considerations 4-15

    4.5.1   Bacteria (*Legionella*) Protection 4-15

    4.5.2   Scalding Prevention 4-16

    4.5.3   Secondary Circulation. 4-17

    4.5.4   Hard Water 4-17

    4.5.5   Hot Water Supply Pipework 4-18

    4.5.6   Wastewater Heat Recovery. 4-18

4.2 Version Control

Version number	Changes	Date
10.01	Initial version	10-Nov-2020

The Domestic Building Service Panel Guide reporting tool can be used to notify the panel of any suggested corrections, or comments. These will be collated and used as the basis for review of forthcoming updates. Please feel free to use the tool, which is located at https://www.dbsp.co.uk/reporting-tool

4.3 System Design (Domestic Hot Water) – Introduction

Note: This section currently focuses on the specification of hot water systems with high (70–90°C) flow temperatures; greater emphasis on the design of hot water systems with lower circulation temperatures will be provided in a future update. Section 4.4.1.2 partially addresses this, but it is currently recommended to seek advice from other publications regarding the design of low flow temperature hot water systems.

There are essentially two main methods of producing domestic hot water. These are either by means of a hot water storage system that stores hot water ready for use, or by instantaneous means such as a combination boiler producing hot water on demand.

In addition, there are also systems that combine both methods, where a limited amount of hot water is stored and additional demand is supplied instantaneously.

Several factors must be considered when choosing which type of hot water system is most appropriate for a given application, and it is essential that the expectations and requirements of the client are fully established. The characteristics of the chosen option, and any limitation that might occur, will be central to this process.

Note: BS 8558:2015 (Guide to the design, installation, testing and maintenance of services supplying water for domestic use within buildings and their curtilages. Complementary guidance to BS EN 806) provides more detailed guidance in these matters.

The main factors to be considered are as follows:

- the likely demands in terms of volume, flow rate and temperature requirements, particularly during periods of simultaneous demand
- the dynamic pressures that will be required, bearing in mind the choice of outlet fittings and the available incoming supply
- the response time, which will depend on both the available power for heating domestic hot water and the flow temperature of the system
- any special requirements for disabilities, etc.
- the potential options for renewable technologies to heat the water, either as a stand-alone measure, or perhaps in combination with conventional technologies (e.g. a 'hybrid' system); both the initial installation and compatibility with regard to future upgrades should be considered.

The first of these requirements will normally be related to the known or anticipated number of occupants of the property. Account must also be taken of the amount of space available. While there is still a large population of vented hot water systems in the UK, the trend is towards dry roof spaces and the elimination of cold water supply cisterns using mains-fed hot water systems, such as unvented cylinders, thermal stores and combination boilers.

If there is to be no cold water storage, then particular attention should be given to the pressure and flow characteristics of the incoming mains, particularly under conditions of maximum demand. It should be stressed that it is dynamic pressure (under flow conditions) and not static pressure that matters. Generally, at least 1 bar dynamic pressure at the outlet is recommended for good performance of mains-fed hot water systems, preferably 1.5 bar.

When considering/advising whether an instantaneous or stored hot water solution will best meet the requirements of a project, due regard should be given to the following:

- The time taken for the hot water to reach the point of delivery from its source. For combination boilers this can be often be optimised through the specification of the boiler location at the design stage, and any delay also mitigated by the boiler manufacturer's 'pre-heat' or 'keep-hot' functionality (for more detail, see section 4.4.2). Again, either by design or through providing secondary circulation for larger properties (see section 4.5.3 below), the hot water delivery time can similarly be reduced to a minimum for stored hot water solutions.

- The flow rate requirements of the client, and the likely need for and frequency of simultaneous draw-off occurrences.
- Is the client vulnerable and/or is there a specific need for the provision of a back-up hot water solution? Many storage options, even some thermal stores, will be able to provide an immersion heater back-up for use in the unlikely event of a heat generator failure.
- The compatibility with renewable technologies. This will depend very much on the client's current and foreseeable needs. Stored hot water will often be compatible with many renewable technologies, such as solar thermal/photovoltaic (PV) cells. Alternatively, the specification could be for a combination boiler with an air-source heat pump (hybrid system) and a suitable control strategy to fulfil the space-heating demand. This can help to realise the overarching benefits of renewables, while negating the hot water requirement for an electrically powered (immersion heater) pasteurisation cycle, which is invariably needed to heat stored water to the 60°C temperature specified by the Health and Safety Executive (HSE) in order to prevent the growth of *Legionella* bacteria (see section 4.5.1).
- For all hot water solutions, the hardness of the water supply in the geographical area should be considered (see section 4.5.4). In hard water areas, thought should be given to the prevention of limescale build-up in pipes, storage vessels and heat exchangers, by treating the incoming mains water to reduce the total hardness, particularly where the limescale level exceeds 200 ppm. Primary circuits should not be filled with softened water unless the manufacturer's instructions for the heat generator and system components specifically permit it.

Finally, while outside the scope of this Guide, the importance of the commissioning of a hot water system should not be overlooked. Some of the important considerations for the commissioning of a heating system are discussed in section 2.5.1.2.

4.4 Hot Water Sources

4.4.1 Hot Water Storage Cylinders

Most hot water storage cylinders are heated indirectly by a heat generator (via an internal heat exchanger) but can also be heated directly by electricity and renewables such as solar.

In new-build or refurbishment projects, the usual first choice of a storage cylinder tends to be a mains-fed unvented product. In some circumstances, a thermal store may be preferred, particularly if combined with a combustion heat generator or solar thermal technology, where it is desired to store thermal energy for space heating in addition to the provision of domestic hot water (see section 4.4.3).

4.4.1.1 Sizing Hot Water Storage Cylinders

Note: as discussed above, this section focuses primarily on the specification of hot water systems with high (70–90°C) flow temperatures; greater emphasis on the design of hot water systems with lower circulation temperatures will be provided in a future update. Section 4.4.1.2 provides a more detailed approach to calculating reheat times for systems with different flow and return temperatures, but otherwise it is currently recommended to seek advice on the design of low flow temperature hot water systems from other publications.

It is important that the cylinder is sized correctly. The size is related not only to the maximum anticipated demand but also the power and availability of the heat source. Space heating requirements for dwellings have decreased due to better building design, and heat generator outputs have followed, which means that recommended cylinder sizes have generally increased.

Provided the cylinder and heat generator are correctly matched in terms of size and capacity and a suitable control system is in place, running out of hot water should only occur in exceptional circumstances.

Note: Cylinder manufacturers generally quote the reheat performance in terms of the number of kilowatts (kW) required to heat the water from cold to hot in 20 minutes or so. These outputs are measured under laboratory conditions, and in most cases it is the size of the heat generator that determines the reheat time. Counter to this, an oversized heat exchanger in the cylinder is generally a good thing, as it lowers the primary return temperature, decreases heat generator cycling and aids combustion efficiency.

Table 4.1 lists recommended minimum hot water storage volumes for various sizes of dwelling; the reheat timings assume a high flow temperature heat generator. The sizing of the heat generator is discussed further in section 5.7.1, where the power requirements and allowances given in Table 4.1 are used.

Note: The Hot Water Association website has a calculator that can be used alongside the information in this Guide.

Table 4.1 Recommended storage volumes

Size of dwelling	Indirect heating (internal heat exchanger)		Direct heating (immersion heater – 3 kW)
	Minimum required nominal capacity of cylinder (litres)	Cylinder coil rating (kW)	Minimum required nominal capacity of cylinder (litres)
1 bedroom	90	9.0	150
2 bedrooms	130	13.0	190
3 bedrooms	150	15.0	210
4 bedrooms	200	20.0	260
4/5 bedrooms (2 bathrooms)	210	20.0	270

> **Example**: For a four-bedroom dwelling with one bathroom, heated by a natural gas boiler, with occupants who use water at a 'medium' rate, a minimum of a 200 litre hot water cylinder should be specified (see Table 4.1).

Note: Normally the thermostat position on indirect cylinders (with an internal heat exchanger) is such that a reheat will be triggered after about 33% of the content has been discharged.

Note: The cylinder coil rating in Table 4.1 is for a combustion heat source with a high flow temperature. Depending on the system control settings and assuming that sufficient output is available to meet the cylinder coil rating, reheat will normally take less than 20 minutes. To calculate the reheat times for low flow temperature heat sources such as heat pumps, see section 4.4.1.2.

Note: Electrically heated cylinders can make use of off-peak or smart tariffs if they are controlled such that when the contents are discharged to the point where there is less than 60 litres of hot water left then a boost is available. To heat the top 60 litres back up to 60°C takes about 60 minutes.

Hot water cylinders should have primary pipework of at least 22 mm diameter, which will ensure low pressure loss and rapid cylinder temperature recovery; increased pipe size may be required for larger cylinders or if specified by the cylinder manufacturer.

If a vented cylinder is to be specified, due perhaps to limitations in the mains water supply or other factors, it is important to choose the correct grade BS 1566 cylinder to suit the maximum static head of the supply cistern.

If an unvented cylinder is to be specified, it should comply with BS EN 12897:2016. Information on unvented cylinders is given in section 4.4.1.3.

Note: Hot water storage products should be energy labelled according to the European regulations, and minimum standards apply (see section 1.5.7). However, this may change since the UK left the EU on 1 January 2021. In the case of indirectly heated cylinders (via an internal heat exchanger), the energy label is based on the standing heat loss of the cylinder. For electric water heating, which is generally unvented cylinders with immersion heaters, the energy label is based on the actual efficiency (i.e. the electricity input vs the hot water output based on specified hot water draw off profiles).

As indirect cylinders (heated via an internal heat exchanger) and electric water heaters use different test criteria, a direct comparison of the two is not possible.

4.4.1.2 Sizing Hot Water Storage Cylinders – Detailed Approach

The approach presented in section 4.4.1.1 is intended for high flow temperature heat generators such as gas, liquid fuel and biomass boilers. This section introduces the calculations behind Table 4.1, which can be used when the situation differs from what has been presented above, be that a higher hot water demand, a lower power heat generator or a low flow temperature system design.

Note: For more detail on the calculation see Annex B to BS 8558:2015.

The reheat time of a hot water cylinder may be calculated using the formula:

$$M = \frac{V_{cyl} \times (T_2 - T_1)}{14.3 \times P} \qquad \text{(Equation 6)}$$

Equation 6 may be rearranged as follows to work out how much heat input (power) is required to reheat a given volume to a given temperature in a given time:

$$P = \frac{V_{cyl} \times (T_2 - T_1)}{14.3 \times M} \qquad \text{(Equation 7)}$$

where:

M is the time taken to heat the cylinder from temperatures T_1 to T_2 in minutes
V_{cyl} is the volume of water to be heated (cylinder volume) in litres
T_1 is the starting temperature of the water in the cylinder in °C
T_2 is the target temperature of the water in the cylinder in °C
P is the rate of heat input to the cylinder in kW

Note: P will be the lower of either the cylinder coil rating or the capacity of heat generator output directed to heating water

> **Example**: using Equation 7, the power required to reheat a 170 litre hot water cylinder from 40°C to 60°C in 20 minutes would be:

$$\frac{170 \times (60 - 40)}{14.3 \times 20} = \frac{170 \times 20}{286} = \frac{3{,}400}{286} = 12 \text{ kW}$$

Note: Equations 6 and 7 ignore heat losses from the cylinder. Assuming the hot water cylinder is insulated to current standards (see section 1.5.7), and that the reheat time is relatively short, these losses will have very little effect.

Note: A heat generator will not be able to heat a cylinder to a temperature (e.g. T_2) higher than the system flow temperature. A heat generator may be able to provide different flow temperatures for different heat calls, allowing the heating system to be designed to operate at a lower temperature than when heating hot water; the timing and control of hot water heating and space heating should be separated (see section 5.11).

Note: As the cylinder temperature approaches the flow temperature of the heating system, the rate at which it is heated will slow. Therefore it is recommended that the hot water heating flow temperature is at least 5°C above the target temperature of the cylinder (T_2).

Table 4.2 gives typical values for the rated power of various common heat generators (P). These values may be used as a starting point in Equations 6 and 7 if a heat generator has not already been selected. The selected cylinder should also have a coil rating of at least the capacity given in the table.

Table 4.2 Typical rated power of various heat generators

Appliance (non-combination)	Typical rated power, P (kW)
Single domestic electric immersion heater	3
Small, high flow temperature heat generator and direct cylinder (1–2 bedrooms)	6
Medium, high flow temperature heat generator and direct cylinder (2–4 bedrooms)	10
Large, high flow temperature heat generator and direct cylinder (4+ bedrooms)	15

It is important to consider the peak demand for hot water consumption. For example, all members of the household may shower as soon as they come home from work, giving a very large peak in demand at around 6 p.m. each day. This kind of scenario will likely not be satisfied by using the standard cylinder sizes presented in Table 4.1.

It is recommended that hot water cylinder loading be detailed in 15-minute intervals for a typical day (loadings for weekdays, weekend days and any other days with a significantly different schedule should be given separately). As part of this process, it is important to allow for water being drawn off at the point of use at a lower temperature than that at which it is stored in the cylinder (see section 4.5.2). The volume of water used from the cylinder after the temperature has been reduced by thermostatic mixing may be calculated by the formula:

$$V_{hot} = \frac{(T_{draw} - T_{cold})}{(T_{hot} - T_{cold})} \times V_{draw}$$

(Equation 8)

Equation 8 may be rearranged as follows to calculate a given quantity of water drawn off via a thermostatic mixing valve (TMV) for given volume at a given temperature in a cylinder:

$$V_{draw} = \frac{[(T_{hot} \times V_{hot}) - (T_{cold} \times V_{hot})]}{(T_{draw} - T_{cold})}$$

(Equation 9)

where

V_{hot} is the volume, in litres, of hot water drawn from the cylinder to supply
V_{draw} is the volume, in litres, of water drawn from the point of use
T_{hot} is the temperature, in °C, of the water in the cylinder
T_{cold} is the temperature, in °C, of the cold water supply
T_{draw} is the temperature, in °C, of the water drawn from the point of use

Example: A hot water cylinder is heated to 60°C, and 150 litres of 45°C water is drawn off to fill a bath via a TMV supplied with cold water at 10°C. Using Equation 8, the volume of water drawn from the hot water cylinder will be:

$$\frac{(45 - 10)}{(60 - 10)} \times 150 = \frac{35}{50} \times 150 = 0.7 \times 150 = 105 \text{ litres}$$

Using information gathered from the client, the design point-of-use outlet information (see Table 4.4) and Equation 8, a profile of hot water use throughout the day can be estimated. Figure 4.1 shows an example of such a profile for a weekday, with two showers in the morning, a shower and a bath in the evening, and various hand-washing and kitchen sink usage throughout the day.

The reheat time and heating power required can be analysed using Equations 6 to 9.

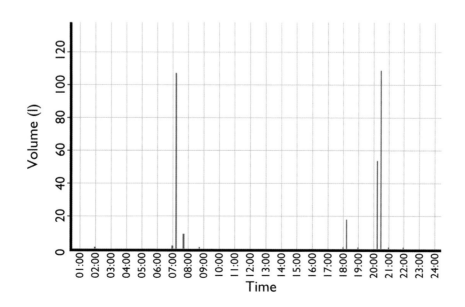

Figure 4.1 Example weekday hot water draw-off at a cylinder

Example: Peak usage in Figure 4.1 is at around 8:00 p.m., when an 8-minute shower is directly followed by a bath. The property has a 120 litre hot water cylinder, and a system design flow temperature of 55°C. How long would it take the heat generators in Table 4.2 to reheat the cylinder sufficiently for a 150 litre bath, assuming the hot water cylinder is fully heated to 50°C prior to the shower?

Use Equation 8 to work out how much hot water is used for the shower (assuming cold water at 10°C):

8 minutes at 12 l/min (see Table 4.4) is 96 litres at the point of use (at 40°C, see Table 4.4)

$$\frac{(40-10)}{(50-10)} \times 96 = \frac{30}{40} \times 96 = 0.75 \times 96 = 72 \text{ litres} \qquad \text{from the cylinder (at 50°C)}$$

Assuming efficient cylinder stratification, there will be 78 litres (= 150 − 72) of hot water at 50°C remaining in the cylinder, the remaining 72 litres being cold water at 10°C.

Use Equation 9 to work out how much of the bath can be filled with the remaining 78 litres of hot water:

$$\frac{[(50\times78)-(10\times78)]}{(45-10)} = \frac{(3{,}900-780)}{35} = \frac{3{,}120}{35} = 89 \text{ litres} \qquad \text{of the bath can be filled (at 45°C, see Table 4.4)}$$

Use Equation 6 to work out how long it would take a medium, high flow temperature heat generator to reheat the further 61 litres of hot water to the 45°C required (note that it is not required to take the temperature all the way up to 50°C):

$$\frac{61\times(45-10)}{14.3\times10} = \frac{61\times35}{143} = \frac{2{,}135}{143} = 15 \text{ minutes}$$

The step above can be followed for each of the heat generators in Table 4.2 to obtain the times given in Table 4.3.

Table 4.3 Time taken to reheat 61 litres of water from 10°C to 45°C for various typical heat generator sizes

Appliance	Time (min)
Single domestic electric immersion heater	50
Small, high flow temperature heat generator and direct cylinder (1–2 bed)	25
Medium, high flow temperature heat generator and direct cylinder (2–4 bed)	15
Large, high flow temperature heat generator and direct cylinder (4+ bed)	10

Note: An additional heat source such as an immersion heater may be required in the scenario given in the example above to ensure that the *Legionella* sterilisation requirements are met if the main heat source is not able to achieve this (see section 4.5.1).

Note: The above approach assumes good cylinder design and stratification. The manufacturer's advice should be followed to ensure this.

4.4.1.3 Unvented Hot Water Cylinders
Note: The specification for unvented hot water cylinders is given here at a high level. It is important that safety and design requirements are followed as required by Part G3 of the Building Regulations 2010 (or the regional equivalent, see Table 1.1). Further guidance and courses on this are available from other sources.

Unvented hot water cylinders are often the system of choice in medium to large new-build projects. This is partially driven by beneficial Dwelling Emission Rate (DER)[1] (calculated in the UK government's Standard Assessment Procedure for Energy Rating of Dwellings (SAP)) calculation efficiencies, due to the ability to integrate renewable energy sources more easily into new-builds, but it is also due to the high kilowatt output requirements for a combination boiler in a large property (see section 4.4.2). However, high-output combination boilers, perhaps with electric showers to service multiple en suite bathrooms, are also commonly specified, particularly if there is not sufficient space to install a cylinder. In refurbishment projects, an unvented cylinder hot water solution is often used, provided of course that the mains water supply is adequate.

With both unvented cylinders and combination boilers, the use of higher pressures provided by a direct mains connection allows for much better performing showers, mixer taps and other fittings, while freeing the loft space of tanks and pipework.

The UK water by-laws prohibit sending expansion water to waste, so all unvented systems have to be fitted with some means of accommodating the increase in water volume as it is heated. There are two categories of unvented system: those having a separate external expansion vessel, and those where the expansion is accommodated internally in the system, which are often referred to as 'bubble tops'. As there is no open vent, there must be at least two levels of overtemperature protection over and above that provided by the control thermostat, in order to stop the cylinder reaching 100°C. This is generally achieved by the use of a non-automatically resetting energy cut-out, in conjunction with a pressure and temperature relief valve.

In addition, there needs to be a non-return valve (double check valve), a pressure-reducing valve and an expansion-relief valve. Expansion and temperature-relief valves must be installed to allow for safe discharge, as per the requirements laid out in Part G3 of the Building Regulations 2010 (or the regional equivalent, see Table 1.1).

An example of an internal expansion (bubble top) unvented hot water cylinder installation is shown in Figure 4.2.

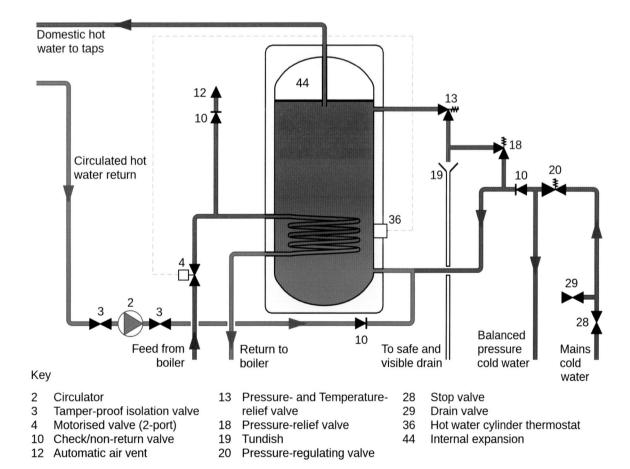

Key

2	Circulator	13	Pressure- and Temperature-relief valve	28	Stop valve
3	Tamper-proof isolation valve			29	Drain valve
4	Motorised valve (2-port)	18	Pressure-relief valve	36	Hot water cylinder thermostat
10	Check/non-return valve	19	Tundish	44	Internal expansion
12	Automatic air vent	20	Pressure-regulating valve		

Figure 4.2 Internal expansion unvented hot water cylinder

---

[1] The actual CO_2 emission rate of self-contained dwellings based on their actual specification.

4.4.2 Combination Boilers

Combination boilers produce hot water instantaneously in response to a hot water tap being opened and a flow of water in the distribution pipework. The advantages of these types of boiler are space saving and continuous hot water on demand. The hot water output is dependent solely on the boiler output. Most combination boiler manufacturers have standardised their product literature to show hot water flow rates calculated using a 35°C temperature rise. This is useful as a means of comparing boiler outputs, but does not always represent the case in the real world, where higher temperature rises might be required for some outlets (for further guidance, see section 4.4.2.1).

Most combination boilers are supplied with a 'keep hot' facility enabled by default, which either involves a small store of primary or secondary water, or uses occasional firing of the boiler to keep the heat exchanger hot, thus improving the response time, although at the expense of slightly increased fuel consumption.

Where a water meter with a non-return valve is installed at the property, it may be necessary to install a mini expansion vessel on the cold mains supply to the combination boiler (check the boiler manufacturer's instructions).

In some dwellings it may be appropriate to use a combination boiler to provide part of the hot water requirement, and install one or more cylinders or electric water heaters elsewhere nearer the point of use.

4.4.2.1 Sizing Combination Boilers

As stated earlier, the required output in kilowatts can be determined for each hot water outlet by looking at the flow rate and temperature requirement. For each outlet there is a recommended design flow rate, but in cases of simultaneous demand this can be reduced to a minimum. These values are outlined in Table 4.4, where it is assumed that the temperature of the incoming cold water is 10°C. It should be noted that in circumstances where lower incoming temperatures occur, such as late winter, the performance will fall below the levels in Table 4.4. In all cases, consideration must be given to individual client requirements, and any contractual specifications (e.g. the terms of any new building warranty provision).

Table 4.4 Output requirements using combination boilers with a cold inlet at 10°C

Hot water outlet	Design flow rate (l/min)	Minimum flow rate simultaneous demand (l/min)	Outlet temperature (°C)	Power required for design flow rate (kW)	Power required for minimum flow rate (kW)
Bath	12	9	40–45	25.1–29.3	18.8–22.0
Shower	12	6	40	25.2	12.6
Washbasin	9	6	40	18.9	12.6
Kitchen sink	12	6	50	33.4	16.7

Note: The use of 40°C or 45°C for the bath temperature will depend on which industry guidance is followed.

Conditions of simultaneous demand can now be considered by looking at likely use combinations, and typical scenarios. Where it is likely that only a single outlet will be used at one time, the highest appropriate value in the 'Power required for design flow rate' column in Table 4.4 will be the total kilowatt output required. Where it is likely that multiple outlets will be used at the same time, the highest combination of the appropriate values from the 'power required for minimum flow rate' column in Table 4.4 should be summed to give the total kilowatt output required. Table 4.5 gives some typical draw-off scenarios.

It should be noted that, in all cases, the effect of obtaining 6 l/min at 50°C from the kitchen tap has been ignored, and the client should be warned that in some cases the specified hot water outlet rates may not be achieved if other outlets are in use.

Table 4.5 Typical draw-off scenarios

Outlet combination (kitchen demand ignored)	Total output required (bath outlet temperature 40°C) (kW)	Total output required (bath outlet temperature 45°C) (kW)
Shower only	25.2	25.2
Bath only	25.1	29.3
Two showers	25.2	25.2
Bath plus shower	31.4	34.6
Three showers	37.8	37.8

Note: 'Bath' refers to the filling of a bath. A shower may be a stand-alone cubicle or en suite, a shower over a bath and fed via a mixer tap, or a shower over a bath but with a separate mixer unit, but all these must be fed by the combination heat generator, not a stand-alone unit (e.g. not an electric shower).

For a combination boiler system, the hot water heating power requirement will typically be significantly higher than that of the space heating power requirement. As such, a heat generator should be selected based on the hot water heating power requirement only.

The draw off scenario that most closely matches the property being designed for should be selected from Table 4.4, and a heat generator selected that is able to deliver the total kilowatt output required.

> **Example 1**: A house has a kitchen with a kitchen sink, a bathroom with a bath and a shower over the bath fed from the mixer tap, and a separate en suite shower. It is assumed that the shower over the bath will be used in preference to the bath being filled. The kitchen sink is discounted, as discussed above, and therefore the worst-case scenario is that both showers will be used at once. Either by summing two allocations of the 'Power required for minimum flow rate' for a shower in Table 4.4, or by reading off the 'Two showers' row in Table 4.5, the property should have installed a combination boiler rated for an output of at least 25.2 kW.

> **Example 2**: For the same house as in Example 1, it is assumed that the bath will be filled in preference to using the shower over the bath. The kitchen sink is discounted as before, so the worst-case scenario is that the bath and one shower will be used at once. Either by summing the allocations of the 'Power required for minimum flow rate' for a shower and a bath in Table 4.4, or by reading off the 'Bath plus shower' row in Table 4.5, the property should have installed a combination boiler rated for an output of at least a 31.4 kW (if the bath outlet temperature chosen is 40°C) or 34.6 kW output (if the bath outlet temperature chosen is 45°C).

Note: Care needs to be taken when selecting the worst-case scenario for simultaneous demand. While the demand in Example 2 above may be worse (higher) than that in Example 1, if the occupants are unlikely to ever choose to run a bath at the same time as someone else is showering, the result will be an oversized and potentially inefficient boiler (research shows that more than half of the UK population prefers showers to baths). Consideration should be given to what is the realistic worst-case scenario.

Note: These are the kilowatt outputs required for domestic hot water appliances (e.g. combination boilers) to achieve the hot water performance characteristics detailed. Once heated to the required store temperature, a typical unvented cylinder system can deliver hot water at 60°C at a flow rate of 30 l/min.

4.4.3 Thermal Stores

The design and specification of thermal stores is beyond the scope of this Guide, but high-level information is included here for completeness.

Note: The design and specification of thermal stores is intended to be covered in a future supplement to this Guide to be published by the Domestic Building Service Panel (https://www.dbsp.co.uk).

Thermal stores are vessels containing primary water that is heated by means of a separate heat generator, direct firing heater or an immersion heater. They are typically used to add storage for space heating by non-automatic heat generators, but they also supply instantaneous hot water. They are often heated to around 82°C, although this can be lower depending on the design flow temperature of the space heating system. If heated to this high a temperature, it is important that a compatible heat generator is specified, as not all heat generators are designed to reach 80°C under normal operating conditions.

Thermal stores include combined primary storage units (CPSUs), which are, in effect, a form of combination boiler but where the hot water performance is provided mainly by stored energy.

Thermal stores can be either vented or unvented, and supply domestic hot water by means of heat transfer using either an internal heat exchanger coil or an external pumped heat exchanger, normally plate to plate.

Like all hot water storage systems, the requirements for thermal stores are covered by Part G3 of the Building Regulations 2010 (or the regional equivalent, see Table 1.1), but unlike unvented secondary systems they do not normally need a temperature-relief valve. There is a wide variety of designs and control configurations of a thermal stores, one of the most popular being the two-circulator type (Figure 4.3).

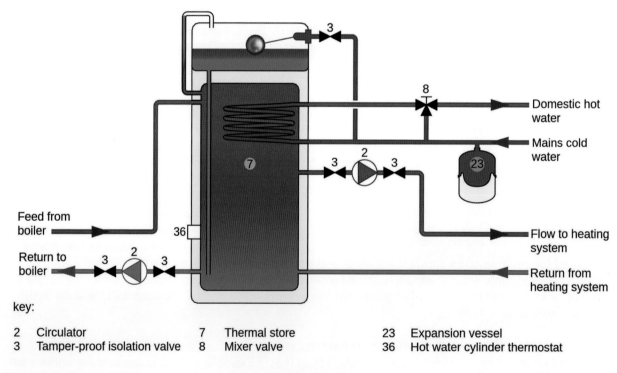

key:

| 2 | Circulator | 7 | Thermal store | 23 | Expansion vessel |
| 3 | Tamper-proof isolation valve | 8 | Mixer valve | 36 | Hot water cylinder thermostat |

Figure 4.3 Thermal store

As the hot water is produced by heat exchange, a thermal store tends to have a declining draw-off temperature profile, whereas an unvented cylinder delivers water more or less at the storage temperature, with a sudden drop off at the end. Therefore, on a like-for-like performance basis, a thermal store needs to be larger than an unvented cylinder.

One major advantage of a thermal store is its versatility to integrate and utilise other energy sources, especially renewables, for space and water heating.

4.5 Other Hot Water Considerations

4.5.1 Bacteria (*Legionella*) Protection

Legionnaires' disease, also known as legionellosis, is a potentially fatal lung infection that is characterised mainly by pneumonia. The disease begins quite abruptly, with high fever, chills, headache and muscle pain. Later symptoms include cough, shortness of breath, high fever, muscle pains and headaches. *Legionella pneumophila* serogroup 1 is the organism most commonly responsible for Legionnaires' disease, although at least 50 other species of *Legionella* have been reported.

Outbreaks of the illness can occur from exposure to bacterial growth in all sorts of premises (both work and domestic) where water is maintained at a temperature high enough to encourage bacterial growth but not sufficiently high to pasteurise the water. The illness is caught by inhaling contaminated small droplets of water (aerosols) from showers, taps, air-conditioning or hot tubs.

Certain conditions increase the risk of an outbreak of *Legionella*:

- a water temperature in all or parts of the system of 20–45°C, which is suitable for the growth of the bacteria
- the creation and dispersal of breathable water droplets (e.g. an aerosol created by a cooling tower, or spray water outlets)
- stored and/or recirculated water
- deposits that provide a source of nutrients for the bacteria and can support its growth (e.g. rust, sludge, scale, organic matter and biofilms).

The risk of infection by *Legionella* increases with age, but some people are at higher risk, including:

- people over 45 years of age
- smokers and heavy drinkers
- people suffering from chronic respiratory or kidney disease
- people with diabetes, lung disease and/or heart disease
- anyone with an impaired immune system.

While there is no specific guidance on *Legionella* for private dwellings, which mostly fall outside the scope of the Health and Safety at Work etc. Act 1974, when designing hot water systems the recommendation is to follow best practice such as that produced by CIBSE (TM13: *Minimising the Risk of Legionnaires' Disease*, 2013) and the HSE (Approved Code of Practice L8: *Legionnaires' Disease. The Control of Legionella Bacteria in Water Systems*, 2013).

Note: Commercial buildings and buildings with shared services or common parts that include the provision of water fall within the scope of the Health and Safety at Work etc. Act 1974. For buildings such as these, the HSE Approved Code of Practice L8 contains the legally enforceable requirements to demonstrate compliance with the Act.

Note: The optimum temperature for the multiplication of *L. pneumophila* in the laboratory is between 32°C and 42°C. The bacteria can survive at higher temperatures, but the survival time decreases from a few hours at 50°C to a few minutes at 60°C; at 70°C the organism is killed virtually instantaneously. Below 37°C the multiplication rate decreases, and it can be considered insignificant below 20°C.

Prevention depends on good design and a managed regular preventive maintenance plan for water systems, which should be carried out and recorded by a competent person. The designer of a heating or hot water system should ensure, as a minimum, that the cold water supply is kept as cold as possible, and that the system is capable of heating any stored water to at least 60°C. The exact pasteurisation routine for a domestic hot water system will differ depending on the circumstances of the building, with the risk from *Legionella* being balanced against the risk from scalding (see section 4.5.2), the requirement to reduce energy consumption (see section 1.5) and the risk level of the occupants of the property.

The assessment of *Legionella* risk is beyond the scope of this Guide, but it should be undertaken by competent persons.

Note: For heat generators that are not always able to achieve the pasteurisation requirements, an electric immersion heater with suitable controls can often be used to ensure that the requirements of the risk assessment are met.

Note: BS 8580:2010 provides guidance on how to undertake a *Legionella* risk assessment (see section 3).

Further reference should be made to the guidance contained in CIBSE TM13, HSE Approved Code of Practice L8 and the related technical guidance document HSG274 Part 2 (*The Control of Legionella Bacteria in Hot and Cold Water Systems*, 2014).

- CIBSE TM13 gives guidance on the appropriate design, installation, commissioning, operation and maintenance procedures necessary to minimise the risk of infection by *Legionella* from water systems within a building. It is available from the CIBSE Knowledge Portal.[2]
- HSE Approved Code of Practice L8 is aimed at duty holders, including employers, those in control of premises and those with health and safety responsibilities for others, to help them comply with their legal duties in relation to *Legionella*.
- HSG274 is in three parts, and provides practical advice and guidance on identifying and assessing sources of risk, preparing a scheme to prevent or control risk, and implementing, managing and monitoring precautions.[3]

Note: For systems designed for use in healthcare environments, the Department of Health and Social Care document HTM 04-01 (*Safe Water in Healthcare Premises*, 2017) should also be referred to.

4.5.2 Scalding Prevention

It may be required to store water either temporarily or constantly at a temperature of 60°C or above. This could be as part of a bacteria (*Legionella*) risk management strategy (see section 4.5.1) or to maximise the storage capacity of a thermal store (see section 4.4.3). While these are important and valid considerations, it is also important to ensure that the water is at a safe temperature at the point of use. While not required in privately owned domestic properties, it is best practice to design a system to prevent a risk of scalding, which can lead to life-changing injuries and can be life-threatening to the young and elderly.

The risk of scalding is typically mitigated by the use of either a TMV at the storage vessel, or separate TMVs at each point of use. A TMV works by blending a proportion of cold water with the hot, to ensure that the output temperature is no greater than the set temperature (for more details see 'Domestic hot water mixer' in section 5.11.3.2).

Note: TMVs certified by the BuildCert TMV2 Scheme should be used in domestic properties.

Note: Many mixer taps and showers have the functionality of a TMV built in, although some are only approved as type-1 TMVs (TMV1) in the BuildCert scheme.

Note: For more information on this subject see the Building research Establishment (BRE) Information Paper IP14/03 (*Preventing Hot Water Scalding in Bathrooms using TMVs*).

The BuildCert TMV scheme recommends the following maximum hot water temperatures at the point of use:

- 46°C for bath fill
- 41°C for showers
- 41°C for washbasins
- 38°C for bidets.

---

[2] Search for TM13 at https://www.cibse.org/knowledge/.
[3] Available from the HSE website: https://www.hse.gov.uk/pubns/books/hsg274.htm.

Note: The temperature should never exceed 46°C.

Note: 46°C is the maximum temperature for water from a bath hot tap, allowing for the margin of error inherent in thermostatic mixing valves, including allowance for temperature loss in metal baths, especially an early cast iron bath in installed in a cold bathroom. However, 46°C is not a safe bathing temperature for adults or children. The British Burn Association recommends 37–37.5°C as a comfortable bathing temperature for children.

Note: In premises covered by the Care Standards Act 2000, the maximum water outlet temperature is 43°C.

4.5.3 Secondary Circulation

On occasion, long pipe runs may be unavoidable and secondary circulation should be considered, particularly in larger domestic applications. Always check the suitability of components (e.g. circulator) and the pipework type for secondary circulation with the manufacturer.

Note: Where long pipe runs are unavoidable, consideration should be given to locating the hot water source centrally in the building and distributing radially, in order to minimise heat loss wherever possible.

Secondary circulation helps to avoid excessive waiting times for hot water and reduces the risk of microbial growth (see section 4.5.1).

It should be noted that secondary circulation involves the use of circulation pumps (and their associated energy demand), and that pipework losses will be increased. Losses can be minimised by proper lagging and, in extreme cases, trace heating. The circulation pump should ideally be linked to a suitable time or proximity control regime in order to avoid unnecessary electricity consumption.

Where possible, siting the storage cylinder in the optimum position (close to the point of use), and minimising pipe diameters to reduce draw-off times, should be considered before specifying secondary circulation.

The circulator selected for the secondary circulation should have the lowest practicable power consumption, integrated facilities to detect the water temperature, pressure sensing and a timer to allow the system to be fully automated.

It is generally not appropriate to use secondary circulation with thermal stores or with cylinders using off-peak electricity.

4.5.4 Hard Water

In hard water areas where the temporary hardness exceeds 200 mg/ml, it is recommended that consideration be given to treating the incoming mains water supply with a suitable base-exchange water softener, so that all equipment is protected, and the client has the advantage of using softened water. If a water softener is to be used, it is necessary to make sure that there is sufficient mains water pressure to overcome the pressure drop of the softener, which can be up to 1 bar. Alternatively, an appropriate in-line scale reducer or ion-exchange unit can be fitted on the cold water supply to the water heater/cylinder, or potentially on the cold mains supply to the property.

Note: Softened water can have a higher sodium content and may not be fit for human consumption. Therefore, a dedicated, unsoftened drinking water branch pipe is typically provided upstream of the softener.

Care must be taken to ensure the suitability of the low-pressure hot water (LPHW) heating system and components for filling and use with softened water, where this is proposed. Particular care is needed where aluminium materials are present, in order to avoid the potential for accelerated system corrosion. Such suitability should be checked for all system components via the appliance/component manufacturer's instructions.

Where the compatibility of all components cannot be confirmed and a water softener is present (or planned), provision needs to be made to ensure the heating system is filled with unsoftened water. This can be achieved either by filling via the softener bypass (a requirement of BS EN 1473: 2016), and giving the client appropriate advice on subsequent, periodic filling, or by providing an unsoftened mains supply pipe branch upstream of the water softener and connected to the heating system filling point (mains-side filling point connection or header tank ball-valve connection).

If softened water is to be used to fill the heating system, subject to satisfactory checks being made in line with the above, an inhibitor suitable for use with softened water should be used. The need for regular checking of the correct inhibitor concentration, plus redosing as appropriate, should be stressed to the user.

HSE guidance is to heat stored hot water at a temperature of 60°C to prevent the growth of *Legionella* bacteria (see section 4.5.1). Heating stored hot water to a higher temperature may elevate the risk of scale formation.

4.5.5 Hot Water Supply Pipework

The length of hot water draw-off pipework to taps and other outlets should be kept to a minimum in order to reduce the amount of cold water drawn off before the hot water arrives (reference should be made to BS 8558:2015).

Note: Hot water outlet flow restrictors, which are often specified for water- and energy-saving purposes and to aid SAP compliance, will impact on draw-off times before a temperature that is acceptable to the user is present at the outlet.

The maximum recommended lengths of pipe are shown in Table 4.6. Where there is more than one size of pipe on a hot water distribution branch, the equivalent length and size should be estimated. When the length of supply pipework branch exceeds the recommended maximum, and the DHW source cannot be relocated, secondary circulation or trace heating should be installed.

Table 4.6 Maximum recommended pipe runs for hot water draw-off

Pipe size (mm)	Maximum length (m)
10, 12	20
15, 22	12
28	8
35 or above	3

4.5.6 Wastewater Heat Recovery

As discussed in section 1.5, energy efficiency is becoming a more central focus of system design. One type of system that is starting to be seen on domestic hot water (DHW) systems is a wastewater heat recovery system (WWHRS). These systems work by recycling the heat energy locked up in the shower drain water. This is energy that would normally leave the building envelope as waste. It works by means of simple heat exchange. The outflowing waste shower water imparts its energy to the incoming cold water main (CWM), typically resulting in a temperature rise of around 15–18°C. This 'pre-heated CWM' is then routed to the cold-side of the thermostatic mixer shower and/or the DHW source (e.g. combination boiler, DHW cylinder, air source heat pump, heat interface unit, etc.).

The WWHRS technology is listed in SAP for reducing energy. There are three recognised installation methods: system A (preheated CWM water to the cold side of the shower and the water heater), system B (preheated CWM water to the cold side of the shower *only*) and system C (preheated CWM water to the water heater *only*). Each of these systems has a slightly different impact on the efficiency of the WWHRS.

By routing preheated CWM water to the cold side of the shower, the ratio of generated DHW to CWM water normally required to achieve a desired shower temperature is automatically adjusted in favour of the cold side, resulting in less generated DHW being used per shower. By also feeding preheated CWM water to the DHW source, the heat generator or cylinder does not have to work as hard to reach the regulated DHW output temperature. In this way, significant energy savings can be made, and householder bills reduced.

Currently, the most efficient WWHRS devices typically take the form of a long vertical copper pipe heat exchanger. Waste water falls as a thin film through the inside of the heat exchanger, running counter-flow to the incoming mains water, which circulates around the outside to ensure maximum heat exchange. Vertical WWHRS devices can typically have a heat recovery efficiency of 55–65%, and so can significantly reduce showering costs and energy consumption.

For bungalows or apartments, a number of horizontal WWHRS systems are available that are either integrated into shower trays or wet-room drain channels, or can be installed directly below a bath or shower tray (on the same floor, rather than the floor below).

As the most efficient systems are vertical, and therefore most suited to showers on the first floor or above, this can make it more difficult to install vertical units in apartments, as, depending on the build, future access may be need to be through a different property.

In addition, some WWHRS are single walled, which means that, to comply with water regulations, the waste trap needs to be downstream of the product, and accessible, in case of any future blockage. In such scenarios, the waste trap may typically be on a different (lower) floor to where it would conventionally be for a shower, with the same potential access issues as before. In mitigation, a WWHRS is a simple fit-and-forget technology, with no electrical components and no pumps or controllers, and so it requires very little maintenance.

5 System Design (Heating)

5.1 Contents

5.1   Contents 5-2

5.2   Version Control 5-4

5.3   Introduction 5-5

5.4   System Layout 5-6

    5.4.1   Typical System Layout 5-6

    5.4.2   Y-Plan Configuration 5-7

    5.4.3   Primary Circuit Radiator 5-8

    5.4.4   Open-Vented Systems 5-9

    5.4.5   One-Pipe Circuits 5-9

    5.4.6   Reverse-Return Layout 5-10

    5.4.7   Reverse Circulation 5-11

5.5   Heat Emitters 5-13

    5.5.1   General 5-13

    5.5.2   Heating System Water Temperature 5-13

    5.5.3   Exposed Pipework Emissions 5-14

    5.5.4   Output Emission Factors 5-15

    5.5.5   Radiator Selection 5-19

    5.5.6   Underfloor Heating 5-19

5.6   Pipework 5-21

    5.6.1   Pipework Sizing Strategy 5-21

    5.6.2   Pipework Sizing Strategy – Approximation 5-21

    5.6.3   Pipe Sizing Design: Fluid Velocity 5-24

    5.6.4   Pipe Sizing Design: Frictional Resistance 5-31

5.7   Sizing the Heat Source 5-36

    5.7.1   Heat Generator/Boiler Sizing Method 5-36

5.8   Circulators 5-38

    5.8.1   Circulator Selection 5-38

    5.8.2   Circulator Position 5-38

    5.8.3   Circulator Sizing 5-39

    5.8.4   Isolating Valves 5-41

    5.8.5   Integral Circulators 5-41

    5.8.6   Circulator Fault Diagnosis 5-41

5.9   Fluid Expansion Compensation 5-44

    5.9.1   Sealed Heating Systems 5-44

    5.9.2   Open-Vented Systems 5-54

5.10 Low-Loss Headers and Manifolds 5-57

    5.10.1   Low-Loss Headers 5-57

    5.10.2   Manifolds 5-57

5.11   System Controls. 5-60

    5.11.1   Introduction 5-60

    5.11.2   Control functions – Inputs 5-61

    5.11.3   Control functions – Outputs 5-66

    5.11.4   Control Functions – Controller .5-73

    5.11.5   Zoned Heating 5-75

    5.11.6   Recommended Control Systems .5-77

5.12   Pipework Insulation 5-79

    5.12.1   Insulation of Heating System Pipework 5-79

    5.12.2   Insulation of Domestic Hot Water Pipework 5-80

    5.12.3   Insulation in Unheated Areas 5-80

    5.12.4   Insulation of Condensate Pipework 5-81

    5.12.5   Installation of Insulation 5-81

5.13   Water Treatment 5-82

    5.13.1   Debris, Corrosion and Limescale. 5-82

    5.13.2   Antifreeze 5-83

    5.13.3   Microbiological Contamination .5-83

5.14   Heat Storage and Buffering 5-84

5.15   System Integration 5-85

5.16   Appendix 5-86

    5.16.1   Worksheet B – Heat Emitters and Pipework – Blank 5-86

    5.16.2   Worksheet B – Heat Emitters and Pipework – Instructions 5-88

    5.16.3   Worksheet C – Water Content of System – Blank. 5-90

    5.16.4   Worksheet C – Water Content of System – Instructions 5-92

5.2 Version Control

Version number	Changes	Date
10.01	Initial version	10-Nov-2020

The Domestic Building Service Panel Guide reporting tool can be used to notify the panel of any suggested corrections, or comments. These will be collated and used as the basis for review of forthcoming updates. Please feel free to use the tool, which is located at https://www.dbsp.co.uk/reporting-tool

5.3 Introduction

Note: This section focuses on the specification of heating systems with high (70–90°C) circulation temperatures. Further advice on the design of systems with lower circulation temperatures will be provided in a later update, and will emphasise the additional attention needed with regard to:

- external temperatures
- building exposure
- intermittency factors
- emitter responsiveness
- controls.

Meanwhile, advice should be sought from other publications regarding the design of low flow temperature heating systems.

The procedure for calculating the heat demand for each room in a property was set out in section 4. In this section, the steps to convert that heat demand into a fully designed heating system are set out.

Firstly, options for various system layouts are discussed in section 5.4, before each of the various components below are discussed in detail:

- heat emitters (section 5.5)
- pipework (section 5.6)
- sizing the heat source (section 5.7)
- circulators (section 5.8)
- fluid expansion compensation (section 5.9)
- system controls (section 5.11)
- pipework insulation (section 5.12)
- water treatment (section 5.13).

Finally, heat storage and the integration of various heat sources and types of heat emitters are discussed in sections 5.14 and 5.15, respectively.

While outside the scope of this Guide, the importance of the commissioning of a heating system should not be overlooked. Some of the important considerations for the commissioning of a heating system are discussed in section 2.5.1.2.

5.4 System Layout

In this section, the typical layout of a heating system (sealed, fully pumped and S-plan configuration) is discussed, along with some less common variations, including Y-plan, open-vented, one-pipe and reverse-return systems. The problem of reverse circulation is also briefly discussed.

5.4.1 Typical System Layout

Figure 5.1 shows a typical fully pumped sealed system, sometimes known as the 'S-plan configuration'. It uses two motorised valves, one to direct the primary water flow through the heating system, and the other to direct the primary water flow through the coil of the domestic hot water cylinder. Operation of the two valves (i.e. when they are open or closed) will be based on the demand for heat, which is controlled by the heating and hot water systems' time and temperature controller (for more details on controls, see section 5.11).

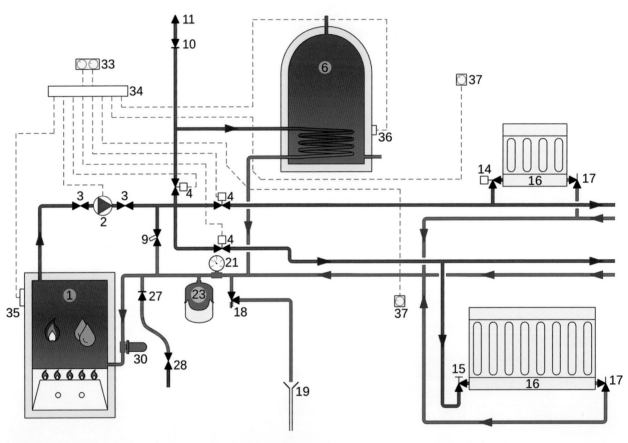

Key:

1	Boiler	14	Thermostatic radiator valve	27	Double check/non-return valve
2	Circulator	15	Wheel valve	28	Stop valve
3	Tamper-proof isolation valve	16	Radiator	30	Filter
4	Motorised valve (2-port)	17	Balancing/lockshield valve	33	Controller
6	Hot water cylinder	18	Pressure-relief valve	34	Wiring terminal box
9	Automatic balancing valve	19	Tundish	35	Boiler control signal
10	Check/non-return valve	21	Pressure gauge	36	Hot water cylinder thermostat
11	Air vent	23	Expansion vessel	37	Wall mounted thermostat

Figure 5.1 A typical fully pumped system (S-plan)

The guidance in Approved Document L1A of the Building Regulations 2010 (or the regional equivalent, see Table 1.1) requires that homes with total floor areas exceeding 150 m^2 have at least two independently controlled space-heating 'zones'. The requirement can be met by the specification of two heating zone valves (or more where appropriate and desired), with a separate zone valve for controlling the hot water; typically, the upstairs and downstairs heating circuits are separated.

It is also common for heating systems in smaller dwellings (total floor area <150 m^2) to be designed for, and installed with, multiple heating zones. This is partly because such a set-up is favourably treated in the UK government's Standard Assessment Procedure for Energy Rating of Dwellings (SAP), but it is also because of the potential for energy reduction due to more control being given to the building occupants; see section 5.11.

Note: An automatic balancing valve is generally required for new S-plan systems with a combustion heat source, except where the heat generator manufacturer specifies that one is built into their product, and that it is sufficiently sized for the system bypass requirements. If one is not already present, it should be provided to such systems at the time of appliance replacement. The automatic balancing valve allows circulation to be maintained at the end of a demand, dissipating residual heat in the appliance if all motorised valves are closed. This is a pump overrun function, which will invariably be incorporated in the appliance. Automatic balancing valves also allow the heat generator's minimum level of circulation to be met when all thermostatic radiator valves have closed down. Automatic balancing valves are discussed further in section 5.11.3.1.

Note: A system filter (see section 5.13.1) should be included to protect the heat generator. It should be located on the return pipework to the heat generator. It should be noted that, when specifying a filter, the associated pressure losses should be taken into account when specifying the pipework (see section 5.6.4).

Note:

- Heat emitter components – wheel valve and balancing/lock shield valve – are discussed further in section 5.5.
- Circulator components – tamper-proof isolation valve and heating circulator – are discussed further in section 5.8.
- Sealed system fluid expansion compensation components – expansion vessel, pressure relief valve, tundish, pressure gauge and air vent – are discussed further in section 5.9.1.
- Control components – cylinder thermostat, room thermostat, wiring terminal box, controller, motorised valve and automatic balancing valve – are discussed further in section 5.11.
- Hot water cylinders are discussed further in section 4.4.1.

5.4.2 Y-Plan Configuration

Similar operation to that described above and shown in Figure 5.1 can be achieved by using a single mid-position valve and a different electrical wiring arrangement, as shown in Figure 5.2; this is sometimes known as a 'Y-plan configuration'. This arrangement was common a few years ago, but is being used less and less today.

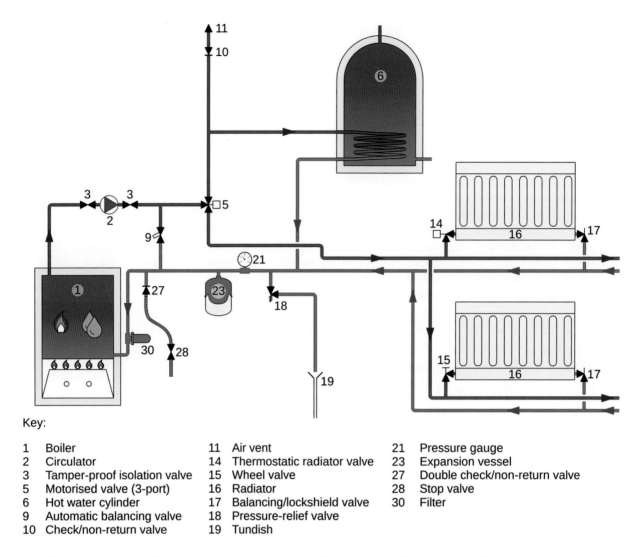

Key:

1	Boiler	11	Air vent	21	Pressure gauge
2	Circulator	14	Thermostatic radiator valve	23	Expansion vessel
3	Tamper-proof isolation valve	15	Wheel valve	27	Double check/non-return valve
5	Motorised valve (3-port)	16	Radiator	28	Stop valve
6	Hot water cylinder	17	Balancing/lockshield valve	30	Filter
9	Automatic balancing valve	18	Pressure-relief valve		
10	Check/non-return valve	19	Tundish		

Figure 5.2 Heating and domestic hot water using a mid-position or diverter valve (Y-plan)

5.4.3 Primary Circuit Radiator

It was previously common practice to have the facility to use a radiator towel rail in a bathroom or a separate heating coil in a cupboard to aid drying after the main heating system has been turned off for the summer (Figure 5.3). This is no longer recommended, as Part L of the Building Regulations 2010 (or the regional equivalent, see Table 1.1) requires separate time and temperature control for space heating and hot water (see section 5.11.6). The same result can be achieved by installing the towel radiator as a separate zone (see section 5.11.5).

Note: This may also be achieved by the use of an electric towel radiator, depending on the client's requirements.

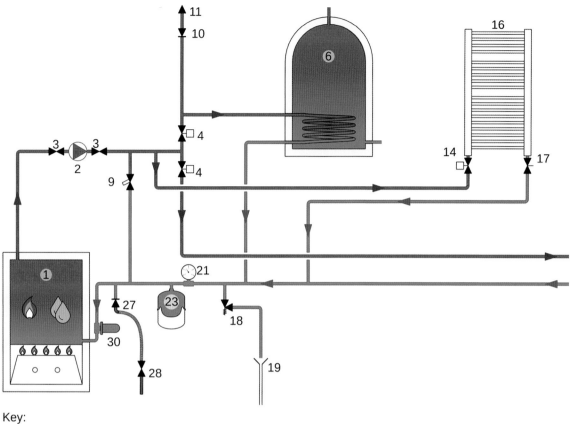

Key:

1	Boiler	10	Check/non-return valve	19	Tundish
2	Circulator	11	Air vent	21	Pressure gauge
3	Tamper-proof isolation valve	14	Thermostatic radiator valve	23	Expansion vessel
4	Motorised valve (2-port)	16	Radiator	27	Double check/non-return valve
6	Hot water cylinder	17	Balancing/lockshield valve	28	Stop valve
9	Automatic balancing valve	18	Pressure-relief valve	30	Filter

Figure 5.3 Domestic heating system layout showing connections for the bathroom radiator to operate in summer and winter. **(NEVER design a system in this way)**

5.4.4 Open-Vented Systems

The sealed approach to fluid expansion compensation has all but replaced the open-vented approach, apart from in certain situations where manufacturers require connection to a non-sealed system (typically liquid fuel boilers, as well as wood and solid-fuel boiler stoves). The open-vented approach is discussed in section 5.9.2.

5.4.5 One-Pipe Circuits

One-pipe circuits are outside the scope of this Guide, and therefore specialist advice should be sought. One-pipe circuits require careful design to take account of the reducing water temperature along the circuit, which reduces radiator outputs and hence affects their sizing. The recommendations in this Guide do not apply to such systems.

5.4.6 Reverse-Return Layout

A reverse-return layout is shown in Figure 5.4. This is a variation of the conventional two-pipe circuit, which has the advantage of equalising the pressure loss to all parts of the system, providing an equal and inherently balanced flow to all parts of the circuit. This is particularly useful when installing two heat generators (Figure 5.5). It is achieved by ensuring that:

- each element (two radiators in the case of Figure 5.4 and two boilers in the case of Figure 5.5) has an equal combined length of flow and return pipework connected between it and a common point
- each element has the same resistance (this is usually achieved by ensuring they are the same age and model)
- each length of pipework is of the same diameter.

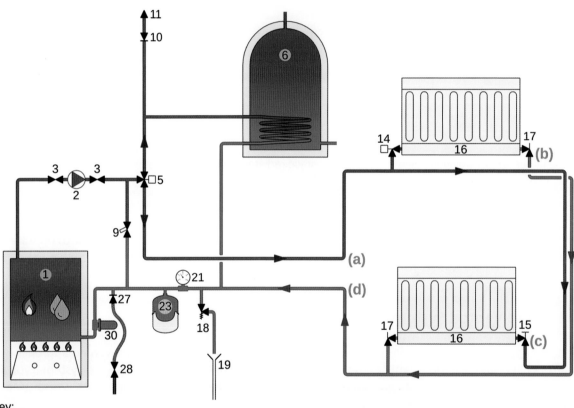

Key:

1	Boiler	11	Air vent	21	Pressure gauge
2	Circulator	14	Thermostatic radiator valve	23	Expansion vessel
3	Tamper-proof isolation valve	15	Wheel valve	27	Double check/non-return valve
5	Motorised valve (3-port)	16	Radiator	28	Stop valve
6	Hot water cylinder	17	Balancing/lockshield valve	30	Filter
9	Automatic balancing valve	18	Pressure-relief valve		
10	Check/non-return valve	19	Tundish		

Figure 5.4 Reverse return heating connection

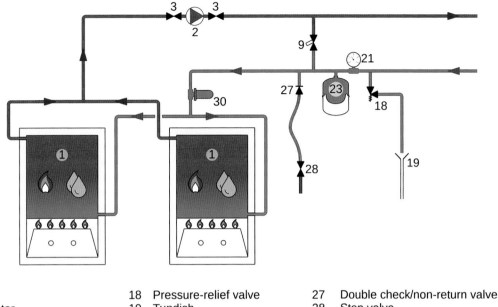

Key:

1	Boiler	18	Pressure-relief valve	27	Double check/non-return valve
2	Circulator	19	Tundish	28	Stop valve
3	Tamper-proof isolation valve	21	Pressure gauge	30	Filter
9	Automatic balancing valve	23	Expansion vessel		

Figure 5.5 Reverse return heat generator connection

Example: The length of pipework in Figure 5.4, between **a** and **d** is the same whether the water must travel via radiator 1 and point **b**, or radiator 2 and point **c**; assuming radiators 1 and 2 are the same model and were installed at the same time, and all pipework is 15 mm diameter. The flow through the two radiators will therefore naturally be the same, without any need for balancing.

This type of layout is generally suited to larger properties, where a room may have multiple radiators of the same model in a room, and multiple heat generators to connect to. It is not usually found in smaller domestic properties.

5.4.7 Reverse Circulation

Reverse circulation (not to be confused with the reverse-return layout discussed above) can cause radiators to heat up when only the water heating circuit should be operating. It can be diagnosed by the temporary reversal of flow and return to some of the radiators, and is the result of the return path for those radiators being shared with the hot water primary circuit. An example of a connection that enables reverse circulation is shown in Figure 5.6. The problem is easily avoided by ensuring that all heating circuits are taken from a common flow, and that all heating returns are joined to a common return located before the return connection from the hot water cylinder, as shown in Figure 5.7.

Note: Figure 5.6 shows connections that promote reverse circulation, and, as such, should never be installed. With circulation to the cylinder and with the heating valve closed, water from the cylinder return is pumped through the upper radiator circuit in reverse, then through the lower circuit in the correct direction. Radiators will heat up even though the heating is switched off. See Figure 5.7 for the correct connection method.

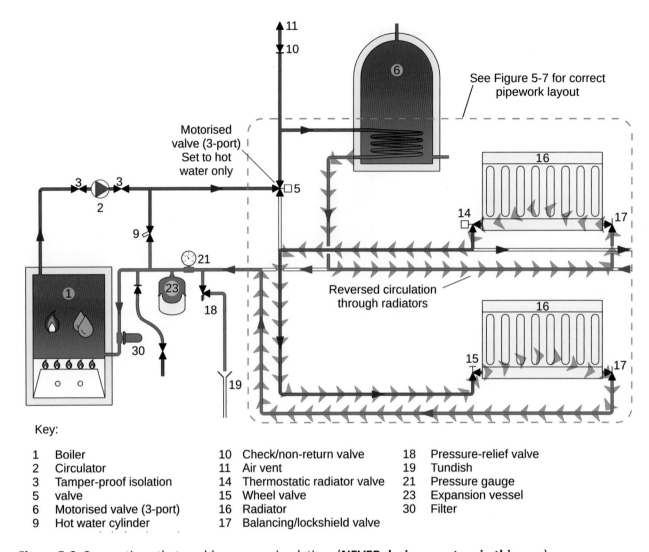

Key:

1	Boiler	10	Check/non-return valve	18	Pressure-relief valve
2	Circulator	11	Air vent	19	Tundish
3	Tamper-proof isolation	14	Thermostatic radiator valve	21	Pressure gauge
5	valve	15	Wheel valve	23	Expansion vessel
6	Motorised valve (3-port)	16	Radiator	30	Filter
9	Hot water cylinder	17	Balancing/lockshield valve		

Figure 5.6 Connections that enable reverse circulation. (**NEVER design a system in this way**)

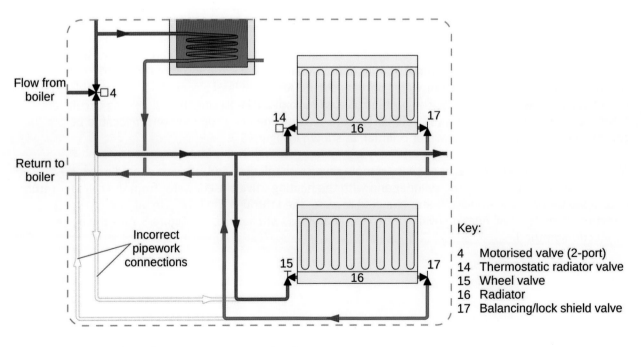

Key:

4	Motorised valve (2-port)
14	Thermostatic radiator valve
15	Wheel valve
16	Radiator
17	Balancing/lock shield valve

Figure 5.7 Connections that prevent reverse circulation

5.5 Heat Emitters

5.5.1 General

Once a basic layout has been established for the system, heat emitters need to be specified for each space. Steel panel radiators remain the most popular type of heat emitter in both Britain and the Republic of Ireland, and therefore are the focus of this section. Other heat emitters, such as fan convectors, floor (trench) convectors, skirting heating or underfloor heating, require special considerations, and are outside the scope of this Guide. For underfloor heating, the *Underfloor Heating Design & Installation Guide* (also published by the Domestic Building Service Panel (https://www.dbsp.co.uk)) should be consulted, otherwise the manufacturer's guidance should be followed.

The process of selecting a radiator is as follows:

1. Select the appropriate water temperatures for the system (section 5.5.2).
2. Calculate the heat inputs to the room from the pipework (section 5.5.3).
3. Calculate the emission factors for the configuration of radiators required (section 5.5.4).
4. Select the required radiator (section 5.5.5).

This section presents the information needed to carry out the above four steps.

5.5.2 Heating System Water Temperature

Selecting the heating system water temperature will depend on the type and size of heat emitters, as well as the type of heat generator. The heat source and heat emitter manufacturers' recommendations should be sought for appropriate water temperatures, but where this information is not available use the values below (section 1.6 gives details and considerations for various types of heat generator).

* Flow temperature:
  - high flow temperature systems, 60–70°C (typically only combustion heat generators)
  - low flow temperature systems, 35–55°C (for heat pumps and combustion heat generators with buffer storage).
* Temperature differential (ΔT):
  - typical design difference between the flow and return water temperatures is 14% of the flow temperature as a minimum.

  Example: A 60°C flow temperature system would typically have as a minimum an 8.4°C temperature differential (60 × 0.14 = 8.4), and therefore a return temperature of 52°C.

Note: Some older existing systems have design temperatures of 82°C flow and 71°C return, which are derived from the old 180/160°F standard.

Two other important factors, which will be used in the calculations below, are:

* *Mean water temperature (MWT)* – The average of the system flow and return temperatures after applying the optimum or appropriate differential for the design.

  Example: A gas condensing boiler with a flow temperature of 70°C and a return temperature of 50°C, would have a MWT of

$$\frac{70+50}{2} = \frac{120}{2} = 60°C$$

* *Mean water to air temperature (MW-AT)* – The difference between the MWT and the room air temperature, as used for emitter sizing.

> **Example**: A gas condensing boiler with a flow temperature of 70°C and a return temperature of 50°C, heating a room at 21°C, would have a MW-AT differential of 60 – 21 = 39°C.

Historically, flow and return water temperatures of 85/65°C (MWT 75°C) were used in the design of older solid fuel systems with gravity circulation, but this was reduced to 82/71°C (MWT 76.5°C) for all gas and liquid fuel appliances with pumped circulation. Currently, efficient condensing boiler systems use 70/50°C (MWT 60°C) to maximise efficient operation, while heat pumps typically operate at 55/47°C (MWT 51°C) or 35/30°C (MWT 32.5°C), the lower values providing improved coefficients of performance (see section 1.6.5). Other examples of systems that are able to operate at a low or very low MWT are those where buffer storage is included in the system (see section 5.14).

For low-MWT emitters, further guidance should be sought from the manufacturers and the companion to this Guide, the *Underfloor Heating Design & Installation Guide* (also published by the Domestic Building Service Panel (https://www.dbsp.co.uk)).

Where different emitters require different temperature differentials within the same system, designers should make use of low loss headers or manifolds with separate subsystem water circulators (see section 5.10).

Note: Designers should be aware that laminar flow conditions resulting from very low flow rates can potentially cause unpredictable heat transmission.

Note: When upgrading a non-condensing boiler in a house that has had cavity wall insulation and double glazing added, the existing radiators will usually be sufficiently oversized to enable a condensing boiler to run with lower return water temperatures, and thus increase the latent heat recovery from the exhaust gases, giving more efficient operation (see section 1.6.2.3). Section 5.5.4.1 describes a methodology for ensuring this is the case if required.

5.5.3 Exposed Pipework Emissions

Where there are exposed pipes within a heated room, their heat output contributes to the heating of the room and should be deducted from the calculated room heat loss (see section 3) before the radiator size is arrived at.

Note: See Table 5.17 in section 5.12.1 for insulated pipes.

Note: For a new installation where the pipework sizes are not already known, the pipework size approximation strategy can be used, as discussed below in Section 5.6.2, or the heat emitter can be sized after the pipework has been correctly sized (see Section 5.6.3 and 5.6.4).

After measuring the length and size of the exposed pipes in a room and the MW-AT under design conditions, the heat output from the exposed pipes may then be calculated using Tables 5.1 and 5.2.

Table 5.1 gives the heat output per metre of pipe run for different pipe diameters against a series of temperature differentials.

Table 5.2 gives factors for the pipe configuration (i.e. whether there is more than one pipe and whether the pipes are run vertically or horizontally). If a room contains more than one type of pipe run (i.e. if there are both horizontal and vertical pipes or if there are pipes of different diameters), it will be necessary to calculate these separately and to add the values together.

The heat input to a room from exposed pipework can then be found by multiplying the appropriate pipework emissions (in W/m) from Table 5.1 by the length of exposed pipework (in m) by the appropriate layout factor from Table 5.2.

Table 5.1 Pipework emissions (W/m) for painted copper pipe

Pipe size (mm)	MW-AT differential (°C)						
	35	39	44	48	52	56	60
8	13	15	17	19	21	23	25
10	16	18	21	23	26	28	30
15	21	24	28	31	35	38	41
22	29	33	38	43	47	52	56
28	35	41	47	53	58	64	69
35	43	49	57	63	70	77	83
42	49	56	65	73	81	89	96
54	61	70	81	90	100	110	119
67	72	82	96	107	118	130	141
76	81	92	107	120	132	145	158
108	108	124	144	161	178	195	212

Table 5.2 Pipe layout factors

Pipe layout	Factor
Single pipe horizontal	1.00
Double pipe horizontal	0.90
Single or double pipe vertical, up to 15 mm diameter	0.75
Single or double pipe vertical, 22 mm diameter and over	0.80

Example: A room has a MW-AT of 39°C, 4.8 m (2 × 2.4 m) of vertical and 1.5 m of horizontal (1 × 300 mm plus 1 × 1.2 m) (single) exposed painted copper 15 mm pipework.

From Table 5.1, the pipework emissions are 24 W/m. From Table 5.2, the vertical pipe layout factor is 0.75, and the horizontal single pipe layout factor is 1.

Therefore:

Vertical: 24 × 4.8 × 0.75 = 86.4 W
Horizontal: 24 × 1.5 × 1 = 36 W
Total: 122.4 W

Worksheet B in section 5.16.1 is provided to assist with this calculation. Step by step instructions for filling in Worksheet B can be found in section 5.16.2.

5.5.4 Output Emission Factors

The output of a radiator can vary considerably from the nominal output stated in the manufacturer's output tables, depending on the conditions under which the radiator is installed. Therefore, the nominal output required to deliver the room heat loss (see section 3) needs to be calculated. The following four factors determine the conversion between the nominal (manufacturer's stated) and the required radiator output.

Note: The output from a radiator is generally more by means of convection rather than by radiation (80/20), despite the name.

- *MW-AT differential factor, f1* (see section 5.5.4.1) – The difference between the mean temperature of the heating water and the room temperature (MW-AT) determines the rate at which the heat from the water can be transferred to the room. This determines the value of factor f1, which is used to adjust the rated output of the emitter from the manufacturer's catalogue rating. The values of f1 given below assume that the catalogue rating is based on a MW-AT differential of 50°C, which is currently used by all European radiator manufacturers. However, the manufacturer's data should be checked in case an older basic temperature (60°C) has been used, in which case a further correction will have to be made to take account of it.
- *Pipe connections factor, f2* (see section 5.5.4.2) – Radiator catalogue data for output is based on pipe connections being made to top and bottom tapings at the same end (TBSE) of the radiator (Figure 5.8). If any other configuration is used, then the factor f2 must be applied. For bottom opposite ends (BOE) connections, which are the most frequently used connections in domestic installations, a connection factor of 0.96 should be applied.
- *Enclosure factor, f3* (see section 5.5.4.3) – The positioning of a radiator (e.g. in a recess) affects its output and determines the value of factor f3. This factor also takes into account the reduced output as a result of encasing a radiator in a cabinet with top and bottom grilles. Low surface temperature enclosure kits have a similar effect and require the application of a factor, which should be obtained from the manufacturer.
- *Finish factor, f4* (see section 5.5.4.4) – The surface finish of a radiator also affects its ability to emit heat, which is accounted for by factor f4. This normally needs to be applied when radiators are painted after installation. Ordinary water- or oil-based paints will not affect the outputs, but metallic paint can cause a reduction in heat emission of 15%, which would result in f4 being set at 0.85.

Manufacturers may provide a different methodology for sizing their radiators, and their literature should be consulted. If none is provided, the methodology presented here can be used.

Each of the four factors (f1 to f4) need to be calculated individually, as laid out below.

5.5.4.1 f1 – MW-AD Differential Factor

Table 5.3 is based on a MW-AT differential of 50°C as required by BS EN 442, and applies to most radiators manufactured since 2000.

Table 5.3 Values of the MW-AT differential factor (f1) for steel panel radiators

MW-AT difference (°C)	0	1	2	3	4	5	6	7	8	9
10	0.123	0.140	0.156	0.174	0.191	0.209	0.227	0.246	0.265	0.284
20	0.304	0.324	0.344	0.364	0.385	0.406	0.427	0.449	0.471	0.493
30	0.515	0.537	0.560	0.583	0.606	0.629	0.652	0.676	0.700	0.724
40	0.748	0.773	0.797	0.822	0.847	0.872	0.897	0.923	0.948	0.974
50	1.000	1.026	1.052	1.079	1.105	1.132	1.159	1.186	1.213	1.240
60	1.267	1.295	1.323	1.350	1.378	1.406	1.435	1.463	1.491	1.520

> **Example**: A room with a MW-AT differential of 34°C would have an f1 factor of 0.606 (from row 30, column 4 in Table 5.3). Therefore, the radiator will only output 60.6% of the output of the manufacturer's stated value in this situation.

If checking for the output of any existing radiators quoted to other MW-AT differential, such as 60°C, the following equation below can be used:

$$f1 = \left(\frac{MW - AT_{actual}}{MW - AT_{catalogue}} \right)^{1.3}$$

(Equation 10)

where

MW-AT$_{actual}$ is the actual MW-AT differential in °C
MW-AT$_{catalogue}$ is the catalogue MW-AT differential in °C (typically 60°C)

Example: A heat pump is replacing a fossil fuel boiler. The heat pump is set up for a 56°C flow and 48°C return. The specified room temperature is 21°C. The manufacturer of the radiator only specifies outputs for their radiators for a MW-AT differential of 60°C.

MWT: $\frac{56 + 48}{2} = \frac{104}{2} = 52°C$

MW-AT: 52 − 21 = 31°C

Using Equation 10:

$$f1 = \left(\frac{31}{60} \right)^{1.3} = 0.517^{1.3} = 0.424$$

This means the radiator will emit only 42.4% of the heat stated in the manufacturer's catalogue, and therefore will need to be at least doubled in size to provide the required comfort conditions.

Note: Should the heat pump in the example above be serving an underfloor heating system and set for optimum performance and a high coefficient of performance (CoP), the MW-AT differential could be as low as 11.5°C (i.e. 35°C flow, 30°C return, giving a mean water temperature (MWT) of 32.5°C.

Any radiators considered to operate at these temperatures would need to be so large as to be unwieldy and uneconomical. Why? Putting these numbers into Equation 10:

$$f1 = \left(\frac{11.5}{60} \right)^{1.3} = 0.117$$

A radiator 8.8 times larger than the correct one according to the manufacturer's stated output would be needed to deliver the same heat output. While not impossible to make allowances for, it may be impractical due to the amount of wall space required. At these operating temperatures, underfloor heating, with its larger surface area, may be more appropriate. Another option would be to use two integrated circuits running at different temperatures, but this solution is beyond the scope of this Guide.

Note: The design and specification of systems integrating circuits running at different temperatures is intended to be covered in the forthcoming companion to this Guide, the *Integration Guide*, also to be published by the Domestic Building Service Panel (https://www.dbsp.co.uk).

Note: For underfloor heating, the exponent 1.3 should be replaced by 1.10, and for a fan convector it should be replaced by 1.05.

5.5.4.2 f2 – Pipe Connections Factor

The appropriate factor from Table 5.4 should be selected for the type of connections to be used on the radiator (see Figure 5.8).

Table 5.4 Values of the pipe connections factor (f2)

Connection type	f2
Top and bottom same end (TBSE)	1.00
Top and bottom opposite ends (TBOE)	1.05
Bottom opposite ends (BOE)	0.96

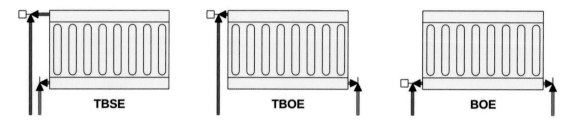

Figure 5.8 Radiator connections

5.5.4.3 f3 – Enclosure Factor

The appropriate factor from Table 5.5 should be selected for the type of enclosure surrounding the radiator.

Table 5.5 Values of the enclosure factor (f3)

Enclosure type	f3
Fixed on plain surface	1.00
Shelf over radiator	0.95
Fixed in open recess	0.90
Encased in cabinet with front or top grille	0.70 or 0.80

5.5.4.4 f4 – Finish Factor

The appropriate factor from Table 5.6 should be selected for the paint finish applied to the radiator

Table 5.6 Values of the finish factor (f4)

Finish	f4
Oil- or water-based paint	1.00
Metallic based paint	0.85

Note: Factor f4 normally needs to be applied when radiators are painted after installation.

5.5.5 Radiator Selection

The heat loss calculated for each room in section 3 provides the basis for sizing the heat emitters, as these must be capable of providing sufficient heat input to match the design heat loss, including any winter reheat allowance for intermittent heating.

Firstly, the total radiator heat output required for a room must be calculated by subtracting the exposed pipework emissions (see section 5.5.3) from the design heat loss (see section3).

To work out which radiator to select from a manufacturer's catalogue, the total radiator heat output required must be divided by the product of the factors f1 to f4:

$$\text{catalogue heat output required} = \frac{\text{total radiator heat output required}}{f1 \times f2 \times f3 \times f4} \qquad \text{(Equation 11)}$$

In most cases this adjustment will result in an increase in the number of watts required between the total radiator heat output and the recommended catalogue output, in order to take into consideration the output emission factors discussed. A radiator (or radiators) can then be selected that will supply at least the adjusted number of watts.

> **Example**: A living room has a design heat loss of 865 W, 122.4 W of pipework emissions, a MW-AT differential of 41°C, TBOE connections, a shelf over the radiator and the radiator has been repainted with water-based paint.
>
> Total radiator heat output required = 865 − 122.4 = 742.6 W
>
> Using Equation 11 and f1 = 0.773 (see section 5.5.4.1), f2 = 1.05 (see section 5.5.4.2), f3 = 0.95 (see section 5.5.4.3) and f4 = 1.00 (see section 5.5.4.4):
>
> $$\text{catalogue heat output required} = \frac{742.6}{0.773 \times 1.05 \times 0.95 \times 1.00} = \frac{742.6}{0.771} = 963.2 \, W$$
>
> The nearest radiator in the manufacturer's catalogue that fits the space required is 600 mm high × 1000 mm wide, and outputs 980 W. This therefore would be the radiator selected.

Note: Different f factors may be needed for different rooms in a house if more than one type of heat emitter is to be used or if the MW-AT differential varies. If the manufacturer's data for the MW-AT differential is not available, the conversion factor equation can be used, if necessary, substituting the power figure accordingly.

Note: Locating radiators under windows to counteract down draughts remains accepted practice (subject to avoiding full-length curtains, which obscure and reduce output), although, as the U-values for windows are continuously increasing, this is less of a consideration than previously.

Note: Radiators are typically specified to have a thermostatic radiator valve (see section 5.11.3.1) on the flow connection and a lockshield valve on the return connection. The lockshield valve allows the radiator to be balanced correctly during commissioning (see section 2.5.1.2). If no thermostatic radiator valve is installed on the flow connection, a simple wheel valve should be installed instead to allow the radiator to be isolated.

Worksheet B in section 5.16.1 is provided to assist with this calculation. Step by step instructions for filling in Worksheet B can be found in section 5.16.2.

5.5.6 Underfloor Heating

While outside the scope of this Guide, as the design principles differ significantly from the procedures given here for panel radiators, some basic information regarding underfloor heating is included below. The design of underfloor heating is covered in the companion to this Guide, the *Underfloor Heating Design & Installation Guide* (also published by the Domestic Building Service Panel (https://www.dbsp.co.uk)).

An underfloor heating system uses embedded warm water pipes to heat the floor surface and the room. Ducted warm air systems are also beyond the scope of this Guide, and specialist advice is required for their design.

Heat transfer from the floor surface is primarily by radiation (50–60% of output) with the balance made up by convection. Radiant heat systems typically provide a greater level of comfort to occupants for the following reasons:

- they create comfort at a slightly lower air temperature (by 1 or 2°C) than is expected from a radiator or convector system, because they heat our bodies directly
- radiant heat leads to limited air convection currents and low temperature stratification (unlike other types of space heating system), both of which are generally pleasing
- extensive experience has proved that if the feet are slightly warmer than the head, optimum comfort is produced.

There is also generally a benefit in terms of fuel economy, due to the lack of higher air temperatures near the ceiling.

By contrast, if an underfloor system is used only for short periods and at infrequent intervals (intermittent heating), competing systems may return lower running costs, particularly when long-lag screed or solid floor systems are used. However, the compensated control of a solid floor system means that the temperature reduces gradually when the system is switched off, rather than rapidly, as with some other systems.

The basic principle of operation of a 'wet' underfloor heating system is that heated water (30–60°C depending on the floor finish) is circulated through plastic or composite pipes buried in the floor, which is designed to be very conductive in order to efficiently transfer the heat from the pipes to the floor surface.

Because the floor surface area is large compared with the size of a steel panel radiator, the floor surface temperature required is very low compared with that of a radiator, and is close to room temperature. Normally the maximum floor surface temperature is below 29°C in all occupied areas so as to achieve an acceptable degree of foot comfort. Lower temperature limits, such as 27°C for vinyl floors, are sometimes required for delicate structures or surface finishes.

It is essential that floor coverings do not provide too great a degree of insulation, or the heat in the underfloor system may not be able to raise the room temperature to its design level. Extra care is required to select a low-resistance underlay for fitted carpets or laminate floor systems.

The design of underfloor heating systems should be undertaken in accordance with BS EN 1264, Parts 1–4, which is the basis of the CIBSE *Underfloor Heating Design & Installation Guide*, where full information on the subject is provided.

5.6 Pipework

In section 5.5 it was shown how to size heat emitters for the property. Now the pipes that carry the heat from the heat generator to the heat emitters need to be sized. Two factors govern the correct size of the pipe, both of which are discussed below. Firstly, the fluid flow velocity through the pipework needs to be sufficiently low so as to not increase noise, which will disturb the occupant. Secondly, the resistance the pipework places on the flow of fluid through it must be low enough that a sensibly sized circulator can be used.

This section presents the information required to assess these two factors and make a sizing decision.

5.6.1 Pipework Sizing Strategy

Heating system pipework must be sized so that each part of the circuit has sufficient circulation to deliver its rated heat output. The flow required for each heat emitter is directly related to its output, and may be calculated using the design temperature difference. The pressure required to achieve sufficient circulation depends on the resistance to flow in the circuit, which is affected by the pipe length and diameter, the number and type of fittings, and the resistance of components, including the heat generator and heat emitters. The designer's task is to ensure that the circuit resistance is low enough for the circulator (pump) to achieve the required flow to all points in the circuit, without undue noise or a tendency to collect air in parts of the system. In particular, the circulator has to be capable of overcoming the resistance of the circuit with the highest resistance – the 'index circuit'– at the same time as providing the necessary flow required by the whole system.

It is recommended that a planned heating system is drawn out prior to starting the pipe sizing calculation process. This may be a scaled isometric drawing such as the one shown in Figure 5.9, a simpler two-dimensional plan or a drawing generated using a computer package. While this Guide recommends the scaled isometric drawing approach, the important element is having an understandable and reliable method of following through the multi-step pipe-sizing process presented in sections 5.6.3 and 5.6.4.

In addition, the data for each section of pipework needs to be recorded as the pipe sizing methodology is being worked through. This may be directly on the drawing for a simple system such as the one shown in Figure 5.9, but separate tables may be required for larger systems. Figure 5.9 shows the pipework layout for a terraced house. The rooms and the individual sections (**a–m**) are identified, and the pipe lengths have been included as measured, but these can also be scaled from the drawing.

Note: The flow and return pipes in Figure 5.9 are shown as a single line, with the scale allowing for the fact that the line measurement is two lengths of pipe.

5.6.2 Pipework Sizing Strategy – Approximation

Sometimes, such as when supplying an estimate to a client, it may be useful to approximate the pipe sizes required before doing the full calculation as set out in sections 5.6.3 and 5.6.4. For this purpose, Tables 5.7 and 5.8 provide approximations for the amount of heat that various sized pipes can carry for a given temperature differential.

Note: The data in Tables 5.7 and 5.8 does not take into account the total circulator pressure available for the system or the temperature drop required by any specific item of equipment, or any specific pipework connection sizes required by items such as the boiler or hot water cylinder.

Note: The information in Tables 5.7 and 5.8 should only be used for pipework on pumped systems.

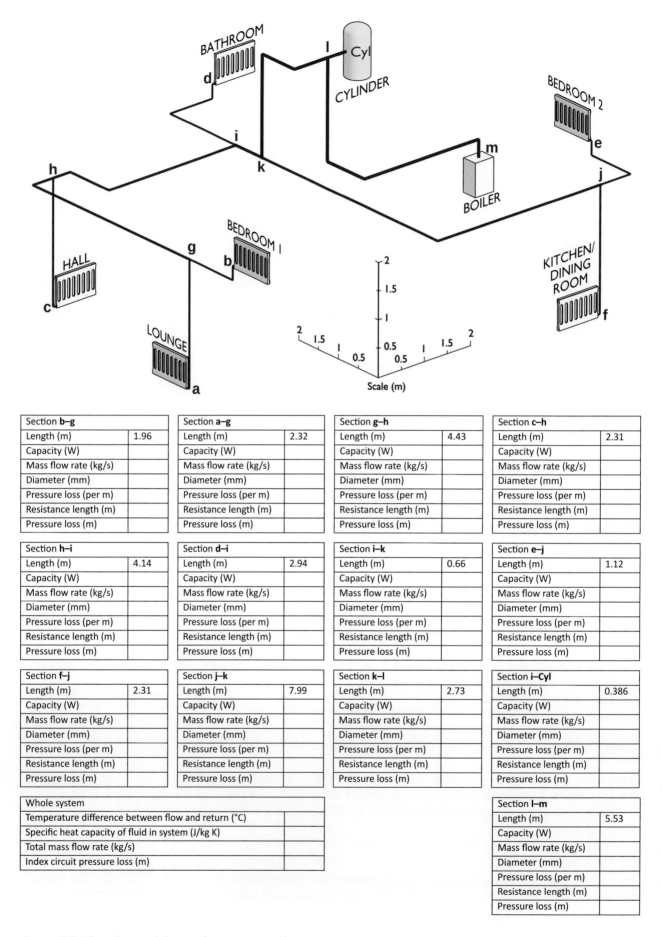

Section **b–g**	
Length (m)	1.96
Capacity (W)	
Mass flow rate (kg/s)	
Diameter (mm)	
Pressure loss (per m)	
Resistance length (m)	
Pressure loss (m)	

Section **a–g**	
Length (m)	2.32
Capacity (W)	
Mass flow rate (kg/s)	
Diameter (mm)	
Pressure loss (per m)	
Resistance length (m)	
Pressure loss (m)	

Section **g–h**	
Length (m)	4.43
Capacity (W)	
Mass flow rate (kg/s)	
Diameter (mm)	
Pressure loss (per m)	
Resistance length (m)	
Pressure loss (m)	

Section **c–h**	
Length (m)	2.31
Capacity (W)	
Mass flow rate (kg/s)	
Diameter (mm)	
Pressure loss (per m)	
Resistance length (m)	
Pressure loss (m)	

Section **h–i**	
Length (m)	4.14
Capacity (W)	
Mass flow rate (kg/s)	
Diameter (mm)	
Pressure loss (per m)	
Resistance length (m)	
Pressure loss (m)	

Section **d–i**	
Length (m)	2.94
Capacity (W)	
Mass flow rate (kg/s)	
Diameter (mm)	
Pressure loss (per m)	
Resistance length (m)	
Pressure loss (m)	

Section **i–k**	
Length (m)	0.66
Capacity (W)	
Mass flow rate (kg/s)	
Diameter (mm)	
Pressure loss (per m)	
Resistance length (m)	
Pressure loss (m)	

Section **e–j**	
Length (m)	1.12
Capacity (W)	
Mass flow rate (kg/s)	
Diameter (mm)	
Pressure loss (per m)	
Resistance length (m)	
Pressure loss (m)	

Section **f–j**	
Length (m)	2.31
Capacity (W)	
Mass flow rate (kg/s)	
Diameter (mm)	
Pressure loss (per m)	
Resistance length (m)	
Pressure loss (m)	

Section **j–k**	
Length (m)	7.99
Capacity (W)	
Mass flow rate (kg/s)	
Diameter (mm)	
Pressure loss (per m)	
Resistance length (m)	
Pressure loss (m)	

Section **k–l**	
Length (m)	2.73
Capacity (W)	
Mass flow rate (kg/s)	
Diameter (mm)	
Pressure loss (per m)	
Resistance length (m)	
Pressure loss (m)	

Section **i–Cyl**	
Length (m)	0.386
Capacity (W)	
Mass flow rate (kg/s)	
Diameter (mm)	
Pressure loss (per m)	
Resistance length (m)	
Pressure loss (m)	

Whole system	
Temperature difference between flow and return (°C)	
Specific heat capacity of fluid in system (J/kg K)	
Total mass flow rate (kg/s)	
Index circuit pressure loss (m)	

Section **l–m**	
Length (m)	5.53
Capacity (W)	
Mass flow rate (kg/s)	
Diameter (mm)	
Pressure loss (per m)	
Resistance length (m)	
Pressure loss (m)	

Figure 5.9 The pipework layout for a terraced house

Table 5.7 Quick sizing for copper pipe (water velocity 0.9 m/s) at the given flow and return water temperature differentials

Pipe diameter(mm)	Approximate load (W)		
	7 ΔT (°C)	11 ΔT (°C)	20 ΔT (°C)
8	1,000	1,500	2,700
10	1,500	2,400	4,300
15	4,000	6,000	11,000
22	8,500	13,000	23,000
28	14,000	22,000	40,000
35	22,000	34,000	62,000
42	34,000	55,000	100,000
54	55,000	90,000	160,000
67	85,000	130,000	235,000
76	108,000	170,000	310,000
108	240,000	360,000	650,000

Table 5.8 Quick sizing for plastic pipe (water velocity 1.2 m/s) at the given flow and return water temperature differentials

EN series 5 pipe diameter (mm)	Approximate load (W)		
	7 ΔT (°C)	11 ΔT (°C)	20 ΔT (°C)
10	1,400	2,100	3,900
12	2,200	3,500	6,400
15	4,000	6,200	11,400
16	4,700	7,300	13,300
18	5,700	9,000	16,400
20	7,200	11,400	20,700
22	8,900	14,100	25,600
25	11,500	18,100	32,800
28	14,400	22,600	41,000
32	19,000	29,800	54,200
40	29,400	46,100	83,900
50	46,000	72,200	131,300
63	73,000	114,700	208,500
75	104,100	163,600	297,500
90	149,600	235,100	427,400
110	223,700	351,500	639,100

> **Example**: To quickly estimate the size of pipework required to supply 2,315 W of heat to a load at a temperature differential of 11°C (the difference between the flow and the return temperatures), either 10 mm copper pipe (from Table 5.7) or 12 mm plastic pipe (from Table 5.8) would be required.

5.6.3 Pipe Sizing Design: Fluid Velocity

As discussed above, the first stage when sizing pipework is to ensure that the fluid flow velocity is sufficiently low so as not to cause unnecessary noise. The smaller the diameter of the pipework, the higher the velocity needs to be to carry sufficient heat to meet the demand on the system. One approach is to use oversized pipework throughout, but this is seen as bad practice, and will end up in higher costs to the customer.

The process for calculating the size of pipework that is sufficient to ensure a sufficiently low velocity is as follows:

1. Calculate the heat required to supply each space, as shown in section 3, plus an allowance for losses throughout the complete system (section 5.6.3.1).
2. Calculate the flow rate required to carry sufficient heat in each section of the system (section 5.6.3.2).
3. Select a suitable pipe size to carry the required flow rate at an acceptable velocity, for each section of the system (section 5.6.3.3).

5.6.3.1 Heat-Carrying Capacity
This section describes how to work out the amount of heat that each section of pipework is required to carry.

Firstly, the total heat loads for all the rooms in the property should be written in the tables for the relevant pipe sections on the system drawing (the calculation of total heat load for a room is given in section 3.5). For the system shown in Figure 5.9 this will be sections **b–g**, **a–g**, **c–h**, **d–i**, **e–j** and **f–j**.

Secondly, if there is any hot water storage, the allowance for this should also be written in the relevant table. Typical hot water heating power requirements for high flow temperature heat generators are given in Table 4.1 (see section 4.4.1.1) for different sizes of dwellings, and a detailed calculation process for other heat generators is given in section 4.4.1.2.

Finally, working backwards through the system from the end points (rooms) to the heat generator, the heat load that each section needs to carry should be evaluated. For example, section **g–h** carries the heat for both sections **b–g** and **a–g**.

Note: The total heat load (see section 3), not the catalogue heat output required or the total radiator heat output required (see section 5.5.5), should be used for pipework sizing.

Note: When a section of pipework passes outside the heated space, such as for connecting to a heat generator (boiler) located in a garage or outdoor enclosure, add up to 10% to the total calculated capacity for that section.

Note: As discussed in section 5.11, the heating controls will often typically prioritise a hot water demand over a heating demand. When this is the case, any pipework sections between the heat generator and any hot water storage that are shared with the heating system may be sized to the larger of the capacity to carry heating or the capacity for hot water demand. This will usually be the hot water capacity.

Note: Pipework supplying a hot water cylinder should never be less than 22 mm diameter.

Example: For the system shown in Figure 5.9, if section **i–k** is calculated to be carrying 4,823 W, the kitchen/dining room and bedroom 2 have been calculated to have heat losses of 1,842 and 754 W, respectively. The system is heated by a gas boiler with flow and return temperatures of 70°C and 50°C. The values to be added to the tables on the system drawing (see Figure 5.9) are as follows:

- Pipework section **e–j** (bedroom 2):

Section	e–j
Length (m)	1.12
Capacity (W)	**754**
⋮	⋮

- Pipework section **f–j** (kitchen/dining room):

Section	f–j
Length (m)	2.31
Capacity (W)	**1,842**
⋮	⋮

- Pipework section **j–k** (carries the capacity of sections **e–j** and **f–j**)

Section	j–k
Length (m)	7.99
Capacity (W)	**2,596**
⋮	⋮

- Pipework section **i–k**:

Section	i–k
Length (m)	0.66
Capacity (W)	**4,823**
⋮	⋮

- Pipework section **k–l** (carries the capacity of sections **j–k** and **i–k**)

Section	k–l
Length (m)	2.73
Capacity (W)	**7,419**
⋮	⋮

- Pipework section **l–m** (carries capacity of sections **k–l** and **l–Cyl**): from Table 4.1 (see section 4.4.1.1), a two-bedroom house requires a capacity of 13,000 W. Therefore, the hot water capacity requirement is used, as it is larger than the capacity of section **k–l** and in this case the control system isolates the heating demand during periods of hot water demand.

Section	l–m
Length (m)	5.53
Capacity (W)	**13,000**
⋮	⋮

5.6.3.2 Flow Rate Requirement

To establish the required mass flow rate (*m*) of water through the pipework to deliver the calculated heat-carrying capacity, the following equation should be used:

$$m = \frac{H}{\Delta T \times \text{SHC}}$$

(Equation 12)

where

 m   is the mass flow rate in kg/s
 H   is the calculated heat-carrying capacity in W
 ΔT is the temperature difference between the flow and the return in °C
 SHC is the specific heat capacity of the fluid in system in J/kg K

Fresh water has a specific heat capacity of 4,187 J/kg K, and is the value that will be typically used for most domestic heating systems. The value will not be changed significantly by the addition of inhibitors; although the manufacturer's specifications should be consulted.

The specific heat capacity of the generic antifreeze propylene glycol is only 2,500 J/kg K, which is significantly lower than that of fresh water. The amount of propylene glycol used depends on the frost protection temperature required, but it is usually in the range of 25–30% of the water content. Thus, a 25% propylene glycol plus 75% water mixture will produce SHC = 3,770 J/kg K on average. Increased pumping resistance in the region of 10% is therefore quite common, as more water needs to be pumped to deliver the same heat-carrying capacity.

Note: Check with the propylene glycol supplier for temperature protection recommendations.

Note: Automotive ethylene glycol antifreeze (SHC = 2,360 J/kg K) is a *toxic* product and should not be used in residential systems because of the requirement for its controlled disposal.

Example: For the system shown in Figure 5.9, assuming a modern condensing system boiler, the flow rate required for bedroom 2 (**e–j**) is (using Equation 12):

H = 754 W

ΔT = 20°C (from section 5.5.2)

SHC = 4187 J/kg K

$$m = \frac{754}{20 \times 4,187} = \frac{754}{83,740} = 0.009 \text{ kg/s}$$

Section	e–j
Length (m)	1.12
Capacity (W)	754
Mass flow rate (kg/s)	**0.009**
⋮	⋮

This calculation should be repeated for each section of pipework, and the mass flow rate values added to the tables on the system drawing (see Figure 5.9).

Note: At this stage it is useful to record the total mass flow rate for the system, as this will be required when selecting the circulator (see section 5.8.1). For the system shown in Figure 5.9, this will be the mass flow rate for pipework section **l–m**.

5.6.3.3 Pipe Size

Once the mass flow rate for each section of pipework is known, an appropriate pipe size can be selected to ensure that the velocity of the fluid is sufficiently low so as not to cause excessive noise or friction. The maximum velocity chosen should be 1.5 m/s, as, above this level, noise will be excessive and the frictional resistance to flow will be significant. Likewise, a velocity of less than 0.5 m/s should not be selected, as this is unlikely to be sufficient to remove pockets of trapped air in a system. It is therefore recommended to select a velocity of around (or slightly below) 1.0 m/s. Tables 5.9 to 5.11 can be used to make this selection.

> **Example 1**: Pipework section **k–l** in Figure 5.9 is copper pipework and the temperature differential is 20°C.
>
> A mass flow rate of 0.0886 kg/s (calculated as in section 5.6.3.2) is off the bottom of the columns for 8 and 10 mm pipe in Table 5.9. Therefore, 15 mm pipework will be suitable; the velocity will be between 0.5 and 1.0 m/s, and therefore noise should not be a problem. Pipework with a diameter of 15 mm is provisionally selected subject to the frictional resistance sizing check in section 5.6.4.

Section	k–l	
Length (m)	2.73	
Capacity (W)	7419	
Mass flow rate (kg/s)	0.0886	
Diameter (mm)	**15**	← Provisional value
⋮	⋮	

> **Example 2**: A system is composed of plastic pipework, has a temperature differential of 11°C and the following capacity and mass flow rate values.
>
> A mass flow rate of 0.24 kg/s is in the column for 16 mm pipework in Table 5.11, but would result in a fluid velocity greater than 1.0 m/s. Therefore, a pipe size of 20 mm will be suitable, because it will result in a velocity between 0.5 and 1.0 m/s and noise should not be a problem. Pipework with a diameter of 20 mm is provisionally selected subject to the frictional resistance sizing check in section 5.6.4.

⋮	⋮	
Capacity (W)	**11,054**	
Mass flow rate (kg/s)	0.24	
Diameter (mm)	**20**	← Provisional value
⋮	⋮	

The above procedure should then be repeated for each section of pipework, and the selected values for the pipework diameter added to the tables on the system drawing (see Figure 5.9).

Note: As discussed above, hot water cylinders should have primary pipework of at least 22 mm diameter, which will ensure low pressure loss and rapid recovery of the cylinder temperature.

Note: At this stage it is useful to note the values of the pressure loss per metre section in the relevant tables (such as in Figure 5.9) by copying the appropriate pressure loss (in metres head of water per metre run of pipe m(hd)/m) from the first columns of Tables 5.9 to 5.11. This is discussed further in section 5.6.4.1.

Table 5.9 Mass flow rate of water (kg/s) in copper pipes (8–35 mm). See notes after Table 5.11

Pressure loss (m(hd)/m)	Mass flow rate (kg/s) at given pipe diameters						Velocity (m/s)
	8 mm	10 mm	15 mm	22 mm	28 mm	35 mm	
				0.3 m/s			
0.008	0.0062	0.0107	0.0357	0.1054	0.2137	0.3861	0.5 m/s
0.009	0.0064	0.0115	0.0382	0.1128	0.2285	0.4126	
0.010	0.0066	0.0122	0.0406	0.1198	0.2426	0.4379	
0.011	0.0068	0.0129	0.0429	0.1265	0.2561	0.4621	
0.012	0.0070	0.0136	0.0452	0.1329	0.2691	0.4853	
0.013	0.0072	0.0142	0.0473	0.1392	0.2815	0.5077	
0.014	0.0074	0.0149	0.0494	0.1452	0.2936	0.5293	
0.015	0.0077	0.0155	0.0514	0.1510	0.3053	0.5503	
0.016	0.0079	0.0161	0.0533	0.1566	0.3166	0.5706	
0.017	0.0082	0.0167	0.0552	0.1621	0.3277	0.5903	
0.018	0.0085	0.0173	0.0571	0.1675	0.3384	0.6096	
0.019	0.0087	0.0178	0.0589	0.1727	0.3489	0.6284	
0.020	0.0090	0.0184	0.0606	0.1778	0.3591	0.6467	
0.021	0.0092	0.0189	0.0624	0.1828	0.3691	0.6646	
0.022	0.0095	0.0194	0.0641	0.1877	0.3789	0.6822	
0.024	0.0100	0.0204	0.0674	0.1972	0.3980	0.7162	
0.026	0.0105	0.0214	0.0705	0.2064	0.4163	0.7490	
0.028	0.0110	0.0223	0.0736	0.2152	0.4340	0.7807	
0.030	0.0114	0.0233	0.0765	0.2238	0.4511	0.8114	1.0 m/s
0.032	0.0119	0.0242	0.0794	0.2321	0.4678	0.8411	
0.034	0.0123	0.0250	0.0822	0.2402	0.4840	0.8701	
0.036	0.0127	0.0259	0.0850	0.2481	0.4997	0.8982	
0.038	0.0131	0.0267	0.0876	0.2557	0.5151	0.9257	
0.040	0.0135	0.0275	0.0902	0.2632	0.5301	0.9525	
0.042	0.0139	0.0283	0.0928	0.2706	0.5448	0.9788	
0.044	0.0143	0.0291	0.0953	0.2778	0.5591	1.0044	
0.046	0.0147	0.0298	0.0977	0.2848	0.5732	1.0296	
0.048	0.0150	0.0306	0.1001	0.2917	0.5870	1.0542	
0.050	0.0154	0.0313	0.1025	0.2985	0.6005	1.0784	
0.052	0.0158	0.0320	0.1048	0.3051	0.6138	1.1022	
0.054	0.0161	0.0327	0.1070	0.3117	0.6269	1.1255	
0.056	0.0165	0.0334	0.1093	0.3181	0.6397	1.1485	
0.058	0.0168	0.0341	0.1115	0.3244	0.6524	1.1710	
0.060	0.0171	0.0348	0.1136	0.3307	0.6648	1.1933	
0.062	0.0175	0.0354	0.1158	0.3368	0.6771	1.2152	
0.064	0.0178	0.0361	0.1179	0.3429	0.6892	1.2368	1.5 m/s
0.066	0.0181	0.0367	0.1199	0.3488	0.7011	1.2580	
0.068	0.0184	0.0373	0.1220	0.3547	0.7129	1.2790	
0.070	0.0187	0.0380	0.1240	0.3605	0.7245	1.2997	
0.072	0.0190	0.0386	0.1260	0.3663	0.7359		
0.074	0.0194	0.0392	0.1280	0.3719	0.7472		
0.076	0.0197	0.0398	0.1299	0.3775	0.7584		
0.078	0.0200	0.0404	0.1319	0.3830	0.7694		
0.080	0.0202	0.0410	0.1338	0.3885	0.7803		
0.082	0.0205	0.0416	0.1356	0.3939	0.7911		
0.084	0.0208	0.0422	0.1375	0.3993	0.8018		
0.086	0.0211	0.0427	0.1393	0.4045	0.8123		
0.088	0.0214	0.0433	0.1412	0.4098	0.8228		
0.090	0.0217	0.0439	0.1430	0.4150	0.8331		
0.092	0.0220	0.0444	0.1448	0.4201	0.8433		
0.094	0.0222	0.0450	0.1465	0.4252			
0.096	0.0225	0.0455	0.1483	0.4302			
0.098	0.0228	0.0461	0.1500	0.4352			
0.100	0.0230	0.0466	0.1517	0.4401			
0.102	0.0233	0.0471	0.1534	0.4450			
0.104	0.0236	0.0477	0.1551	0.4498			
0.106	0.0238	0.0482	0.1568	0.4546			
0.108	0.0241	0.0487	0.1585	0.4594			
0.110	0.0243	0.0492	0.1601	0.4641			
0.112	0.0246	0.0497	0.1617	0.4688			
0.114	0.0249	0.0502	0.1634	0.4735			
0.116	0.0251	0.0507	0.1650	0.4781			
0.118	0.0253	0.0512	0.1666	0.4827			
0.120	0.0256	0.0517	0.1681	0.4872			
0.130	0.0268	0.0541	0.1759				
0.140	0.0280	0.0565	0.1834				
0.150	0.0291	0.0587	0.1906				
0.160	0.0302	0.0609	0.1977				
0.170	0.0313	0.0631	0.2045				
0.180	0.0323	0.0651	0.2112				
0.190	0.0333	0.0672	0.2177				
0.200	0.0343	0.0692	0.2240				

Table 5.10 Mass flow rate of water (kg/s) in copper pipes (42–159 mm). See notes after Table 5.11

Pressure loss (m(hd)/m)	Mass flow rate (kg/s) at given pipe diameters							Velocity (m/s)
	42 mm	54 mm	67 mm	76 mm	108 mm	133 mm	159 mm	
					0.3 m/s			
0.0007	0.1626	0.3348	0.6161	0.8601	2.2831	4.0501	6.4924	
0.0008	0.1756	0.3613	0.6645	0.9273	2.4602	4.3626	6.9908	
0.0009	0.1879	0.3864	0.7104	0.9909	2.6277	4.6580	7.4620	
0.0010	0.1996	0.4103	0.7540	1.0515	2.7871	4.9391	7.9102	
0.0012	0.2215	0.4548	0.8351	1.1631	3.0832	5.4606	8.7383	
0.0014	0.2419	0.4963	0.9108	1.2673	3.3590	5.9464	9.5101	0.5 m/s
0.0016	0.2612	0.5354	0.9820	1.3655	3.6185	6.4031	10.2358	
0.0018	0.2801	0.5723	1.0494	1.4585	3.8639	6.8355	10.9230	
0.0020	0.2973	0.6075	1.1135	1.5471	4.0974	7.2466	11.5776	
0.0022	0.3138	0.6427	1.1778	1.6320	4.3206	7.6396	12.2031	
0.0024	0.3296	0.6748	1.2363	1.7136	4.5442	8.0167	12.8034	
0.0026	0.3449	0.7058	1.2927	1.7921	4.7492	8.3966	13.3813	
0.0028	0.3597	0.7358	1.3473	1.8680	4.9474	8.7452	13.9394	
0.0030	0.3740	0.7649	1.4002	1.9453	5.1395	9.0830	14.4796	
0.0032	0.3879	0.7931	1.4515	2.0168	5.3259	9.4110	15.0036	
0.0034	0.4016	0.8209	1.5021	2.0863	5.5097	9.7347	15.5389	
0.0036	0.4149	0.8480	1.5521	2.1540	5.6899	10.0485	16.0355	
0.0038	0.4279	0.8747	1.5998	2.2200	5.8629	10.3528	16.5196	
0.0040	0.4410	0.9004	1.6464	2.2845	6.0318	10.6499	16.9923	
0.0042	0.4534	0.9254	1.6919	2.3475	6.1970	10.9404	17.4542	
0.0044	0.4655	0.9499	1.7365	2.4092	6.3586	11.2246	17.9062	
0.0046	0.4773	0.9739	1.7802	2.4696	6.5170	11.5029	18.3489	1.0 m/s
0.0048	0.4890	0.9975	1.8231	2.5289	6.6722	11.7758	18.7829	
0.0050	0.5004	1.0206	1.8651	2.5871	6.8245	12.0436	19.2086	
0.0052	0.5116	1.0434	1.9064	2.6442	6.9741	12.3065	19.6267	
0.0054	0.5226	1.0657	1.9470	2.7003	7.1210	12.5648	20.0374	
0.0056	0.5335	1.0877	1.9869	2.7555	7.2656	12.8188	20.4413	
0.0058	0.5441	1.1093	2.0262	2.8099	7.4078	13.0687	20.8385	
0.0060	0.5546	1.1305	2.0648	2.8633	7.5477	13.3147	21.2296	
0.0062	0.5650	1.1515	2.1029	2.9160	7.6856	13.5570	21.6147	
0.0064	0.5752	1.1722	2.1405	2.9679	7.8215	13.7957	21.9941	
0.0066	0.5853	1.1926	2.1775	3.0191	7.9554	14.0310	22.3682	
0.0068	0.5952	1.2127	2.2140	3.0696	8.0875	14.2631	22.7371	
0.0070	0.6050	1.2325	2.2500	3.1195	8.2178	14.4921	23.1010	
0.0072	0.6147	1.2521	2.2856	3.1687	8.3465	14.7181	23.4602	
0.0074	0.6242	1.2714	2.3207	3.2172	8.4735	14.9413	23.8149	
0.0076	0.6337	1.2905	2.3554	3.2652	8.5990	15.1617	24.1651	
0.0078	0.6430	1.3094	2.3897	3.3126	8.7230	15.3794	24.5112	
0.0080	0.6522	1.3281	2.4236	3.3595	8.8455	15.5947	24.8532	
0.0082	0.6614	1.3465	2.4571	3.4058	8.9667	15.8074	25.1913	
0.0084	0.6704	1.3648	2.4903	3.4516	9.0865	16.0178	25.5256	
0.0086	0.6793	1.3829	2.5231	3.4970	9.2050	16.2260	25.8563	
0.0088	0.6882	1.4007	2.5555	3.5418	9.3222	16.4319	26.1835	
0.0090	0.6969	1.4184	2.5876	3.5862	9.4383	16.6357	26.5072	
0.0092	0.7056	1.4359	2.6194	3.6302	9.5531	16.8374	26.8277	
0.0094	0.7141	1.4533	2.6509	3.6737	9.6669	17.0371	27.1450	
0.0096	0.7226	1.4705	2.6821	3.7168	9.7795	17.2348	27.4592	
0.0098	0.7311	1.4875	2.7130	3.7595	9.8911	17.4307	27.7703	1.5 m/s
0.0100	0.7394	1.5043	2.7436	3.8018	10.0016	17.6248	28.0786	
0.0120	0.8190	1.6653	3.0356	4.2055	11.0559	19.4754		
0.0140	0.8929	1.8145	3.3063	4.5795	12.0322			
0.0160	0.9621	1.9544	3.5599	4.9298	12.9464			
0.0180	1.0276	2.0865	3.7994	5.2607				
0.0200	1.0898	2.2121	4.0271	5.5751				
0.0220	1.1493	2.3321	4.2446	5.8755				
0.0240	1.2064	2.4473	4.4532	6.1636				
0.0260	1.2614	2.5582	4.6540	6.4409				
0.0280	1.3145	2.6652	4.8479					
0.0300	1.3659	2.7689	5.0356					
0.0320	1.4158	2.8694						
0.0340	1.4642	2.9671						
0.0360	1.5114	3.0622						
0.0380	1.5575	3.1549						
0.0400	1.6024	3.2454						
0.0420	1.6463							
0.0440	1.6893							
0.0460	1.7314							
0.0480	1.7727							
0.0500	1.8132							
0.0520	1.8530							
0.0540	1.8920							
0.0560	1.9305							

Table 5.11 Mass flow rate (kg/s) of water in plastic pipes (10–63 mm). See notes after the table

Pressure loss (m(hd)/m)	Mass flow rate (kg/s) at given pipe diameters									Velocity (m/s)
	10 mm	12 mm	16 mm	20 mm	25 mm	32 mm	40 mm	50 mm	63 mm	
			0.3 m/s			0.5 m/s				
0.008	0.0152	0.0253	0.0557	0.1026	0.1882	0.3672	0.6701	1.2205	2.2664	
0.009	0.0163	0.0271	0.0597	0.1097	0.2013	0.3925	0.7160	1.3036	2.4199	
0.010	0.0174	0.0288	0.0634	0.1166	0.2137	0.4165	0.7596	1.3826	2.5658	
0.011	0.0184	0.0304	0.0670	0.1231	0.2256	0.4395	0.8014	1.4581	2.7053	
0.012	0.0194	0.0320	0.0704	0.1294	0.2370	0.4616	0.8414	1.5306	2.8391	
0.013	0.0203	0.0335	0.0738	0.1354	0.2480	0.4829	0.8800	1.6005	2.9680	1.0 m/s
0.014	0.0212	0.0350	0.0770	0.1413	0.2587	0.5035	0.9173	1.6679	3.0924	
0.015	0.0221	0.0365	0.0801	0.1470	0.2690	0.5234	0.9534	1.7332	3.2128	
0.016	0.0229	0.0378	0.0831	0.1525	0.2790	0.5428	0.9884	1.7965	3.3297	
0.017	0.0237	0.0392	0.0861	0.1578	0.2887	0.5616	1.0225	1.8581	3.4433	
0.018	0.0246	0.0405	0.0889	0.1630	0.2982	0.5799	1.0556	1.9181	3.5538	
0.019	0.0253	0.0418	0.0917	0.1681	0.3074	0.5978	1.0880	1.9766	3.6616	
0.020	0.0261	0.0431	0.0945	0.1731	0.3165	0.6152	1.1196	2.0336	3.7669	
0.021	0.0269	0.0443	0.0971	0.1780	0.3253	0.6323	1.1504	2.0895	3.8698	
0.022	0.0276	0.0455	0.0997	0.1827	0.3339	0.6490	1.1807	2.1441	3.9704	
0.024	0.0290	0.0479	0.1048	0.1920	0.3507	0.6814	1.2393	2.2500	4.1657	
0.026	0.0304	0.0501	0.1097	0.2009	0.3669	0.7126	1.2958	2.3520	4.3537	
0.028	0.0317	0.0523	0.1145	0.2095	0.3825	0.7427	1.3503	2.4505	4.5351	1.5 m/s
0.030	0.0330	0.0544	0.1191	0.2178	0.3977	0.7719	1.4031	2.5459	4.7107	
0.032	0.0343	0.0565	0.1235	0.2259	0.4123	0.8003	1.4543	2.6384	4.8811	
0.034	0.0355	0.0585	0.1278	0.2338	0.4266	0.8278	1.5041	2.7282		
0.036	0.0367	0.0604	0.1321	0.2415	0.4405	0.8546	1.5526	2.8158		
0.038	0.0379	0.0623	0.1362	0.2490	0.4541	0.8808	1.5999	2.9011		
0.040	0.0390	0.0642	0.1402	0.2563	0.4673	0.9063	1.6460	2.9844		
0.042	0.0401	0.0660	0.1441	0.2634	0.4803	0.9313	1.6911	3.0658		
0.044	0.0412	0.0678	0.1480	0.2704	0.4930	0.9557	1.7353			
0.046	0.0423	0.0695	0.1518	0.2773	0.5054	0.9796	1.7785			
0.048	0.0433	0.0712	0.1555	0.2840	0.5176	1.0031	1.8209			
0.050	0.0444	0.0729	0.1591	0.2906	0.5295	1.0261	1.8625			
0.052	0.0454	0.0746	0.1627	0.2971	0.5413	1.0487	1.9033			
0.054	0.0464	0.0762	0.1662	0.3034	0.5528	1.0710	1.9434			
0.056	0.0474	0.0778	0.1696	0.3097	0.5641	1.0928				
0.058	0.0483	0.0794	0.1730	0.3159	0.5753	1.1143				
0.060	0.0493	0.0809	0.1764	0.3219	0.5863	1.1355				
0.062	0.0502	0.0824	0.1797	0.3279	0.5971	1.1563				
0.064	0.0511	0.0840	0.1829	0.3338	0.6078	1.1769				
0.066	0.0520	0.0854	0.1861	0.3396	0.6183	1.1971				
0.068	0.0529	0.0869	0.1893	0.3453	0.6287	1.2171				
0.070	0.0538	0.0883	0.1924	0.3510	0.6389	1.2368				
0.072	0.0547	0.0898	0.1955	0.3566	0.6491	1.2563				
0.074	0.0556	0.0912	0.1985	0.3621	0.6590					
0.076	0.0564	0.0926	0.2015	0.3675	0.6689					
0.078	0.0573	0.0939	0.2045	0.3729	0.6786					
0.080	0.0581	0.0953	0.2075	0.3783	0.6883					
0.082	0.0589	0.0967	0.2104	0.3835	0.6978					
0.084	0.0597	0.0980	0.2132	0.3887	0.7072					
0.086	0.0605	0.0993	0.2161	0.3939	0.7165					
0.088	0.0613	0.1006	0.2189	0.3990	0.7257					
0.090	0.0621	0.1019	0.2217	0.4040	0.7349					
0.092	0.0629	0.1032	0.2244	0.4090	0.7439					
0.094	0.0637	0.1044	0.2272	0.4140	0.7528					
0.096	0.0645	0.1057	0.2299	0.4188	0.7617					
0.098	0.0652	0.1069	0.2325	0.4237	0.7705					
0.100	0.0660	0.1082	0.2352	0.4285						
0.102	0.0667	0.1094	0.2378	0.4333						
0.104	0.0675	0.1106	0.2404	0.4380						
0.106	0.0682	0.1118	0.2430	0.4427						
0.108	0.0689	0.1130	0.2456	0.4473						
0.110	0.0697	0.1142	0.2481	0.4519						
0.112	0.0704	0.1153	0.2506	0.4565						
0.114	0.0711	0.1165	0.2531	0.4610						
0.116	0.0718	0.1176	0.2556	0.4655						
0.118	0.0725	0.1188	0.2581	0.4700						
0.120	0.0732	0.1199	0.2605	0.4744						
0.130	0.0766	0.1255	0.2725							
0.140	0.0799	0.1308	0.2840							
0.150	0.0831	0.1360	0.2952							
0.160	0.0862	0.1411	0.3060							
0.170	0.0892	0.1459								
0.180	0.0921	0.1507								
0.190	0.0950	0.1554								
0.200	0.0978	0.1599								

Note: The pipe sizes listed in Tables 5.9 to 5.11 are nominal diameters (as typically listed by manufacturers), which for copper pipe are the outer diameters of the pipe (the wall thicknesses used are: 8 and 10 mm pipe, 0.6 mm; 15 mm pipe, 0.7 mm; 22 and 28 mm pipe, 0.9 mm; 35, 42, 54 and 67 mm pipe, 1.2 mm; 76, 108 and 133 mm pipe, 1.5 mm; 159 mm pipe, 2 mm). The nominal diameters for plastic pipe are inner diameters. For pipes of other dimensions, the manufacturer's literature should be consulted.

Note: The mass flow rates listed in Tables 5.9 to 5.11 were calculated using the following parameters: water density, 983.2 kg/m^3; dynamic viscosity, 0.000466 N s/m^2; absolute roughness, 0.0015 mm. Low flow temperature systems, as well as those with certain additives such as inhibitors or antifreeze, may have a different water density and dynamic viscosity. Plastic pipe, particularly multi-layer pipe, may have an absolute roughness higher or lower (due to low-resistance inner layers) than the value used here. Corrosion of or build-up on the inside of the pipe of old or poorly maintained pipes will also affect the absolute roughness. For situations that differ significantly from those used here, the manufacturer's literature should be consulted.

Note: The pipe pressure losses in Tables 5.9 to Table 5.11 are expressed in metres head of water per metre run of pipe (m(hd)/m). Other sources may express pressure loss in different units, such as pascals per metre (Pa/m).

Note: Always use compatible units in any calculation (1 m head of water = 9,807 Pa).

5.6.4 Pipe Sizing Design: Frictional Resistance

As discussed above, the second step in working out the size of pipework is to ensure that the resistance the pipework places on the flow of the fluid is low enough that a sensibly sized circulator can be used. In section 5.6.3, a pipe size was selected that ensures a sufficiently low velocity not to create excessive noise. This now needs to be checked to ensure that the selected pipe size does not offer excessive resistance, as this will increase the electricity consumption of the pump, the wear on the pump and the cost of the pump required.

The process for calculating whether the selected pipework size offers sufficiently low resistance is as follows:

1. identify the resistance for each item in the system (pipework, heat generator, radiators, large valves, etc.) – see sections 5.6.4.1 to 5.6.4.3
2. identify the index circuit – see section 5.6.4.4
3. determine the suitability of the existing or selected pump, repeating steps 1–3 with a different pipework sizes if necessary – see section 5.8.3

5.6.4.1 Pipework Pressure Loss
The pressure loss in metres of head lost per metre run of pipe for various pipe sizes is given in Tables 5.9 to 5.11, together with values of the mass flow rate and the maximum velocity.

> **Example**: For the system shown in Figure 5.9, consider that pipework section **k–l** is composed of copper pipe.
>
> With a mass flow rate of 0.0886 kg/s and a pipe size of 15 mm, reading from column 1 of Table 5.9, the pressure loss per metre of pipework is 0.040 m(hd)/m (as 0.0886 kg/s is larger than the nearest mass flow rate value of 0.0876 kg/s, the next largest pressure loss is selected).

Section	k–l
Length (m)	2.73
Capacity (W)	7419
Mass flow rate (kg/s)	0.0886
Diameter (mm)	15
Pressure loss (per m)	**0.040**
⋮	⋮

The above procedure should then be repeated for each section of pipework, and the pressure loss values obtained added to the tables on the system drawing (see Figure 5.9).

Note: For low temperature heat pump systems the viscosity of the thermal transfer fluid increases (becomes thicker) as the temperature falls, and, as such, the pumping resistance can often increase by 50%. This is outside the scope of this Guide, and specialist knowledge should be sought.

5.6.4.2 Fixtures and Fittings Resistance
The pressure loss in the system due to the resistance of fixtures and fittings needs to be accounted for.

For larger items, such as heat generators, heat emitters and filters, as well as certain valves and fittings, the manufacturer's information should provide the value of the pressure loss across the item. This is discussed further in section 5.6.4.3.

For fittings where no manufacturer's information is available, Table 5.12 can be used to estimate the equivalent length of additional pipework to provide the same resistance to the flow.

Table 5.12 Equivalent length of copper pipework (m) for fittings (add 20% if velocity exceeds 1 m/s) for given pipework diameters

Fitting	Equivalent Length of straight pipe (m) for the given pipe diameter				
	10 mm	15 mm	22 mm	28 mm	35 mm
Straight valve	0.5	0.5	0.6	0.6	0.8
Angle valve	2.0	2.0	4.5	6.0	N/A
Press fit/capillary elbow	1.7	1.4	1.3	1.3	1.2
Tee branch – press fit	1.7	1.5	1.5	1.7	2.0
Tee branch – capillary	0.6	0.7	1.0	1.3	1.5
Radiator heat emitter	Assume 1 m of pipe per metre of radiator length				

Example: For the system shown in Figure 5.9, pipework section **f–j** comprises:

- copper pipe
- 2 angle valves: 2 × 0.5 m = 1 m
- 6 capillary elbows: 6 × 1.7 m = 10.2 m

Values for 10 mm pipe fittings used, as 8 mm fittings are not given in Table 5.12.

Radiator resistance is not included here, as the pressure loss is known from the manufacturer's specification (see section 5.6.4.3).

Therefore, the resistance length for this section is 1 + 10.2 + 2.31 = 13.5 m.

Section	f–j
Length (m)	2.31
Capacity (W)	1842
Mass flow rate (kg/s)	0.022
Diameter (mm)	8
Pressure loss (per m)	0.0902
Resistance length (m)	**13.5**
⋮	⋮

The above procedure should then be repeated for each section of pipework, and the values of the resistance length added to the tables on the system drawing (see Figure 5.9).

5.6.4.3 Pressure Loss

Once the resistance length has been calculated for a section, the pressure loss due to the pipework and the fittings can be calculated by multiplying the resistance length by the pressure loss per metre.

Finally, the pressure losses from larger items such as heat generators, heat emitters and filters, as well as certain larger valves and fittings, need to be accounted for. The pressure losses for these items should be provided in the manufacturer's specifications.

Note: Pressure losses across items are often provided in units of kilopascals; 1 kPa is equivalent to approximately 0.102 m of head loss.

To obtain the total pressure loss for the section, the pressure losses calculated for the pipework and fittings should be added to those obtained from the manufacturers' specifications for any specific items.

Example: For the system shown in Figure 5.9, pipework section **f–j**, with a radiator pressure loss (from manufacturer) of 0.026 m.

Pressure loss for pipework and fittings = 0.092 × 13.5 = 1.24 m

Total pressure loss for pipework section = 1.24 + 0.026 = 1.27 m

Section	f–j
Length (m)	2.31
Capacity (W)	1842
Mass flow rate (kg/s)	0.022
Diameter (mm)	8
Pressure loss (per m)	0.092
Resistance length (m)	13.5
Pressure loss (m)	**1.27**

The above procedure should then be repeated for each section of pipework, and the values of the resistance length added to the tables on the system drawing (see Figure 5.9).

Note: For existing systems up to 45 kW output that are being upgraded, where no manufacturer's information is available and a full survey is not possible, an allowance of 33–50% extra pipework length for the resistance of standard radiators and fittings should be made for the whole system.

5.6.4.4 Identifying the Index Circuit

When considering the frictional resistance (pressure loss) of the circuit, it is important to remember that it is the sum of the resistances for the most resistive circuit in the system that should be considered, not the sum of all the resistances throughout the system. For example, in a house with two rooms, where the total resistance of all the sections of pipework from the heat generator to room 1 is greater than the total resistance of all the sections of pipework from the heat generator to room 2, the circuit from the heat generator to room 1 is the index circuit, and so only the sum of its resistances will be used to size the circulator.

Note: When discussing index circuits, a circuit is the route that the system fluid will take from the heat generator to each of the heat emitters. For example, in the system shown in Figure 5.9, the route from the boiler (**m**) to the lounge (**a**) is a circuit, and the route from the boiler (**m**) to bedroom 1 (**b**) is another circuit, despite both circuits sharing pipework sections for most of their routes.

Identifying which circuit is the index circuit can be difficult and will often require the testing of several candidates (if not all circuits). Typically, the index circuit will be either the one with the longest run or the one with the most contorted path, so these circuits should be considered first. However, this may not always be the case, for example if the designer has oversized the pipework in these sections.

Example: Figure 5.10 shows the system drawing with all the tables completed with the data calculated in sections 5.6.3–5.6.4.3. Candidates for the index circuit and their corresponding resistances are:

Section	f–j
a–m	7.66
b–m	6.88
c–m	5.19
d–m	3.00
Cyl–m	0.34
e–m	5.27
f–m	6.22

For the system as described, the index circuit is, therefore, **a–m**, which has a total pressure loss of 7.66 m.

Note: In Figure 5.10 the value for the mass flow rate for section **c–h** is off the bottom of the table, therefore the next highest value is used.

Note: At this stage it is useful to record the pressure loss for the index circuit, as this will be required when selecting the circulator (see section 5.8.1).

Note: In section 5.8 we will discuss circulator selection, where it may be found that the above resistance is too high for the chosen circulator, and therefore the circulator required may be too expensive. If this is the case, then the above process can be repeated but using a section of pipe with a high-pressure loss increased to the next size up. Care should be taken that the pipe size increases from the load to the heat generator, and that the velocity remains in the target range of 0.5–1.5 m/s (as discussed in section 5.6.3.3).

Note: If a specific circulator is to be used, such as when expanding an existing system, the pressure loss of the index circuit along with the total mass flow rate for the system (from section 5.6.3.2) should now be checked against the circulator manufacturer's specification (see section 5.8.1). If either the index circuit pressure loss or the total mass flow rate for the system is outside the specification for the circulator, the selected pipework sizes may need to be altered to bring the system within the operating range of the circulator.

There may be other occasions when it will be necessary to make further changes. For example, the pressure loss in a section of pipe may turn out to be unduly high, or the size of the heat generator connecting pipework does not conform to the manufacturer's requirements. In such cases, the size must be altered, and the total resistance recalculated. Otherwise, pipe sizing is now complete.

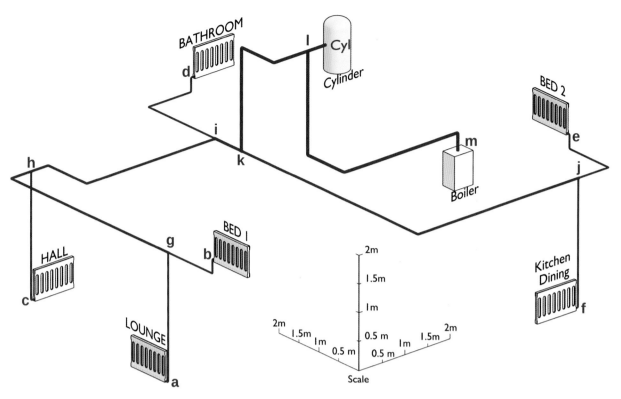

Section b–g	
Length (m)	1.96
Capacity (W)	823
Mass flow rate (kg/s)	0.0098
Diameter (mm)	8
Pressure loss (per m)	0.024
Resistance length (m)	13.05
Pressure loss (m)	0.31

Section a–g	
Length (m)	2.32
Capacity (W)	2930
Mass flow rate (kg/s)	0.0350
Diameter (mm)	10
Pressure loss (per m)	0.062
Resistance length (m)	17.75
Pressure loss (m)	1.10

Section g–h	
Length (m)	4.43
Capacity (W)	3753
Mass flow rate (kg/s)	0.0448
Diameter (mm)	10
Pressure loss (per m)	0.094
Resistance length (m)	15.75
Pressure loss (m)	1.48

Section c–h	
Length (m)	2.31
Capacity (W)	420
Mass flow rate (kg/s)	0.0050
Diameter (mm)	8
Pressure loss (per m)	0.008
Resistance length (m)	14.17
Pressure loss (m)	0.11

Section h–i	
Length (m)	4.14
Capacity (W)	4173
Mass flow rate (kg/s)	0.0498
Diameter (mm)	10
Pressure loss (per m)	0.114
Resistance length (m)	19.93
Pressure loss (m)	2.27

Section d–i	
Length (m)	2.94
Capacity (W)	650
Mass flow rate (kg/s)	0.0078
Diameter (mm)	8
Pressure loss (per m)	0.016
Resistance length (m)	11.81
Pressure loss (m)	0.19

Section i–k	
Length (m)	0.66
Capacity (W)	4823
Mass flow rate (kg/s)	0.0576
Diameter (mm)	10
Pressure loss (per m)	0.150
Resistance length (m)	12.90
Pressure loss (m)	1.94

Section e–j	
Length (m)	1.12
Capacity (W)	754
Mass flow rate (kg/s)	0.009
Diameter (mm)	8
Pressure loss (per m)	0.020
Resistance length (m)	14.61
Pressure loss (m)	0.29

Section f–j	
Length (m)	2.31
Capacity (W)	1842
Mass flow rate (kg/s)	0.0220
Diameter (mm)	8
Pressure loss (per m)	0.092
Resistance length (m)	13.5
Pressure loss (m)	1.24

Section j–k	
Length (m)	7.99
Capacity (W)	2596
Mass flow rate (kg/s)	0.0310
Diameter (mm)	8
Pressure loss (per m)	0.17
Resistance length (m)	24.11
Pressure loss (m)	4.10

Section k–l	
Length (m)	2.73
Capacity (W)	7419
Mass flow rate (kg/s)	0.0886
Diameter (mm)	15
Pressure loss (per m)	0.040
Resistance length (m)	15.51
Pressure loss (m)	0.62

Section i–Cyl	
Length (m)	0.386
Capacity (W)	13000
Mass flow rate (kg/s)	0.1552
Diameter (mm)	22
Pressure loss (per m)	0.016
Resistance length (m)	5.586
Pressure loss (m)	0.09

Whole system	
Temperature difference between flow and return (°C)	20
Specific heat capacity of fluid in system (J/kg K)	4187
Total mass flow rate (kg/s)	0.2508
Index circuit pressure loss (m)	7.66

Section l–m	
Length (m)	5.53
Capacity (W)	13000
Mass flow rate (kg/s)	0.1552
Diameter (mm)	22
Pressure loss (per m)	0.016
Resistance length (m)	15.87
Pressure loss (m)	0.25

Figure 5.10 The pipework layout for a terraced house with completed data

5.7 Sizing the Heat Source

Note: The sizing and selection of heat generators are outside the scope of this Guide. This section and section 1.6 are provided for general background information only. For specific details it is recommended that you seek the advice of manufacturers and others.

This section presents general information on how to select the size of a heat generator for a property.

The heat generator (e.g. combustion boiler, heat pump or electric boiler) must have enough output to meet the maximum load, which includes the radiators, the domestic hot water cylinder (if required) and the heat losses from the distribution pipework.

As discussed previously, the generator should not be oversized, however, because this can cause excessive cycling, which in turn reduces efficiency and increases running cost. This is despite most modern appliances being capable of operating efficiently under part-load conditions.

5.7.1 Heat Generator/Boiler Sizing Method

The required total output for space heating is obtained by summing all the individual heat loads in a property, and adding an allowance for hot water heating if required.

Note: The total heat load (calculated in section 3 and used in section 5.6.3.1), not the catalogue heat output required or the total radiator heat output required (see section 5.5.5), should be used when selecting the size of a heat generator.

5.7.1.1 Combination Boilers/Heat Sources
For heat sources that produce instantaneous hot water, the power required for water heating will normally exceed that for space heating. As such, the appliance should be sized to the water heating power requirement, as discussed in section 4.4.2.1.

Note: If the heat generator itself does not have such control, the control system (see section 5.11.4) needs to be configured to ensure that there cannot be concurrent space heating and hot water demand.

5.7.1.2 System Boilers/Heat Sources
Note: This section focuses on the sizing of heat generators for heating systems with high (70–90°C) flow temperatures, and cases it is assumed that the heat generator can efficiently modulate its output over a wide range (gas and electric boilers, as well as some liquid fuel boilers). Further advice on the design of systems with lower circulation temperatures (e.g. heat pumps) and systems that are not able to widely modulate efficiently (heat pumps and biomass) will be provided in a later update to this Guide. Meanwhile, advice should be sought from manufacturers and others regarding the selection of heat generators for these types of systems.

For system heat generators, consideration should be given to the demand required for space heating as well as any attached domestic hot water system.

The demand for space heating will be the sum of the heat-carrying capacities of the end-point sections of pipework (rooms) in a system (as discussed in section 5.6.3.1).

The demand from any attached domestic hot water system will depend on the calculation method used. The recommended cylinder coil ratings (and therefore heat generator requirements) for high flow temperature heat generators for different sizes of dwellings are given on Table 4.1 (see section 4.4.1). If the detailed sizing method laid out in section 4.4.1.2 has been used, the full calculated hot water heating demand should be used.

The power required to rapidly heat the entire contents of the hot water cylinder is high (see sections 4.4.1.1 and 4.4.1.2), but such a provision is unlikely to be required at the same time as the maximum space heating load, as it generally should be programmed or timed to be non-coincident. In such a case, the heat generator can be sized to the larger of the space heating or the hot water load.

If it cannot be guaranteed that there will not be a coincident heating and hot water demand, for example in a case where there is a constant hot water demand throughout the day, the heat generator should be sized to the total demand from both the hot water and the space heating. For typical domestic situations where the heat generator is of the high flow temperature type and the property is insulated to a reasonable level, this will not be required, as the time for which the indoor temperature will be reduced while the heat generator is diverted to heating water will be limited.

Note: For small or highly insulated properties, the hot water heating demand may be significantly higher than the space heating demand. For some combustion heat generators this may mean the efficiency of combustion is compromised when providing space heating. In this situation the manufacturer's advice should be sought, or alternative heat generator types identified.

Note: It is not necessary to make a further allowance for intermittent heating as this is already included in the heat loss calculation for the individual rooms.

Note: If the heat generator has been sized to meet only the heating or only the hot water demand, the heating and hot water system controller (see section 5.11.4) must be configured to ensure there is not a concurrent space heating and hot water demand if this is not ensured by the heat generator itself.

> **Example**: A small bungalow has the following heat carrying capacity requirements for the pipework sections associated with its rooms: living room, 324 W; kitchen, 231 W; bedroom 1, 312 W; bedroom 2, 297 W; bathroom, 123 W. A gas combustion boiler and domestic hot water cylinder are to be installed. Controls will be used to ensure that domestic hot water and space heating demands are not met concurrently.
>
> Total output for space heating = 324 + 23 + 312 + 297 + 123 = 1,287 W (see section 5.6.3.1)
>
> Cylinder coil rating – two bedrooms and one bathroom, 130 litre cylinder = 13,000 W (13 kW) (see Table 4.1 in section 4.4.1.1)
>
> The hot water demand is higher than the space heating demand, and therefore this value will be used to size the heat generator. The controls will ensure non-concurrent domestic hot water and space heating demands.
>
> Required heat generator size = 13 kW

Note: The above example may lead to inefficient operation of the heat generator when it is only in use for space heating, as it is being oversized during this phase of operation. The designer may wish to consider specifying a longer reheat time (see section 4.4.1.2), with the client's consent.

5.8 Circulators

Two factors govern the selection of an appropriate circulator (pump): the maximum amount of fluid that must be circulated, and the resistance to circulation that the system places on the fluid. Both of these values were calculated in sections 5.6.3.2 and 5.6.4.4.

This section presents the information required to select an appropriate circulator, based on these values.

5.8.1 Circulator Selection

Heating system circulators are either integral to the heat generator or are installed in the flow pipework from the heat generator. They are used to move water at a defined rate to the emitters and hot water cylinders. Current legislation requires that circulators provided in new or existing systems in dwellings meet a minimum standard of an energy efficiency index (EEI) no greater than 0.27. The EEI has been mapped to a scale of A++ to G for the energy labelling of circulators, thus making it easy to differentiate between the energy consumption of different circulators.

Inverter-driven variable-speed circulators are generally recommended. These incorporate an electronic control circuit that can continuously adjust the pumping power to maintain a pressure appropriate for the demands on the system (e.g. when thermostatic radiator valves are used to restrict the flow to individual radiators). This avoids the steep rise or fall in pressure that occurs when the flow is restricted through a fixed-speed pump. The benefits of inverter-driven variable-speed circulators include easier initial set-up, reduced noise and reduced electricity consumption in use.

5.8.2 Circulator Position

Where the circulator is positioned in a system depends on several factors. Consideration should be given to the following:

- The circulator should be installed to maintain a positive pressure at all points around the system, as shown in Figure 5.11.
- When fitted to an open-vented system, the circulator should be located with the cold feed neutral point on the suction side of the pump (see section 5.9.2.2).
- The circulator must be subjected to not less than the minimum static pressure specified by the manufacturer. The minimum static pressure is defined as one-third of the maximum pressure developed by the circulator under no water flow conditions. For most domestic circulators this is between 1.7 and 2.0 m of head of water.
- The circulator should not be located at the lowest part of a system, where it is possible for sediment to collect, nor at the highest point, where air can be a problem.
- When installing the circulator, the manufacturer's instructions regarding the orientation of the installation should be followed. Usually the circulator is placed with its motor shaft in a horizontal position so that there is no undue load on the bearings, and should be fixed either into a vertical pipe such that the water is flowing upward, or in a horizontal position. It is often difficult to remove trapped air from the impeller casing, and for this reason a circulator should not be installed facing vertically downwards.

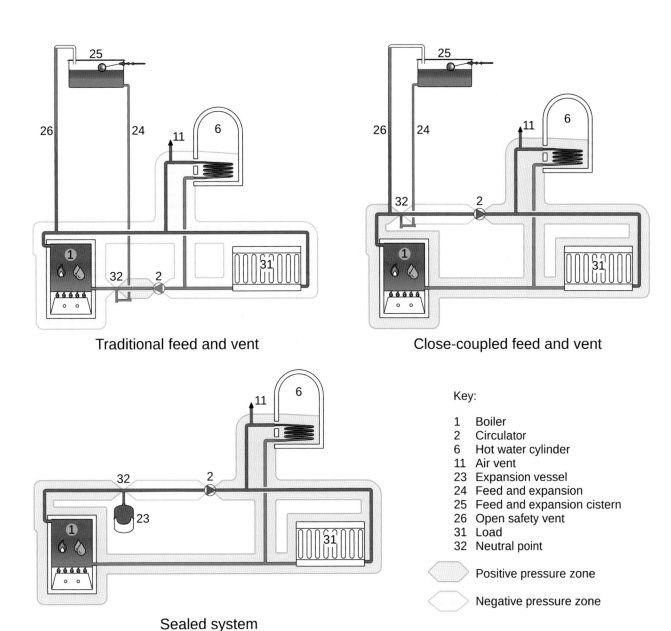

Traditional feed and vent

Close-coupled feed and vent

Sealed system

Key:

1   Boiler
2   Circulator
6   Hot water cylinder
11 Air vent
23 Expansion vessel
24 Feed and expansion
25 Feed and expansion cistern
26 Open safety vent
31 Load
32 Neutral point

   Positive pressure zone

   Negative pressure zone

Figure 5.11 Systems under positive and negative pressure

5.8.3 Circulator Sizing

Advice should be sought from the circulator manufacturer for specific model selection. This section discusses the general principles of selection.

Figures 5.12 and 5.13 show performance charts for typical fixed- and variable-speed circulators. These charts show the relationship between the circulator flow rate and the pressure against which the circulator is operating. These charts will be provided by the manufacturer.

The pressure loss calculations used to size the pipework provide the necessary basis for specifying the circulator. The total flow rate from section 5.6.3.2 and the index circuit resistance from section 5.6.4.4 should be superimposed on the circulator performance chart for comparison with the circulator characteristics. The operating point should be between the middle and the top of the operating range of the circulator. If it is near the bottom of the range a smaller circulator should be considered, and likewise if it is near the top of the range a larger circulator should be considered.

Note: The operating range for a fixed-speed circulator will lie along a series of curves, whereas for a variable-speed circulator there will be an area that the operating point should be within (see Figures 5.12 and 5.13).

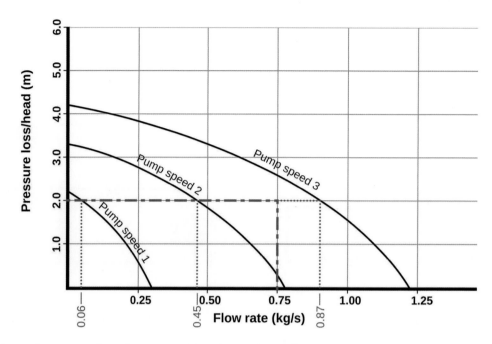

Figure 5.12 Performance chart for a typical fixed-speed circulator

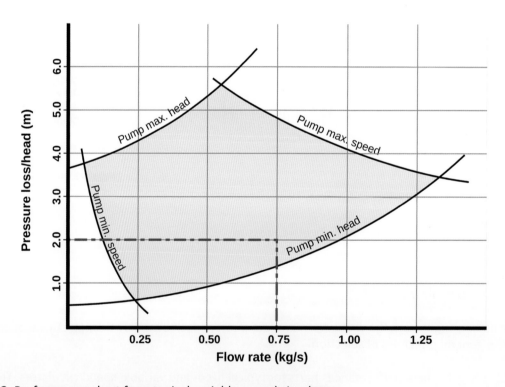

Figure 5.13 Performance chart for a typical variable-speed circulator

Note: Fixed-speed circulators normally have several fixed speed settings. The lowest setting that can generate enough flow at the design pressure should be chosen.

If the circulator is too small or on too low a setting, then the flow rate will be less than required. This will cause the system to not deliver the required heat output. If the circulator is set too high, excessive noise will occur and the amount of electricity consumed by the circulator itself will increase. In both cases the flow and return temperatures will not be as designed.

Example 1: For a system with a required mass flow rate of 0.75 kg/s and a pressure loss of 2 m, the fixed-speed pump described by the performance chart in Figure 5.12 would be suitable if speed 3 is used.

Speed 1 would deliver 0.06 kg/s with a pressure loss of 2 m.

Speed 2 would deliver 0.45 kg/s with a pressure loss of 2 m.

Speed 3 would deliver 0.87 kg/s with a pressure loss of 2 m.

Example 2: For a system with the same requirements as in Example 1, the variable-speed circulator described by the performance chart in Figure 5.13 may be suitable. The operating point is within the circulator's operating range, but it is near the low end, and as such a smaller circulator may be considered. Without selecting a smaller circulator, in a low-flow condition, such as where several thermostatic radiator valves have shut down flow due to the rooms being up to temperature, the circulator will be operating outside its operating range.

5.8.4 Isolating Valves

An isolation valve should be installed either side of the circulator to allow its removal for maintenance purposes. These isolating valves should never be used to regulate the performance of the circulator.

Consideration should also be given to installing isolation valves for other system components, particularly those that require regular maintenance, such as system filters.

Note: Isolation valves should not be fitted where they can affect the correct performance of safety devices such as pressure-relief valves, expansion vessels or cold feeds (see sections 5.9.1 and 5.9.2). Where this is an issue, lockshield or other valve types that require a specific key or tool to operate may be considered.

5.8.5 Integral Circulators

Most sealed system and combination gas and liquid fuel boilers are supplied complete with circulators already piped and electrically wired as part of the package. In such cases, the circulator is usually an important part of the operating sequence of the boiler. The boiler may also incorporate an automatic balancing valve and have an overrun requirement as part of the control function (see 'Automatic balancing valve' in section 5.11.3.1).

Boilers of this type tend to use a high proportion of the available circulator pressure to circulate the water through the heat exchanger, and this will determine the pressure available to be used to circulate water through the rest of the system. Cases where the integral circulator has insufficient capacity for the system, a low-loss header and a second circulator for radiator circuits may be considered, but are beyond the scope of this Guide; they are discussed briefly in section 5.10.

Note: On no account add a second circulator in series with the integral circulator.

5.8.6 Circulator Fault Diagnosis

The focus of this Guide is the design of domestic heating systems, but, for reference, this section discusses some of the common faults associated with circulators, and the symptoms which can be used to diagnose them.

5.8.6.1 Sediment

System design faults and lack of maintenance can often be diagnosed from the sediment found in the circulator. This is usually either black encrustation (ferric oxide) or a red sediment (ferrous oxide), as shown in Figure 5.14.

Figure 5.14 Circulator sediment

Black ferric oxide is often the result of the system not having been flushed out correctly on completion of the installation, leaving extraneous matter in the water and causing the residue to form gases which have to be vented out of the system.

Red ferrous oxide is caused by air entering the system, possibly being entrained on the suction side of the circulator or from the feed and expansion cistern on an open-vented system (see section 5.9.2). This can be avoided by correct design, or by specifying a sealed system. It is commonly the result of incorrect positioning of the feed and expansion pipe in relation to the circulator, or a blockage/restriction caused by system corrosion at the point where the cold feed connects to the system, resulting in failure to maintain a positive pressure at all points in the system. In such circumstances the circulator is likely to fail, often followed by leaking radiators and heat exchangers.

5.8.6.2 Noise

Noise in a heating system can often be difficult to trace, especially if it is emanating from the circulator, as noise can be transmitted and amplified along the pipework to remote parts of the installation.

A heat generator operating at an inadequate flow rate can be heard to 'kettle', a description derived from the characteristic noise it makes. If allowed to operate in this manner for too long before remedial action is taken, it will probably have a deposit of calcium in the heat-transfer coil, which will be extremely difficult, if not impractical, to remove.

Air trapped in the heat generator heat exchanger can be another source of noise. The manufacturer's instructions for all equipment should be followed to ensure all air is purged on commissioning and no gases can build up in a section from which they cannot be vented.

Pipework noise also commonly occurs as a result of the expansion of pipework over joists, or where the pipe has been left touching other pipes or a part of the building structure. Care must always be taken to ensure the pipework is correctly bracketed, is not in tension or compression, and does not carry the weight of components such as the circulator.

Allowance must be made for pipework to expand and contract without coming into contact with other pipes or the building structure. Felt pads or similar should be fitted in notches in joists where pipes will move during expansion and contraction.

5.9 Fluid Expansion Compensation

Water expands as it heats up, and so a heating system needs to be designed to accommodate that expansion. The traditional way to do this was an open-vented system, but, these days, sealed systems have all but replaced them. However, some heat generator manufacturers require an open-vented system, and customers may have an existing system that needs extending or improving, and therefore they are included here for completeness.

This section presents the information required to specify the fluid expansion compensation components for a sealed or open-vented heating system.

5.9.1 Sealed Heating Systems

5.9.1.1 Introduction
A sealed heating system eliminates many corrosion risks, as there is only a minimal possibility of the ingress of air during normal operation of the system, due to the system being wholly above atmospheric pressure. When a sealed system is installed together with an unvented domestic hot water cylinder, or in conjunction with a combination heat generator, there is no need for cisterns or pipework in the roof space. This considerably reduces the risk of frost damage and condensation in the roof space. Sealed systems are also particularly advantageous in flats and bungalows, where it may not be possible to obtain adequate static pressure from a cistern, and there likely isn't space for one anyway. For these reasons it is recommended that where the heat generator manufacturer allows it, a sealed heating system is used rather than a traditional open-vented system.

5.9.1.2 System Components
Figure 5.15 shows a typical sealed system. The system must be provided with a diaphragm expansion vessel complying with BS EN 13381, a pressure gauge, a means for filling, making-up and venting, and a non-adjustable safety valve. Heat generators used in sealed systems should be approved for this purpose by the manufacturer, and must incorporate a high-limit thermostat. It is most important that the manufacturer's instructions are followed when installing the components of a sealed system.

5.9.1.2.1 Expansion vessel
The main component of a sealed heating system is the expansion vessel (Figure 5.16). This accommodates the increased water volume when expansion takes place as the system heats up, and maintains a positive pressure in the system when it cools back down. The expansion vessel contains a flexible diaphragm, which is charged on one side initially with nitrogen but is then topped up as required with air.

The expansion vessel should be located close to the suction side of the circulator to ensure that there is positive pressure in all parts of the system pipework. This will eliminate the possibility of air ingress through valve glands, etc. The vessel should be connected in such a manner as to minimise natural convection currents, in order to maintain the lowest possible temperature at the diaphragm. The pipe connecting the expansion vessel to the heat generator should have a diameter of not less than 15 mm, and must not contain any restriction such as isolating valves.

Note: Some appliances, such as combination boilers, may contain an inbuilt expansion vessel. If so, the sizing of the connecting pipe/hose will be bespoke to the appliance.

It is important that the expansion vessel has enough volume to accommodate the expansion that would occur if the system water were heated from 10°C to 110°C. Consequently, it is important that the system volume is estimated with reasonable accuracy (see section 5.9.1.4).

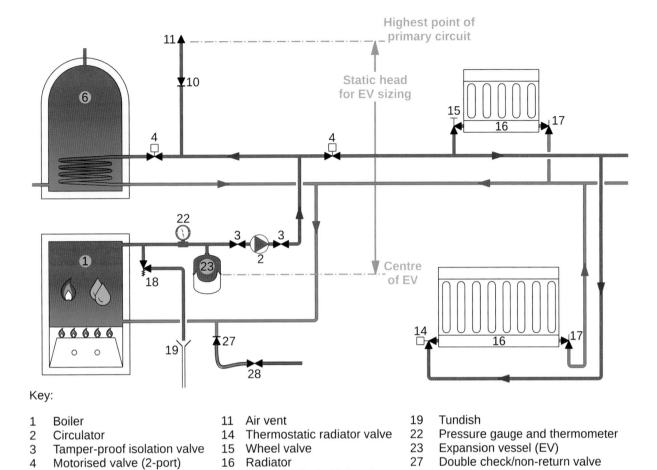

Figure 5.15 Sealed heating system components

Key:

1	Boiler	11	Air vent	19	Tundish
2	Circulator	14	Thermostatic radiator valve	22	Pressure gauge and thermometer
3	Tamper-proof isolation valve	15	Wheel valve	23	Expansion vessel (EV)
4	Motorised valve (2-port)	16	Radiator	27	Double check/non-return valve
6	Hot water cylinder	17	Balancing/lockshield valve	28	Stop valve
10	Check/non-return valve	18	Pressure-relief valve		

Figure 5.16 Expansion vessel

The initial charge pressure in the expansion vessel should be in accordance with the manufacturer's instructions, and must always exceed the static pressure of the heating system at the level of the vessel (Figure 5.17). Prior to connecting the expansion vessel to the system, the pipework should be flushed and tested. Following connection of the vessel, the system, when cold, should be pressurised to above the initial nitrogen pressure in the vessel (typically by 0.2 bar). This will result in a small displacement of the diaphragm, as illustrated in Figure 5.18. When the system is operational, the expansion water will move into the vessel and compress the nitrogen, so that when the operating temperature is reached the system pressure will rise and the diaphragm will be displaced to accommodate the additional volume (Figure 5.19). BS 7206:1990 and BS 4814:1990 define the practical acceptance volume of the vessel as what it will accept when the gauge pressure rises to 0.35 bar below the safety valve setting.

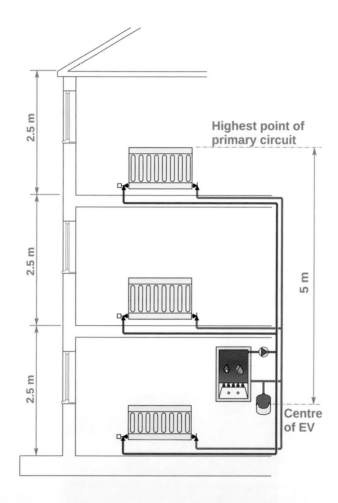

Figure 5.17 Static system pressure at the expansion vessel in a three-storey house (0.5 bar)

Note: 1 m = 0.1 bar.

If the initial system water pressure is too high or the nitrogen fill pressure in the vessel is too low, the diaphragm will be displaced too far into the vessel, which will then be unable to accommodate the volume of expansion water. This will result in an increase in the system pressure and the safety valve will lift, resulting in a loss of system water, which will have to be replaced.

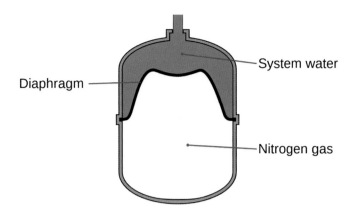

Figure 5.18 Expansion vessel (cold)

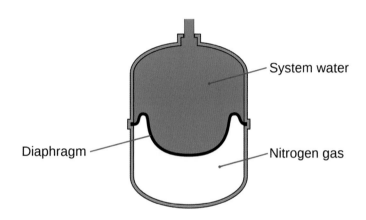

Figure 5.19 Expansion vessel (hot)

5.9.1.2.2 Safety pressure relief valve

All sealed systems must have a non-adjustable safety valve set to lift at a gauge pressure not exceeding 3 bar (300 kPa) (Figure 5.20). Safety valves must also have a manual testing device, valve seating materials that will prevent sticking in a closed position, and provision for connecting a full-bore discharge pipe. The valve should be connected to the flow pipe, close to the heat generator, with no intermediate valves present; alternatively, it may be integrated, by design, within the heat generator (e.g. boiler). The discharge pipe should be either metallic or made of a material that the heat generator and/or pipe manufacturer deems acceptable for the application, based on its ability to withstand the maximum temperatures and pressures that could arise in fault conditions. Discharge pipes should fall continuously throughout their length, and discharge in a way that will not cause danger to people in or about the building, damage to premises, or discharge onto electrical wiring or equipment.

Note: Some appliances with an integrated pressure relief valve may permit the primary discharge pipe to rise to a height above the appliance, before a secondary relief valve, from which the discharge pipework should then fall continuously. This facilitates flexibility in terms of the appliance location where it is not feasible for the pipe to fall immediately away from the appliance to outside (e.g. basement installations). The manufacturer's instructions and advice should be followed closely.

Figure 5.20 Pressure-relief valve

Figure 5.21 Tundish

For high-level terminations that are impractical to run to a lower level, bespoke pipe fittings are available to direct any discharge safely back towards the external structure.

It is important that any pressure loss from the system is apparent, necessitating either a means to establish this visually (e.g. a tundish, see Figure 5.21), a conspicuous external termination point (or it can be evidenced via the heat generator display or gauge) or an audible alarm (from the heat generator or system).

Internal termination to foul drainage pipework may be possible with the use of specialist dry-trap tundish fittings. These must be approved by the heat generator manufacturer, and the manufacturer's instructions for their installation should be followed. Care should be taken to ensure that the downstream connecting waste pipes are of a suitable material for the likely temperature and pressure of discharge under fault conditions. Heat generator manufacturers may also permit the combination of pressure relief discharge pipework and pipework carrying the heat generator condensate. The manufacturer's instructions should be consulted for permissibility and specifics.

5.9.1.2.3 Pressure Gauge and Thermometer

A pressure gauge is provided so that the pressure may be checked, and the system charged to the correct pressure when commissioning or topping up (Figure 5.22). The pressure gauge must be readable from the system filling position. A thermometer, which may be combined with the pressure gauge, shows the temperature of the flow water from the heat generator. Care should be taken to ensure that the thermometer is fitted to the heat generator itself or the flow pipe, not to a non-circulating pipe, and that the thermometer pocket does not restrict the bore of the pipework.

Figure 5.22 Pressure gauge and thermometer

5.9.1.2.4 Filling Loop

Filling and pressurising the system is normally achieved by a temporary direct connection from the cold water supply main through a special filling loop (Figure 5.23). This is an arrangement of fittings that incorporates a BS 1010 stop valve, a double check valve with a test point, and a flexible pipe, which should be disconnected and removed after use and protective caps fitted over the ends of the stop and check valves

Note: Always refer to the heat generator manufacturer's instructions for details on integrated or alternative state-of-the-art filling methods.

Note: Larger systems may utilise an automatic pressurisation unit. This is beyond the scope of this Guide, and specialist advice should be sought.

Figure 5.23 Filling loop

5.9.1.2.5 Water Top-up

Sealed systems do not lose water due to evaporation, so, provided there are no leaks, top-up water should not usually be required except during the initial period of operation when air in the fill water is being removed from the system. Lost water can be replaced by refilling and pressurising through the filling loop.

5.9.1.2.6 Automatic Air Vents

Provision must be made for venting air from sealed systems, using either automatic (Figure 5.24) or manual (Figure 5.25) air vents. Automatic air vents should be fitted at the highest points of the system, and should be float operated. Hygroscopic types of radiator automatic air vent should not be used because they allow continuous evaporation of small quantities of water. The automatic vent incorporated in some heat generators is often sufficient when combined with a manual air vent fitted at the highest point in the system. Automatic air vents can be obtained that have an integral shut-off valve, which allows cleaning to be carried out without draining down the system.

Figure 5.24 Automatic air vent

Figure 5.25 Manual air vent

An air separator with an automatic air vent is an optional item to be considered on larger domestic systems to assist in commissioning and for the easy removal of air (Figure 5.26). It is usually fitted on the flow pipe between the heat generator and the circulator, and creates a neutral point by significantly slowing the fluid velocity, thereby allowing the air to separate out.

Figure 5.26 Air separator

5.9.1.3 Sealed Heat Generator Systems
Heat generators with sealed system components already fitted within the casing, or with casing extensions to hide the components from view, are readily available and provide a compact alternative to installing separate components. Care must be taken to establish if an integral expansion vessel can accommodate the system water expansion. An additional expansion vessel may be required external to the heat generator.

5.9.1.4 Expansion Vessel Sizing
The expansion vessel must be sized according to the total volume of the water in the system, not estimated using 'rules of thumb'.

5.9.1.4.1 Fluid Volume
To calculate the size of the expansion vessel required, first work out the total volume of fluid in the system, as follows:

- The water content of the heat generator and other principal components will be available from manufacturers' data sheets.
- Heat emitter manufacturers usually show water content in terms of section or unit length.
- Hot water cylinder manufacturers usually only publish the surface area of the heating coils in cylinders. Table 5.13 gives the estimated water content of the primary coils of various sizes of cylinder, which may be used where no information is available from manufacturers.
- Pipework water content can be estimated using Table 5.14.

Example: A heating system that has the following specification will have the water content given below:

- Boiler: 1.6 litres (manufacturer's figure)
- Radiators (3 × 1.2 m, 1 × 0.9 m and 1 × 0.6 m radiators; manufacturer's figure 5.15 l/m):

  5.1 × 5.15 = 26.27 litres

- Hot water cylinder (125 litres): 2.3 litres (from Table 5.13)
- Pipework (20 m of 8 mm diameter, 40 m of 10 mm diameter, 10 m of 22 mm diameter):

  (20 × 0.036) + (40 × 0.055) + (10 × 0.320) = 0.72 + 2.2 + 3.2 = 6.12 litres (from Table 5.14)

Total = 1.6 + 26.27 + 2.3 + 6.12 = 36.29 litres

5.9.1.4.2 Sizing

Once the total fluid content of the system has been calculated, Table 5.15 can be used to find the minimum expansion vessel capacity.

Table 5.13 Water content of hot water cylinder heating coils

Cylinder capacity (litres)	Water content of primary heating coil (litres)
96	1.7
125	2.3
145	2.7
175	3.2
225	4.1

Table 5.14 Water content of copper pipes

Nominal pipe size (mm)	Water content per meter (litres)
8	0.036
10	0.055
15	0.145
22	0.320
28	0.539
35	0.835
42	1.232

Table 5.15 Capacities of expansion vessels

Safety valve pressure setting (bar)	3.0			2.5			2.0	
Vessel charge and initial system pressure (bar)	0.5	1.0	1.5	0.5	1.0	1.5	0.5	1.0
Total water content of system (litres)	Select an expansion vessel with a nominal volume not less than that given below (litres)							
25	2.1	2.7	3.9	2.3	3.3	5.9	2.8	5.0
50	4.2	5.4	7.8	4.7	6.7	11.8	5.6	10.0
75	6.3	8.2	11.7	7.0	10.0	17.7	8.4	15.0
100	8.3	10.9	15.6	9.4	13.4	23.7	11.3	20.0
125	10.4	13.6	19.5	11.7	16.7	29.6	14.1	25.0
150	12.5	16.3	23.4	14.1	20.1	35.5	16.9	30.0
175	14.6	19.1	27.3	16.4	23.4	41.4	19.7	35.0
200	16.7	21.8	31.2	18.8	26.8	47.4	22.6	40.0
225	18.7	24.5	35.1	21.1	30.1	53.3	25.4	45.0
250	20.8	27.2	39.0	23.5	33.5	59.2	28.2	50.0
275	22.9	30.0	42.9	25.8	36.8	65.1	31.0	55.0
300	25.0	32.7	46.8	28.2	40.2	71.1	33.9	60.0
Multiplying factors for other system volumes	0.0833	0.109	0.156	0.094	0.134	0.237	0.113	0.2

Note: The safety valve pressure setting will usually be specified by the heat generator manufacturer.

Note: The initial charge pressure should be in accordance with the expansion vessel manufacturer's instructions, and must always exceed the static pressure of the heating system at the level of the vessel (see section 5.9.1.2.1).

Example 1: For the system specified in the example in section 5.9.1.4.1, the total system fluid volume was 36.29 litres. The boiler manufacturer has specified a 3 bar safety valve pressure setting, and a vessel charge pressure of 1.5 bar is being used.

From Table 5.15, the smallest total water content of the system listed above the calculated volume is 50 litres. Reading from the 3 bar safety valve and 1.5 bar vessel charge column, a 7.8 litre expansion vessel is required. As it is unlikely that a 7.8 litre expansion vessel can be sourced, the next largest size available should be used.

Example 2: For a biomass boiler system with a total water content of 625 litres (which includes a small buffer vessel), the manufacturer has specified a 2.5 bar safety valve pressure setting, and a vessel charge pressure of 1 bar is being used.

The total water content of the system is greater than listed in Table 5.15, therefore the multiplying factors given at the bottom of the table will be used. The minimum size of expansion vessel required is 625 × 0.134 = 83.8 litres.

Note: Never select an expansion vessel that is smaller than the calculated size.

Worksheet C in section 5.16.3 is provided to assist with this calculation. Step by step instructions for filling in Worksheet B can be found in section 5.16.4.

The specification and sizing of a sealed system and determination of the required fluid expansion compensation is now complete.

5.9.2 Open-Vented Systems

While rarely designed or specified nowadays for new systems, there remains a significant number of already installed open-vented systems in UK homes. These are rapidly declining in number, due to the popularity of combination boilers, increased consumer and developer appetite for 'room in roof' provision, and/or 'dry lofts'. However, open-vented systems may still be encountered, and in cases of retrofit heating design projects it is possible that site suitability and/or client requirements may dictate that an open-vented system is retained in some circumstances.

For example, where existing heating pipework is buried in concrete-screeded floors, rendering visual inspection impractical, there could be concern about retaining such pipework for use with the typically higher pressures it would be subjected to under sealed system conditions (normally 1–2 bar). It is important that such considerations are discussed fully with the client before any work commences.

Note: Some heat generator manufacturers specify the use of an open-vented system for their appliance.

5.9.2.1 System Components

Open-vented systems are characterised by the following component parts:

- *Feed and expansion (F&E) cistern* (often referred to as the 'header tank') – This accommodates expansion of the system volume upon heating, and provides system make-up water to offset evaporation, removal of air, etc. (Figure 5.27). The cistern will be located at a high point of the system, frequently the loft, to provide a minimum pressure (head) of water for the circulation pump and heat generator to operate effectively.
- *Feed and expansion pipe* (often referred to as the 'cold feed') – This connects the F&E cistern to the main primary circuit, allowing top-up of system make-up water (as above), and transmits the thermal expansion of the system volume upon heating to the F&E cistern (Figure 5.27).
- *Open safety vent pipe* ('open vent' and erroneously referred to as the 'expansion pipe') – This provides an additional path for the expanded water to rise through, while facilitating the removal of air from the system, and providing a route for rapid temperature and pressure relief of the system under fault conditions (e.g. system water rapidly approaching boiling point in the event of failure of the heat generator temperature controls) (Figure 5.27).

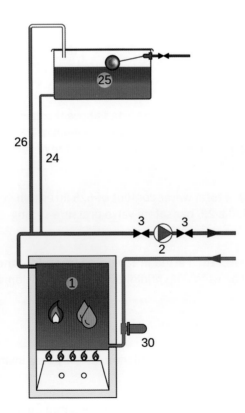

Key:

1   Boiler
2   Circulator
3   Tamper-proof isolation valve
24   Feed and expansion
25   Feed and expansion cistern
26   Open safety vent
30   Filter

Figure 5.27 Open safety vent pipe

Table 5.16 gives recommended sizes for feed and expansion components.

All components of the feed and expansion arrangements in contact with water should be able to withstand the temperature of boiling water, especially the float of the float-operated valve. The float should be made of copper or a similarly heat-resistant material.

Note: If non-metal components are used, they should be marked with a stamp stating that they are suitable for use with water at or above 110°C.

Table 5.16 Feed and expansion components – recommended sizes

	Heat generator output (kW)		
	Up to 25	25–45	45–60
Cistern nominal capacity (litres)	45	70	90
Feed and expansion pipe diameter (mm)	15	22	22
Open safety vent pipe diameter (mm)	22	28	28
Overflow pipe diameter (mm)	22	28	35

5.9.2.2 Pipework Arrangements

The open-safety-vent and cold-feed pipes can both form part of the circulatory system, providing there are no obstructions such as valves, etc., between the heat generator and the F&E cistern. Ensure that the specific requirements of the heat generator and circulator manufacturers are observed regarding the positioning of the cold feed and open safety vent pipes.

'Close coupled' cold feed and open safety vent pipes

Close coupling of the cold feed and open safety vent pipes is accepted practice with most types of high and low resistance automatically controlled heat generators. The connections should be made into a straight horizontal run of the flow pipe, immediately before the circulator. The distance between the connections should be no greater than 150 mm, in order to minimise the pressure difference between the cold feed and the open vent pipes, and hence reduce the vertical movement of water in the open safety vent pipe.

Poor initial design, installation and/or maintenance in this area is often a root cause of issues associated with problematic open-vented systems, such as air entrainment and subsequent system corrosion.

Note: Figure 5.28 shows a close coupled feed and vent. Where these are separated (e.g. the vent on the flow and the feed on the return), the positioning of the circulator is important (see Figure 5.11).

Combined cold-feed and open-vent pipe

A single combined cold-feed and open-vent pipe can be fitted to heat generators that incorporate an overheat thermostat in addition to the normal operating thermostat, and where the heat generator manufacturer permits this. Combined cold-feed and open-vent pipes should be at least 22 mm in diameter (Figure 5.29).

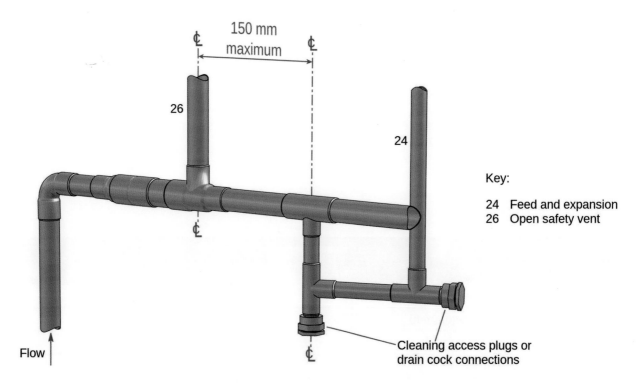

Figure 5.28 Connections for the open safety vent and the cold feed and expansion

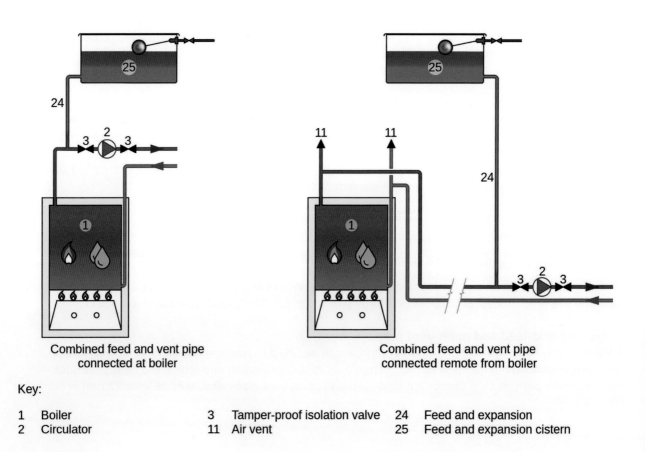

Figure 5.29 Combined feed and vent pipe arrangements (only to be used where a heat generator has an overheat thermostat and with the manufacturer's approval)

5.10 Low-Loss Headers and Manifolds

Low loss headers and manifolds are outside the scope of this Guide, but a summary of their specification is included here for information. For further details, specialist advice should be sought.

Note: The design and specification of low-loss headers and manifolds are intended to be covered by the forthcoming companion to this Guide, the *Integration Guide*, also to be published by the Domestic Building Service Panel (https://www.dbsp.co.uk).

5.10.1 Low-Loss Headers

Larger systems may benefit from having more than one heat generator. Such a case would be if the circulator(s) required to overcome the hydraulic resistance of the heating circuits may impose too great a circulation through the heat generator. This would decrease the temperature differential across the heat generators, raising the return temperature and negating the condensing benefit.

The use of a low-loss header (Figure 5.30) enables the flow rate through the heat generators to be set according to the manufacturer's instructions, thereby maintaining the design flow rate and temperature differential across the heat generators. The diameter of the header should be derived from the combined areas of the flow pipe connections plus 10%, or be sized to ensure a maximum velocity of 0.1 m/s.

Subject to the control regime employed, one or more of the heat generators maintains the design temperature in the low-loss header, from which the system circulators feed the heating and domestic hot water demands as required.

The low-loss header is the neutral pressure point of the system, so the circulators are installed to pump away from it, maintaining a positive pressure in the heat generators and the system. Also, because it is a neutral point, the low-loss header makes an ideal location for an automatic air vent; as the flow velocity is so low, any gases entrained in the fluid will be able to separate out.

Figure 5.30 depicts a sealed system. If an open-vented system is employed, the open safety vent is connected to the top of the low-loss header, and the cold feed and expansion are connected to the bottom of the low-loss header.

When specifying the pipe sizes and circulators for a low-loss header, each circuit supplying and being supplied by the low-loss header should be treated as a separate system and sized individually; the low-loss header being a neutral point in the system should mean that none of the circuits are able to interact with each other.

Where a heat generator manufacturer supplies a horizontal low-loss header, the manufacturer's instructions should be followed.

5.10.2 Manifolds

Manifolds are regularly used in underfloor heating systems, but are beginning to be used more regularly with radiator systems. Similar in look to a low-loss header, but with the difference that the flow and return are separated, the main function of a manifold is to connect and balance flow to multiple circuits (Figure 5.31).

Note: An underfloor heating manifold may need additional temperature blending (see 'Mixer valves' in section 5.11.3.2) to reduce the flow temperature, depending on the design and the manufacturer's requirements.

The advantage of distributing flow to multiple circuits via a manifold is that it makes balancing very simple (see 'System balancing' in section 2.5.1.2). The manifold is sized in a similar way to a low-loss header, and, as such, creates neutral points from which all the circuits separate off and then merge back into. This means the pressure from the circulator is evenly distributed between the circuits.

A radiator system designed to operate in this way, with each room supplied from a separate outlet from the manifold, has the advantage that commissioning and balancing are greatly simplified. The mass flow rate for each circuit (as calculated in section 5.6.3.2) just needs to be set at the manifold (manifolds are often supplied with inbuilt flow setters). The disadvantage of this type of system is that it is likely to require extra pipework, and the cost of the manifolds can be significant.

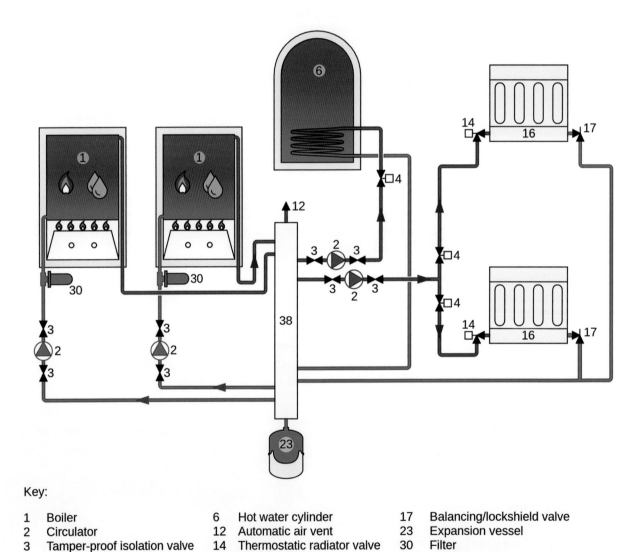

Key:

1	Boiler	6	Hot water cylinder	17	Balancing/lockshield valve
2	Circulator	12	Automatic air vent	23	Expansion vessel
3	Tamper-proof isolation valve	14	Thermostatic radiator valve	30	Filter
4	Motorised valve (2-port)	16	Radiator	38	Low-loss header

Figure 5.30 Multiple heat generators connected via a low loss header

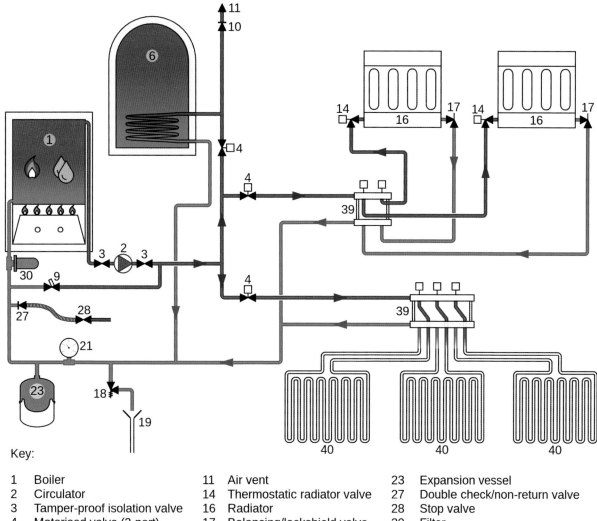

Figure 5.31 Multiple heating circuits connected by a manifold

Key:

1	Boiler	11	Air vent	23	Expansion vessel
2	Circulator	14	Thermostatic radiator valve	27	Double check/non-return valve
3	Tamper-proof isolation valve	16	Radiator	28	Stop valve
4	Motorised valve (2-port)	17	Balancing/lockshield valve	30	Filter
6	Hot water cylinder	18	Pressure relief valve	39	Manifold
9	Automatic balancing valve	19	Tundish	40	Underfloor loop
10	Check/non-return valve	21	Pressure gauge		

5.11 System Controls

If the procedures described in this Guide are followed, they should result in a system that can heat the dwelling under design conditions. However, most of the time much less heat output is required. Controls are therefore needed to ensure that the desired temperatures are achieved in each room, as and when required, under all conditions, including those when little or no additional heat is required.

The selection of appropriate controls also plays a key part in the overall running costs of a heating or hot water system. The cost benefits of controls should not be underestimated, as upgrading controls on older heating systems can save up to 15% on energy bills.

Finally, control systems also have an important role in reducing the risk of condensation or mould occurring in unused rooms by providing a constant minimum level of heating.

Note: As discussed above, this section focuses on the specification of heating systems with high (70–90°C) flow temperatures; greater emphasis on the design of heating systems with lower flow temperatures will be provided in a future update. Controls are key to the effective operation of low flow temperature heating systems, as for such systems it is the water temperature at the heat generator that principally determines the systems efficiency. Factors such as intermittency and emitter responsiveness need to be given particular consideration when selecting and commissioning control systems for low flow temperature heating systems. It is therefore recommended that advice is sought from other publications regarding the design of low flow temperature heating control systems.

5.11.1 Introduction

A heating control system is usually broken down into three distinct functions:

- *Inputs* – The sensors and settings that feed data into the control system.
- *Controller* – The 'brains' of the control system, which will make decisions based on the inputs to control the outputs.
- *Outputs* – The actuators that implement the decisions of the control system and affect the operation of the heating system.

Control systems can vary significantly in complexity. A basic system may have only two inputs (a room temperature sensor and a room set-point temperature), two outputs (a heat generator and a pump) and a thermostat (controller). The thermostat simply switches the heat generator and the pump on when the room temperature drops below the room set-point temperature, and back off again when it rises above this temperature. Such a basic level of control is not recommended. A more complex system may have multiple inputs and outputs for each room, as well as hot water and multiple heat generators, and the controller may have advanced functionality, such as weather compensation, start-up optimisation and internet connectivity. While the latter is straying outside the scope of this Guide, both examples can, at their core, be broken down into the three distinct functions of inputs, outputs and controller.

Note: Advanced control systems integrating multiple types of heat generator and heat emitter will be covered in the forthcoming companion to this Guide, the *Integration Guide*, also to be published by the Domestic Building Service Panel (https://www.dbsp.co.uk).

This section introduces most of the common elements of each of the three functions of a control system, before setting out the minimum and recommended combinations that may be needed for various types of heating system.

5.11.2 Control functions – Inputs

There are two common types of inputs found on a domestic heating system: temperature and time. These two are then split further into specific types of time or temperature input, which in turn will be related to the physically installed devices. Not all are required, but most will need to be considered depending on the requirements of the system, the customer and regulations.

5.11.2.1 Temperature

There are four types of temperature input that may be considered in a domestic heating control system:

- *Internal temperature* (air and water) – The actual temperature of the air in the space, or the water in the cylinder, that is being heated.
- *Set-point temperature* (air and water) – The target temperature of the air in the space, or the water in the cylinder, that is being heated.
- *Outdoor temperature* – The actual temperature outside the heated envelope of the house.
- *Fluid temperature* – The temperature of the fluid in the pipes of a wet heating system.

Note: As discussed in section 3.5.3.1, although air temperature is not the only parameter that defines a person's thermal comfort, it is the easiest to influence and control, and, as such, is the parameter that is almost universally used.

The above four types of temperature input are commonly found in the heating system devices described below.

Room thermostat

Room thermostats (Figure 5.32) are probably the most commonly found domestic heating control input devices. They integrate the inputs of internal air temperature with the set-point temperature for the space in which it is located. The design temperatures for various types of room were discussed in section 3.5.3, but individuals will have their own personal preference.

The thermostat also integrates a basic level of the control function of the system, in that it decides to switch the heating on or off based on the internal air temperature and set-point inputs. Previous practice was to control a house solely off a single thermostat (in such cases the thermostat represented the entire control function), but this is no longer recommended, and time and temperature control should be used (see section 5.11.6).

Figure 5.32 Room thermostat

Where multiple rooms are being heated as one zone (see section 5.11.5), it is recommended that the thermostat be located in (and therefore able to measure the air temperature of) the space that is primarily occupied during the period of heating. For a two-zone system this will typically mean the living room and bedroom. For multi-zone heating systems, or where more advanced functionality is required, the thermostat functionality will be built into the controller (see section 5.11.4), and therefore only a room temperature sensor (see below) is needed in each room.

Care should be given to ensuring that the thermostat is so located that it is able to take an accurate measure of the room's air temperature (at approximately shoulder height, and away from heat emitters, windows, vents and corners of the room).

Note: Wireless room thermostats are readily available, increasing the flexibility of possible positioning.

Note: Building occupants should be reminded that turning a thermostat up to a higher setting will not make the room heat up any faster but may cause the room to overheat and waste fuel. How quickly the room heats up depends on the heat generator size and setting, and the radiator size.

Room temperature sensor

For more advanced control systems, the set-point temperature input for a zone (see section 5.11.5) heating control will be integrated in the system controller; this allows for different set-points at different times of the day or different days of the week. Therefore, a room air temperature sensor (Figure 5.33) is required, rather than a thermostat.

The exact type of room temperature sensor used will often depend on the controller (see section 5.11.4). Primarily it will depend on the communication protocol (analogue or digital) used to send the temperature data back to the controller. The type of heat emitter used in the room may also affect the choice of room temperature sensor. A radiant-based heating system may use a black bulb sensor rather than an air sensor, and underfloor heating may have a floor-temperature sensor.

Note: Control systems for underfloor heating are covered in the companion to this Guide, the *Underfloor Heating Design & Installation Guide*, also published by the Domestic Building Service Panel (https://www.dbsp.co.uk).

As for a room thermostat, the room temperature sensor should be located in the space that is primarily occupied during the period of heating, and in a position that allows it to take an accurate measurement of the internal air temperature of the space it is in.

Figure 5.33 Room temperature sensor

Hot water thermostat

Similar in functionality to a room thermostat, for systems including stored hot water, the hot water thermostat controls the temperature of the water for reasons of comfort, safety and health. It integrates the inputs of the current temperature of the water with the set-point temperature, and then at a basic level controls the source of heat (on or off) based on this data. Similarly, while previous practise was to control the off temperature only, it is now recommended that both time and temperature control are used. When selecting the set-point temperature, consideration needs to be given to ensuring the sterilisation of water to prevent bacterial growth (see section 4.5.1), and also to the safety implications of the prevention of scalding (see section 4.5.2) and boiling.

For direct heating of hot water by an immersion heater, the hot water thermostat will likely be built into the head of the heater. Otherwise, the thermostat is likely to be an external clamp-on type. Versions that use a pre-installed pocket in the cylinder are preferred due to their increased accuracy, but are less common (Figure 5.34). It is important to ensure that the sensor (the rear of the thermostat for the clamp-on type) makes good thermal contact with the metal of the cylinder. It is also important to consider the positioning of the thermostat on the cylinder. With a well-stratified hot water cylinder (i.e. where there is a clear boundary between the hot water at the top of the cylinder and the cold water at the bottom, and very little mixing is occurring in the cylinder), the height of the thermostat will limit or maximise the amount of stored hot water. For secondary or backup heat sources it may be desirable to locate the thermostat higher on the cylinder to ensure that only the minimum amount of water is heated (and therefore the minimum amount of energy is used). For primary heat sources, a lower height on the cylinder for the thermostat may be desirable to ensure that the full design hot water load is met.

Figure 5.34 Hot water cylinder thermostat

Hot water temperature sensor

As for space heating, on more advanced control systems the hot water set-point temperature input will be integrated into the system controller. This allows for different set-points at different times of the day or days of the week, for example to allow for the cylinder to be sterilised regularly to prevent bacterial growth, but kept at a less energy-intensive temperature in between. Therefore, a water temperature sensor (Figure 5.35) is required, rather than a thermostat.

The sensor will typically be installed in a dedicated pocket or port built into the hot water cylinder by the manufacturer. Care should be taken that the sensor is installed correctly to the manufacturer's recommendations, to ensure that an accurate measure of the water temperature is taken.

Figure 5.35 Hot water cylinder temperature sensor

Outdoor temperature sensor

For some of the more advanced functionalities of controllers (see section 5.11.4), it is important to know the outdoor air temperature. This can allow, for example, the controller to supply a lower level of heating on a warmer day, when less is required.

The sensor must be protected from both direct sunlight and rainfall to ensure the accuracy of measurements. Typically, this requires that the sensor be installed on a north-facing external wall, under the cover of the eaves of the roof, but in a position where free circulation of air can occur (i.e. away from the corners of walls). The sensor should also be positioned away from any nearby potential sources of heat, such as boiler flues. Outdoor air temperature sensors will usually be supplied with an enclosure such as the one shown in Figure 5.36.

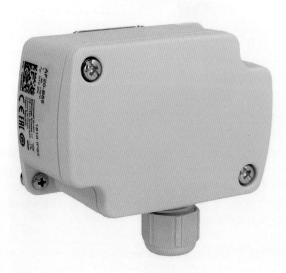

Figure 5.36 Outdoor temperature sensor

Pipe/flow temperature sensor

For some of the more advanced functionalities of controllers (see section 5.11.4), it is important to know the temperature of the water in a wet heating system. This can allow, for example, a controller to supply different temperature water to different emitters that are designed for different flow temperatures.

The pocket-type temperature sensor (Figure 5 37) is the recommended type, but clamp-on variants are also available which fix to the outside of the pipe. The pocket type will usually give a significantly more accurate measurement due to the sensor measuring in the middle of the flow rather than at the surface. Due to laminar flow in pipes, the temperature at the surface of the pipe will be the temperature of the static boundary layer of fluid, rather than the temperature of the fluid moving in the middle of the pipe. The pocket-type sensor takes more work to install than the clamp type, as a special fitting including the pocket is required to be cut into the pipework. For both types, the manufacturer's instructions should be followed to ensure correct installation and location.

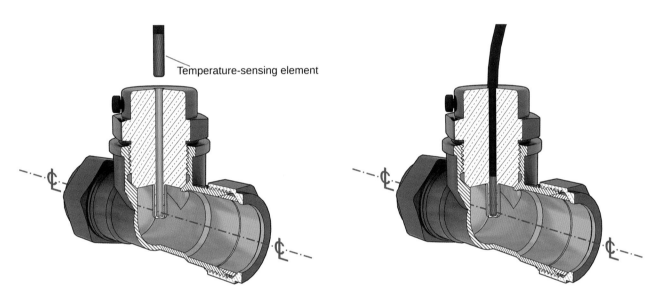

Temperature-sensing element

Figure 5.37 Pipe temperature sensor – pocket type

5.11.2.2 Time

There are two types of time input that may be considered in a domestic heating control system.

Current time

This is a sometimes overlooked input, but it is critical to the correct operation of intermittent space heating or hot water. It is important to ensure that the time can be easily updated by the user; for some smart and internet-connected controllers, the time may be set automatically.

Start/stop time (air and water)

The time period over which the space and water temperatures are maintained at the set-point. There should be the ability to separately define this time for each zone (see section 5.11.5) in the heating system. This is particularly important with regard to reducing energy consumption by heating spaces only when they are occupied, rather than controlling indoor spaces by temperature alone. It may just define which hours over a 24-hour period are heated and which are not, but ideally the periods should be defined separately for each day of the week, and even each season of the year. Consideration should be given to the complexity of the programming of this for the user.

More complex control systems may also allow different set-point temperatures to be associated with different time periods. This can allow for a reduced temperature to be maintained at certain times (e.g. at night), reducing the risk of condensation forming on cold surfaces and improving comfort by reducing dwelling warm-up times. This can also reduce the need for additional heat generator capacity in situations where there is intermittent use or occupancy, by not allowing the building to cool down completely.

Consideration needs to be given to the reheat time of the space (see section 3.5.5), including the emitter responsiveness (this is particularly important for low flow temperature heating systems). For a basic system this will mean setting the heating start time early enough that the appropriate indoor temperature is reached by the desired time, which will vary depending on the type of system and the outdoor weather conditions due to the time of year. Starting the system too early will waste energy, but starting it too late will lead to discomfort. Advanced control functionality such as optimum start/stop (see section 5.11.4) is designed to take care of this automatically.

The above two types of time input are commonly integrated into the controller rather than being separate devices.

5.11.3 Control functions – Outputs

There are two common types of outputs found on a domestic heating system: flow rate and flow temperature. Flow-rate control in domestic systems is typically binary (flow or no flow), but some advanced control systems may use variable flow-rate control; this is beyond the scope of this Guide and specialist advice should be sought. Both of these outputs can be split further into specific types of flow rate and flow temperature output, which will in turn be related to the physically installed devices. Not all the devices described below are required, but most will need to be considered, depending on the requirements of the system, the customer and regulations.

5.11.3.1 Flow Rate
The following heating system components are associated with the control system output of flow rate.

Thermostatic radiator valve
While generally not integrated electronically, thermostatic radiator valves (TRV) (Figure 5.38) are an important part of a well-functioning heating control system. TRVs are designed to sense the air temperature around them and regulate the flow of water through the heat emitter to which they are fitted. They in effect give room-by-room control over the air temperature set-point to a system in which multiple rooms are being controlled as a single zone (see section 5.11.5).

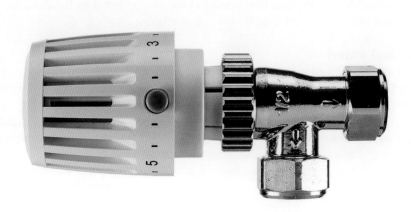

Figure 5.38 Thermostatic radiator valve

Also available are versions with a digital head (Figure 5.39) that give room by room control of the start/stop time as well as temperature control. Finally, there are also versions that include wireless communication to the controller, allowing the heat generator to be called only when one or more room requires it. These TRVs allow relatively simple retrofit of zone control to older properties where improved zone control is essential to energy efficiency.

The head of a TRV should be as far away from the heat emitter and hot pipework as possible, and not blocked by furniture. This is to ensure that it is measuring an accurate sample of the space temperature. This requirement is, unfortunately, often superseded by customers' aesthetic considerations. Where possible, options such as mounting the TRVs horizontally (hot pipes should not be run below) or at the top of a radiator, with a TBOC configuration (ensuring they are not covered by curtains, see section 5.5.4.2), or specifying a remote sensor head should be considered.

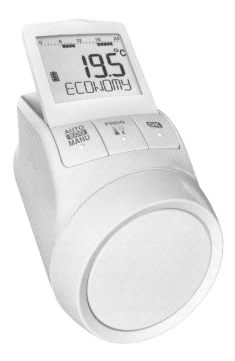

Figure 5.39 Digital thermostatic radiator valve head

Note: The heat emitter in the room containing a room thermostat or temperature sensor should not normally have a TRV installed (see 'Room thermostat' in section 5.11.2.1).

Note: Gravity circulated heating systems should have at least one radiator in the circuit without a TRV installed.

Note: As for room thermostats, building occupants should be reminded that turning a TRV to a higher setting will not make the room heat up any faster, but may cause the room to overheat and waste fuel. How quickly the room heats up depends on the heat generator size and setting, and the radiator size.

Note: Pre-settable TRVs are also available which can help with system balancing (see 'System balancing' in section 2.5.1.2). Typically, during commissioning an insert will be installed in the valve, which will limit the flow rate through the radiator accordingly; the appropriate insert can be selected by following the manufacturer's instructions, or possibly via the manufacturer's app. The balancing valve (see below), can then be used to isolate the radiator without affecting the balancing of the system.

Note: If no TRV is installed on a radiator, a simple wheel valve should be installed instead to allow the radiator to be isolated.

Note: TRVs should be paired with a balancing valve (otherwise known as a lockshield or decorator's valve) (Figure 5.40), the sole purpose of which is to balance the system (see 'System balancing' in section 2.5.1.2), and occupants should be encouraged not to change its setting.

Figure 5.40 Radiator balancing (lockshield) valve

Return temperature limiting valve

The return temperature limiting valve is visually similar to the TRV, but is usually installed on the return side of the radiator, although it is also available as inline versions. The valve performs the function of limiting the water temperature returning back to the heat generator, by cutting off the flow when the temperature exceeds a certain value. This can be particularly useful with condensing boilers, as it ensures the boiler is always operating in condensing mode, thus maximising its efficiency. However, a return temperature limiting valve does not provide the same local temperature control functionality as a TRV, and so a TRV (see above) or a manifold (see section 5.10.2) and manifold actuator will also be required.

Motorised valve

Typically used in either a two- or three-port configuration, motorised valves take an electronic signal from a controller and switch the flow to a circuit on or off. They consist of an electronic actuator mounted on a mechanical valve body. The three-port type (Figure 5.41) is commonly found in Y-plan systems (see section 5.4.2), where the valve is used to switch the flow between the heating circuit and the hot water circuit. (The use of Y-plan systems is becoming less common.) The more common two-port type (Figure 5.42) simply switches the flow on or off in a single circuit, and is the type used on S-plan systems (see section 5.4.1) and systems with multiple zones (see section 5.11.5). Related to the two-port type are actuators for manifolds (Figure 5.43 and section 5.10.2), which take an electronic signal to switch the flow on or off to an individual circuit supplied by the manifold.

Figure 5.41 Motorised valve – three port

Figure 5.42 Motorised valve – two port

Figure 5.43 Manifold actuator

Motorised valves typically open when they receive power, and then automatically close when the power is removed; there is also often a manual override to open them. Varieties that allow for variable flow rates are available, but these are beyond the scope of this Guide. Care should be taken to ensure that the actuator is compatible with the controller that is intended to be used. The manufacturer's instructions should always be followed when installing a motorised valve.

Note: Motorised valves are available that are closed when they are powered, and open automatically when the power is removed. They are less common, but which type is required should be clearly specified.

Pressure-independent control valve
With a well-balanced heating system and with all the TRVs open, the correct flow rate will be delivered to each heat emitter. If one or more heat emitters is shut off (either by manual intervention or by the room achieving its target temperature), the same flow rate must now be split between the remaining heat emitters; this assumes a fixed-speed circulator – a variable-speed circulator (see section 5.8) will partially alleviate the problem by reducing the flow rate as the system pressure increases. This will result in the system being out of balance, and the remaining radiators will give out higher levels of heat than required. Pressure-independent control valves overcome this problem by allowing the installer to pre-set the desired flow rate through the valve, which will then be maintained whatever the pressure in the system.

Valves of this type are commonly found in commercial installations, and they are growing in popularity in the domestic sector, as they make system balancing very simple. The system balancing procedure described in section 2.5.1.2 is not needed with a pressure-independent control valve. Instead the installer simply needs to pre-set the valve with the flow rate calculated in section 5.6.3.2 to deliver the required heat output to the zone. Typically installed as an inline valve for a heating zone, they are also available in the form of a TRV, providing both the local temperature control as well as the pressure-independent control functionality. Inline pressure-independent control valves can usually be fitted with a manifold-type actuator, and can therefore provide the same functionality as a motorised two-port valve, partially offsetting the additional cost.

Note: Variable-speed circulators (see section 5.8) are highly recommended for systems with pressure-independent control valves installed.

Circulator

The circulator or circulators (see section 5.8) are important output devices for the control system. Within the scope of this Guide, it is expected that circulators will be selected to provide the maximum required flow rate (see section 5.6.3.2) for a circuit. The control system will then switch the flow on or off as required by actuating the appropriate combination of motorised valves and circulators.

Note: Some modern inverter-driven circulators will have their own inbuilt control system that will actually reduce the flow rate if the system does not require the maximum flow rate (constant-pressure mode); this will occur if one or more zone valves or TRVs have shut the flow down.

Note: It is important to consider any manufacturer-specified minimum flow rates (this is primarily covered under the 'Automatic balancing valve' section below). Some modern inverter-driven circulators may provide the option to specify a minimum flow rate as part of their inbuilt control system.

Automatic balancing valve

An automatic balancing valve (sometimes known as an 'automatic bypass valve') is often integrated into the heat generator if required. The manufacturer's literature should be consulted to confirm if this is the case, or if an external valve is required.

As for TRVs, while generally not integrated electronically into the heating control system, an automatic balancing valve may be an essential component to ensure the correct operation of certain heat generators.

The need for a balancing valve depends on the heat generator and the control system. Some heat generators require a minimum flow rate to be maintained through their heat exchangers. They may also require circulator overrun to dissipate heat when the heat generator is switched off. For example, after combustion has finished, the system controls may shut down or restrict flow, but the circulator may still be operating, especially in systems using TRVs and two-port valves. In each case, a balancing valve is needed to provide a circulation path.

Where the heat generator manufacturer specifies a balancing valve, Approved Document guidance (see Table 1.1) suggests that an automatic balancing valve should be used, particularly with TRVs or zone valves. This type of valve is set when the system is commissioned such that under normal working conditions it is closed. In operation, the valve opens when the pressure increases in response to reduced flow through the circuit, short-circuiting the flow and return to the heat generator (Figure 5.44).

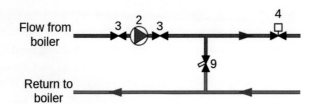

Key:

2	Circulator
3	Tamper-proof isolation valve
4	Motorised valve (2-port)
9	Automatic balancing valve

Figure 5.44 Automatic balancing valve arrangement

The minimum flow rate of water required through the heat generator balancing valve when all other circuits are closed is specified by the heat generator manufacturer, probably in terms of the temperature drop across the heat exchanger. The actual flow rate can vary between 10 l/min (0.17 kg/s) and 40 l/min (0.67 kg/s). An automatic balancing valve should be selected that meets the requirements specified.

Note: Where a low water content heat generator is used, an automatic balancing valve must be fitted directly after the circulator between the main flow and return pipes. You should refer to the manufacturer's instructions, including those on sizing. A minimum pipe diameter of 15 mm is typically required for heat generators up to 19 kW output, and 22 mm for larger generators.

Check/one-way valve
Another mechanical-only device for controlling the flow of fluid in a circuit is the check (or one-way) valve (Figure 5.45). This valve allows flow in one direction, but prevents it in the other. Valves of this type are often found in the filling loop on sealed heating systems (see section 5.9.1.2.4) to prevent contaminated water from the heating system backflowing into the cold water supply. They are typically also found on gravity circulation systems and systems with buffer storage, to prevent flow thermo-syphoning.

Figure 5.45 Check valve

Note: There are two types of check valve. One is spring loaded and the other uses a gravity closed gate. The former should only be used on a gravity system when the manufacturer explicitly states it is suitable, as the minimum flow required to open such a valve may be higher than a gravity circuit is able to deliver.

5.11.3.2 Flow temperature
The following two heating system components are associated with the control system output of flow temperature.

Mixer valves
Mixer valves are not commonly found in domestic heating systems, but their use is increasing. Generally outside the scope of this Guide, they are included here for completeness. Specialist advice should be sought on their use.

Note: The specification of mixer valves is intended to be covered in the forthcoming companion to this Guide, the *Integration Guide*, also to be published by the Domestic Building Service Panel (https://www.dbsp.co.uk).

The primary purpose of a mixer valve is to provide a lower flow temperature to a section of a heating circuit. This may be in a system that integrates two different types of heat emitter, with two different design flow rates (e.g. a heating system with both radiators and underfloor heating). Mixer valves may also be used by controllers that implement weather compensation (see 'Weather compensator' in section 5.11.4) on a system where the heat generator is not able to adjust its output temperature, or where buffer storage is used.

Domestic Heating Design Guide

Mixer valves typically come in one of three forms: a purely mechanical (thermostatic) device with a wax cartridge, similar to a TRV (Figure 5.46); a valve body with an attached electrical actuator and a separate pipe temperature sensor, both of which are controlled via the heating system central controller (sometimes similar in appearance to a three port mixer valve, see Figure 5.41); and a stand-alone combined actuator, pipe temperature sensor and a controller, which can be mounted onto a valve body. All three forms function in the same way; they blend return water (cooler) with the flow in order to achieve the desired output flow temperature.

Figure 5.46 Mechanical (thermostatic) mixer valve

DHW mixers

Often known as a 'thermostatic mixing valve' or 'anti-scald valve', a domestic hot water (DHW) mixer allows water to be stored and distributed at a higher temperature to allow for sterilisation to prevent the growth of bacteria (see section 4.5.1), while complying with recommendations limiting the temperature of water at the point of use (see section 4.5.2).

The DHW mixer valve is functionally and visually similar to the thermostatic mixer valves discussed above, but is designed to control to a different output temperature (Figure 5.47). It is important to make sure that the output temperature is tamper proof.

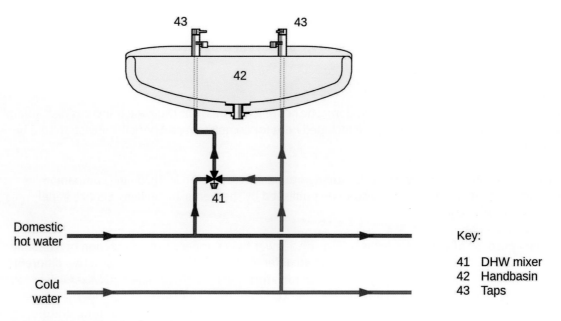

Key:
41   DHW mixer
42   Handbasin
43   Taps

Figure 5.47 DHW mixer valve function

5.11.4 Control Functions – Controller

The last component of the control system is the controller (Figure 5.48). This is where all the inputs feed into and the outputs are driven from. Some controllers have a separate remote wiring box that allows simpler connections of the various inputs and outputs. As discussed above, in the past a very basic control system may have just switched a circulator on and off based on the inputs to a thermostat, but these days it is important to have tighter control of heat generation and distribution. A controller therefore typically brings together the heating and hot water temperature and time inputs for each heating zone and hot water cylinder (if required), combining these with control logic to operate the required outputs in order to minimise energy losses while maximising comfort.

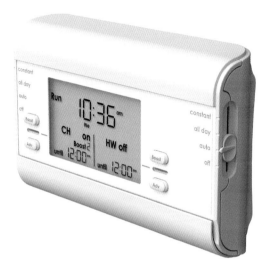

Figure 5.48 Multi-channel heating controller

Note: If the heat generator has been sized to meet only the heating or hot water demand (see section 5.7) and this is not ensured by the heat generator itself, the controller must be configured to ensure there is not a concurrent heating and hot water demand.

Beyond this basic level of control, there are various other functionalities that the controller may offer to further improve comfort and reduce energy consumption. These are discussed below. Not all are required, but most will need to be considered depending on the requirements of the system, the customer and regulations.

Frost protection

It is important to protect a heating system from freezing in the event that the outdoor temperature drops low enough while the building is unoccupied.

For automatic heat generators, this is typically a setting on the controller that calls for heat if any indoor space temperature sensors measure below a certain value; this would occur even if the time element of the control strategy is not calling for heat. Typically, a value of around 4°C is used for frost protection.

For non-automatic heat generators such as solid fuel appliances, other methods of frost protection should be considered, such as electric boilers, immersion heaters or trace heating. These methods may also be considered for automatic LPG and liquid fuel heat generators where the period the building may be unoccupied for could be greater than the level of fuel stored on site. Integrating these secondary heat sources is beyond the scope of this Guide, and specialist advice should be sought.

Heat generator interlock

Typically integrated into most modern heat generators, the interlock is a feature that prevents the heat generator from consuming energy by keeping itself warm when no output is being demanded.

Weather compensator

Weather compensation interacts intelligently with the heat generator to reduce water temperatures according to the outside temperatures; this increases efficiency without compromising user comfort. The premise is that a building will have a lower overall heat loss when it is warmer outdoors than when it is cooler, and therefore less heat needs to be supplied to meet this reduced heat loss. This means that the heat generator is better able to maintain a steady internal temperature by adjusting its output to account for changes in the weather.

Weather compensators require an input from an outdoor temperature sensor, which feeds weather data to the heat generator. This may be done directly to the heat generator, or via a controller that is able to integrate with the heat generator. The heat generator or controller will then use weather compensation curves such as the one shown in Figure 5.49 to select the appropriate flow temperature for the current outdoor temperature. You should seek the manufacturer's advice for specific curves to be used for the controller or heat generator installed.

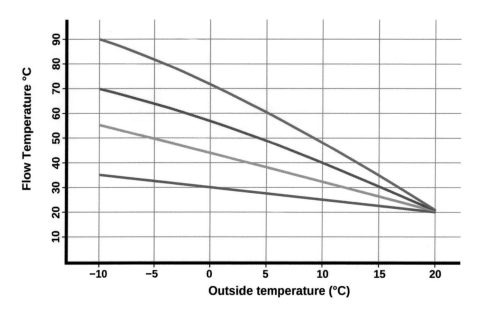

Figure 5.49 Graphical representation of weather compensation heating curves (different curves for different types of system)

Integrated systems with thermal storage and heat generators that are not able to vary their output temperature are also able to employ weather compensation through utilising the output of a mixer valve. This is beyond the scope of this Guide, and therefore specialist advice should be sought.

Optimum start/stop

A controller with an optimum start functionality will optimise the start time of the system through a self-learning process, whereby it recalls previous data and relates it to the current conditions. This means that the controller will ensure that the property will reach the desired comfort level at the start of the occupancy period, and not before. This has the effect of minimising the amount of work the heat generator has to do, and reduces energy use by delaying the start time when the weather is mild.

Customers should be advised that optimum start requires a change in mindset when programming the start time of a heating system. Without an optimum start functionality, the start time of a system is usually set at an estimated point in time before the heat is actually desired, to give a warm-up period to allow the space or building to heat up. With optimum start, the start time of the system should be exactly when the heat is required, as the warm-up period will be calculated by the system.

As well as optimum start, some controllers will have optimum stop functionality. This works in reverse to optimum start, in that it is able to learn the characteristics of how long it takes a building to cool down based on the outdoor temperature. This is then used to switch the heating off earlier than programmed, utilising the period of time the building takes to cool to reduce energy consumption.

Note: The optimum start functionality of a system will take time to learn the characteristics of the building. Customers should be made aware of this.

Note: Optimum start and weather compensation can negatively affect each other's performance if they are not implemented correctly. They should only be used at the same time if both are functions of the same device, and if the manufacturer states that they can both be enabled.

Anti-cycling control/hysteresis/narrow temperature differential

Older mechanical thermostats suffered from a lack of accuracy in their ability to control to a specific temperature, resulting in a wide window of temperatures delivered. The system would significantly overshoot the set-point temperature before switching off, and then significantly undershoot it before coming back on. While not significantly increasing the actual amount of energy consumed, this phenomenon, known as 'hysteresis', does affect comfort, as humans are sensitive to changes in indoor conditions. Modern electronic indoor temperature sensors are able to sense significantly more accurately, and so are able to control the temperature within a much tighter window. This may reduce energy consumption slightly, as a more constant temperature leads to greater overall comfort, and therefore occupants tend to set the indoor set-point temperature lower.

However, control systems have to balance the narrowness of the control window, as a very narrow window will result in lots of very short cycles of demand. This is a significant issue with combustion heat generators, as their start-up and shut-down phases are significantly less efficient than their steady-state phase. Modern control systems will typically have an electronically defined hysteresis of around 1°C, although this may need to be increased for buildings that have high levels of heat loss.

Self-learning/occupancy detection

The occupancy detection functionality is a feature that is starting to be found in a number of so-called 'smart' thermostats. The objective is to heat a space only when it is occupied, thereby reducing energy consumption. Each manufacturer's implementation will differ, and may use a combination of presence detection using sound, light levels, air temperature or passive infra-red levels, possibly with location data from a smartphone, along with other techniques. The system will typically take this data and use machine learning to forecast when people will be present in the house.

Note: Intermittent heating such as this works well in low thermal mass, well-insulated buildings. For buildings with a high thermal mass and high rates of ventilation heat loss, it can be difficult to heat the space up fast enough for such systems to work effectively.

Load compensation

Load compensation is a functionality that reduces the output of a heat generator as the indoor air temperature for the space being heated nears the set-point temperature. This requires that the heat generator is able to modulate its output, but if this is the case the load compensation function ensures that a more constant indoor air temperature is achieved, thereby reducing cycling and improving comfort.

Smart/remotely accessible

The term 'smart thermostat' generally refers to a thermostat that is connected to the internet, and with which the occupant can remotely control the indoor air temperature set-point via a smartphone app or a web page. This gives the user greater control over the heating system, potentially minimising the amount of time for which the space is heated but not occupied.

5.11.5 Zoned Heating

As discussed in section 5.4.1, Approved Document L1A of the Building Regulations 2010 (or the regional equivalent, see Table 1.1) recommends that homes with a total floor area in excess of 150 m^2 utilise at least two independently controlled space heating 'zones'. It is also common for heating systems in smaller dwellings (total floor area <150 m^2) to also be designed for, and installed with, multiple heating zones.

The typical arrangement is to separate the upstairs and downstairs heating circuits, so that the living areas can be heated only during the day and the bedrooms only at night. Designers may also want to segregate a system even further, particularly if an area has a significantly different temperature- or time-demand profile (e.g. bathrooms). Ideally, each room or space in a building would be given independent time and temperature control, but this can have significant cost implications for the client.

Note: In the Republic of Ireland the equivalent area is 100 m^2.

Zoning can be achieved by specifying a room indoor air temperature thermostat or temperature sensor and a motorised valve or manifold actuator for each of the heating zones, as well as separate pipework to the relevant emitters. A controller with sufficient channels for each of the heating zones, plus hot water if required, will also be needed. Figure 5.50 shows a multi-zone heating system, with the various control elements and their connections indicated.

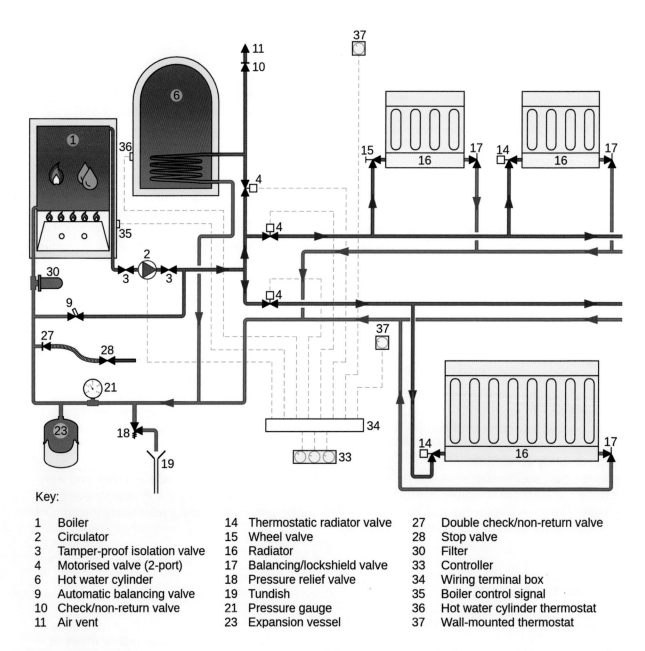

Key:

1	Boiler	14	Thermostatic radiator valve	27	Double check/non-return valve
2	Circulator	15	Wheel valve	28	Stop valve
3	Tamper-proof isolation valve	16	Radiator	30	Filter
4	Motorised valve (2-port)	17	Balancing/lockshield valve	33	Controller
6	Hot water cylinder	18	Pressure relief valve	34	Wiring terminal box
9	Automatic balancing valve	19	Tundish	35	Boiler control signal
10	Check/non-return valve	21	Pressure gauge	36	Hot water cylinder thermostat
11	Air vent	23	Expansion vessel	37	Wall-mounted thermostat

Figure 5.50 Heating and domestic hot water system with one zone valve for hot water and two zone valves for heating circuits

5.11.6 Recommended Control Systems

The recommended minimum control packages for various types of system are described below.

All wet systems must have at least:

- interlock
- anti-cycling control
- thermostatic radiator valves
- frost protection, where necessary to protect the appliance, system and dwelling.

5.11.6.1 Existing Semi-gravity Systems

Note: When upgrading, it is preferable to convert systems to fully pumped operation, but where this is impractical the following should be adopted. (New systems must always be fully pumped.)

All existing semi-gravity systems must have at least:

- space heating time and temperature control
- domestic hot water heating time and temperature control.

This will usually take the form of:

- a two-channel controller
- a room indoor space thermostat or temperature sensor
- a hot water cylinder thermostat or temperature sensor
- a circulator
- a check valve to prevent gravity circulation in the radiator circuit
- a two-port motorised valve fitted on the gravity circuit to the hot water cylinder.

Note: Motorised valves in gravity primary circuits must be fitted so that their operation does not interfere with the route of the open safety vent (OSV) or feed and expansion (F&E) pipes to the heat generator. In order that interlock may be achieved, the motorised valve actuator must have a single-pole double-throw (SPDT) auxiliary switch.

5.11.6.2 Fully Pumped System (Non-combination)

All fully pumped (non-combination) systems must have at least:

- space heating time and temperature control
- domestic hot water heating time and temperature control.

This will usually take the form of:

- a two or more channel controller (one channel for each zone, plus one for domestic hot water)
- room indoor space thermostats or temperature sensors (one thermostat or sensor for each zone)
- a hot water cylinder thermostat or temperature sensor
- a two-port motorised valve (one valve for each zone, plus one for domestic hot water)
- a circulator
- an automatic bypass valve (except where one is incorporated in the heat generator).

5.11.6.3 Combination Systems

All combination systems must have at least:

- space heating time and temperature control.

This will usually take the form of:

- a one or more channel controller (one channel for each zone)
- room indoor space thermostats or temperature sensors (one room thermostat or sensor for each zone)
- a two-port motorised valve (one valve for each zone)
- a circulator (except where one is incorporated in the heat generator)
- an automatic bypass valve (except where one is incorporated in the heat generator).

Since April 2018 in England, gas combination boilers must also be fitted with one of the following advance features under the Boiler Plus standard:

- flue gas heat recovery system (see section 1.6.2.4)
- weather compensation
- load compensation
- smart thermostat with automation and optimisation.

5.12 Pipework Insulation

Energy efficiency standards require that heating pipes should be insulated unless their heat loss contributes to the useful heating requirement of a room or space. In addition, water regulations require that pipes and fittings in an unheated area shall, as far as is reasonably practicable, be protected against damage from freezing and other causes. This section discusses the considerations surrounding the insulation of pipework.

5.12.1 Insulation of Heating System Pipework

Pipes should be insulated unless they contribute to the useful heat requirement of a heated room or space. Taking that further, if there is a possibility that the space they pass through (or an adjoining space to the void they pass through) might be maintained at temperatures different to those they are supplying, insulating the pipes should be considered if possible. As stated in the *Domestic Building Services Compliance Guide* (2018) (or the regional equivalent, see Table 1.1), reasonable provision should be made to limit heat losses from pipes.

The thickness of insulation recommended in Approved Document L of the Building Regulations 2010 (or the regional equivalent, see Table 1.1) is related to the thermal conductivity of the insulation material, provided that the thermal conductivity does not exceed 0.045 W/m K. The relationship between insulation thickness and thermal conductivity must to comply with the requirement for a maximum permissible heat loss (Table 5.17) when the water temperature is 60°C and the ambient still air temperature is 15°C.

All pipes connected to hot water storage vessels, including the open safety vent pipe and the primary flow and return to the heat exchanger, should be insulated for at least 1 m from their points of connection or to the point at which they become concealed.

Table 5.17 gives the insulation thickness required for various values of thermal conductivity, each satisfying the maximum permissible heat loss recommended in Approved Document L (or the regional equivalent, see Table 1.1). The transfer of heat between hot pipes and cold pipes should be avoided where possible by maintaining adequate separation between them. Where hot and cold pipes must run adjacent to each other, they should be insulated to minimise heat transfer.

Table 5.17 Minimum thickness of pipework insulation (mm)

Outside diameter of pipe on which insulation thickness has been based (mm)	Thermal conductivity at 40°C (W/m K)					Maximum permissible heat loss (W/m)*
	0.025	0.030	0.035	0.040	0.045	
8.0	5	7	9	12	16	7.06
10.0	6	8	11	15	20	7.23
12.0	7	10	14	18	23	7.35
15.0	9	12	15	20	26	7.89
22.0	11	14	18	23	29	9.12
28.0	12	16	20	25	31	10.07
35.0	13	17	22	27	33	11.08
42.0	14	18	23	28	34	12.19
54.0	15	19	24	29	35	14.12

*Water temperatures of 60°C for hot water with ambient still air temperatures of 15°C (high emissivity facing: 0.95)

Note: Common forms of pipe insulation have the following approximate thermal conductivities (at 40°C); specifications will vary between manufacturers, therefore test data should be consulted: phenolic foam (foil backed), 0.025 W/m K; nitrile rubber insulation, 0.03 W/m K; mineral wool (foil backed), 0.035 W/m K; EDPM rubber, 0.04 W/m K; polyethylene foam, 0.045 W/m K.

Note: The tinted rows in Table 5.17 indicate those pipe diameters for which a limit of 1.5 times the pipe diameter (at 0.040 W/m K) has been applied for practicality reasons; for more details, see *TIMSA Guidance for Achieving Compliance with Part L of the Building Regulations* (2006).

5.12.2 Insulation of Domestic Hot Water Pipework

The *Domestic Building Services Compliance Guide* (2018) (or regional equivalent, see Table 1.1) requires primary circulation pipes for domestic hot water services to be insulated throughout their length; this means any pipework carrying heat from the heat generator to a hot water cylinder. Consideration should also be given to insulating pipework carrying water from the heat generator or cylinder to the point of use, over and above the required first 1 m from the cylinder. Systems with secondary circulation should always be insulated throughout their length.

5.12.3 Insulation in Unheated Areas

Insulation is required by water regulations to reduce the likelihood of frost damage to pipes and fittings, including cold water service pipes and heating system pipes. This applies to all cold water fittings located within the building but outside the thermal envelope, and to those outside the building. Insulation should comply with BS 5422:2009 and be installed in accordance with BS 5970:2012.

Where low temperatures persist, insulation will only delay the onset of freezing. The efficiency of insulation is dependent on its thickness and thermal conductivity in relation to the size of pipe, the time of exposure, the location and possibly the wind-chill factor. The thickness of insulation is designed to provide protection for a period of up to 12 hours. Where protection is required for longer periods, or the premises are left unoccupied, this should be provided by a frost thermostat set to activate the heating system when the air temperature drops to a pre-selected level, or by draining down. Self-regulating trace heating conforming to BS 6351, in conjunction with a nominal thickness of thermal insulation, can also be used as a method of protection against freezing.

Hot water fittings outside the thermal envelope, where water is likely to be static for a period, should be protected against freezing. In these low temperature conditions, insulation applied to hot water pipes for energy-conservation purposes is usually of insufficient thickness (see section 5.12.1).

For cold water services, two conditions are identified:

- *Normal conditions* – Unheated rooms within the thermal envelope of the heated accommodation, such as store rooms or roof spaces below the roof insulation.
- *Extreme conditions* – Outside the normal heated envelope of the building, such as roof spaces above the roof insulation.

Typical insulation thicknesses to manufacturers' recommendations are given in Table 5.18.

Table 5.18 Thickness of insulation for cold water pipes to prevent freezing

External diameter of pipe (mm)	Thickness of insulation (mm)	
	Within the insulated envelope of the dwelling – normal conditions	Outside the insulated envelope of the dwelling – extreme conditions
15	25	32
22	19	25
28	19	19
35	13	13

5.12.4 Insulation of Condensate Pipework

Insulation used for external condensate pipes and sink or washing machine waste pipes (which may be carrying the heat generator condensate externally to a foul gulley/drain or soakaway) should be weatherproof and have a UV-resistant finish. A minimum of 19 mm thick insulation is recommended for external pipes having an outer diameter of 32 mm. Insulation should comply with BS 5422:2009 and be installed in accordance with BS 5970:2012.

Pipes carrying heat generator condensate, installed within the building but outside of the thermal envelope, should be treated as if they were external, and the same requirements applied.

5.12.5 Installation of Insulation

Thermal insulating materials should be of the closed-cell type, comply with BS 5422:2009 and be installed in accordance with BS 5970:2012. Insulation should be neatly fitted with formed mitred joints at elbows and tees, and should cover all valves and fittings. The manufacturer's approved adhesives should be used on all butt and seam joints.

5.13 Water Treatment

The primary objectives of water treatment should be to maintain the performance of the appliance to provide consistent, on-demand heating while reducing household energy use and carbon equivalents, and guarding against component breakdown. Cleaning and water treatment should be used to preserve, or restore and maintain energy efficiency and system effectiveness. It does so by:

- removing installation and corrosion debris, oils, greases and flux residues in the case of new systems, and corrosion debris and scale for existing systems, and/or microbiological foulants in both cases
- minimising the corrosion of system metals, without adversely affecting non-metals, such as plastics and rubber
- inhibiting the formation of magnetite sludge and other corrosion products
- inhibiting the formation of limescale
- inhibiting the growth of microbiological organisms
- protecting against freezing.

BS 7593:2019 gives recommendations on good practice for the preparation of the circulating water in open-vented or sealed heating systems in individual domestic premises during initial commissioning or recommissioning following major remedial work (e.g. boiler replacement), and the ongoing water treatment to ensure appliance and system protection and continued efficiency in operation.

5.13.1 Debris, Corrosion and Limescale

A correct water treatment and system protection regime is designed to maintain the maximum efficiency of the system. Heating systems should be treated with an approved chemical inhibitor to limit system corrosion debris, which collects as sludge, and limescale, both of which restrict heat transfer (and therefore energy efficiency) and threaten system components.

The ongoing maintenance of the water regime is an important consideration, and the concentration of additives (e.g. inhibitor) should be checked after commissioning and annually thereafter in order to ensure that energy efficiency and ongoing protection are maintained. This check should also include an assessment of water cleanliness and servicing of the in-line filter. To mitigate against potential chemical degradation, corrosion and scale inhibitor should be re-dosed at 5-year intervals. Alternatively, a full laboratory analysis of the system water should be undertaken to verify ongoing corrosion and scale inhibition.

Unless the manufacturer's instructions state otherwise, products from different manufacturers should not be mixed.

All newly installed and refurbished systems need to be thoroughly flushed and cleaned using a chemical product formulated specifically for heating systems. This is in order to remove installation debris from the system that would otherwise obstruct heat transfer and threaten the system components. It is also required to add a corrosion and scale inhibitor to the cleaned system before putting it into regular use. An in-line filter (Figure 5.51) also needs to be installed in the system water circuit to maintain system cleanliness and efficiency, and to avoid any potential debris circulating in the system water. This should be done in accordance with BS 7593:2019 and the instructions of the heat generator manufacturer.

This procedure must also be followed when replacement or extension work is carried out on a system. This is crucial for removing any corrosion debris that would continue to restrict heat transfer in the system and jeopardise the new heat generator or part of the system.

Figure 5.51 In-line filter

5.13.2 Antifreeze

For systems that are not used over the winter months (i.e. in second homes) and which might be exposed to very low temperatures, a suitable inhibited antifreeze product should be considered.

In addition to pipework insulation (see section 5.12.3), antifreeze may also be considered for systems where a portion of the pipework runs outside the heated envelope of the property, and there is a risk that the system may not be operating during a period where there is a risk of freezing.

5.13.3 Microbiological Contamination

Controlling microbiological organisms by using a biocide is fundamental to maintaining a healthy heating system to restrict microbial growth. If a heating system is left untreated there is a risk that the remaining system water, flux residues, debris and contaminated by-products within the system can cause problems.

Bacteria, fungi and slimes cause restricted flow and blockages, and are liable to foul many parts of the system. Bacteria can thrive in both open-vented and sealed systems, especially those fouled with corrosion and other debris – particularly beneath deposits where the temperature might be lower and there is an absence of oxygen. Even the high temperature in the appliance heat exchanger might not be sufficient to kill all microorganism.

Contaminants can give rise to microbiological corrosion of system metals, especially in underfloor heating and other systems that operate at low temperatures (below 60°C), as well as open-vented systems and those with stagnant or low-flow areas.

Water treatment should be applied to all primary systems except for single-feed indirect hot water cylinders. After the system has been cleaned to remove debris, sludge and contaminants, an inhibitor is added to the system water using a chemical product formulated specifically for heating.

5.14 Heat Storage and Buffering

The specification of buffer vessels and other methods of storing heat generated by the heat generator for the purpose of space heating is beyond the scope of this Guide, and, as such, specialist advice should be sought.

Note: This topic is intended to be covered in the forthcoming companion to this Guide, the *Integration Guide*, also to be published by the Domestic Building Service Panel (https://www.dbsp.co.uk).

5.15 System Integration

The integration of multiple types of heat generator and multiple types of heat emitter is beyond the scope of this Guide, and, as such, specialist advice should be sought.

Note: This topic is intended to be covered in the forthcoming companion to this Guide, the *Integration Guide*, also to be published by the Domestic Building Service Panel (https://www.dbsp.co.uk).

5.16 Appendix

5.16.1 Worksheet B – Heat Emitters and Pipework – Blank

See next page.

Worksheet B – Heat Emitters and Pipework

Stage 1 - Job information

Room | 1.1   Job | 1.2   Page | 1.3   of   1.4

Stage 2 - Room information

Design room temp. (°C)	2.1	Design flow temp. (°C)	2.3	Mean water temp. (MWT) (°C)	2.5
Room heat loss (W)	2.2	Design return temp. (°C)	2.4	Mean water to air temp. (MW-Air) (°C)	2.6

Stage 3 - Pipework emissions

Diameter (mm)	Length (m)	Pipework emissions per length (W/m)	Pipe layout factor	A Pipe emission (W)
8	3.x2	3.x3	3.x4	3.x5
10	3.x2	3.x3	3.x4	3.x5
15	3.x2	3.x3	3.x4	3.x5
22	3.x2	3.x3	3.x4	3.x5
28	3.x2	3.x3	3.x4	3.x5
other 3.x1	3.x2	3.x3	3.x4	3.x5
other 3.x1	3.x2	3.x3	3.x4	3.x5
other 3.x1	3.x2	3.x3	3.x4	3.x5

Total pipe emission (W) | 3.6

Stage 4 - Radiator output factors

Net heat output required from radiator (W) | 4.1

	Mean water to air differential factor (f1)	Pipe connections factor (f2)	Enclosure factor (f3)	Finish factor (f4)	Output emission factor (f)
Radiator 1	4.x2	4.x3	4.x4	4.x5	4.x6
Radiator 2	4.x2	4.x3	4.x4	4.x5	4.x6
Radiator 3	4.x2	4.x3	4.x4	4.x5	4.x6
Radiator 4	4.x2	4.x3	4.x4	4.x5	4.x6

Stage 5 - Radiator selection

	Proportion of net heat output required from radiator (W)	Radiator listed output required (W)	Manufacturer listed part #	Water content (litres)	output (W)	Actual calculated output (W)
Radiator 1	5.x1	5.x2	5.x3	5.x4	5.x5	5.x6
Radiator 2	5.x1	5.x2	5.x3	5.x4	5.x5	5.x6
Radiator 3	5.x1	5.x2	5.x3	5.x4	5.x5	5.x6
Radiator 4	5.x1	5.x2	5.x3	5.x4	5.x5	5.x6

DBSP - DHDG -V2020.0

5.16.2 Worksheet B – Heat Emitters and Pipework – Instructions

Work through the following steps, calculating or entering data as required.

Stage 1 – Worksheet information

1.1	Name of the room the worksheet is for
1.2	Job name that the worksheet is part of
1.3	Page number of the worksheet
1.4	Total number of pages of worksheets for the job

Stage 2 – Room information

2.1	Value from cell 2.1 in worksheet A
2.2	Value from cell 5.9 in worksheet A
2.3	Design flow temperature for the heating system (see section 5.5.2)
2.4	Design return temperature for the heating system (see section 5.5.2)
2.5	Add the values from cells 2.3 and 2.4, and divide the sum by 2 (see section 5.5.2)
2.6	Subtract the value from cell 2.1 from cell 2.5 (see section 5.5.2)

Stage 3 – Exposed pipework emissions (see section 5.5.3)

The procedure for all pipe sizes is the same. Therefore, the steps have been combined.

3.x1–3.x5	If an element is not required, enter 0 for all cells

Note: If additional pipe sizes are used other than 8–28 mm, one or more of the other rows may be used.

3.x1	If required, additional pipe size diameter
3.x2	Total exposed length of the relevant diameter of the pipework in the room
3.x3	Relevant pipework emissions (see section 5.5.3 and Table 5.1)
3.x4	Relevant pipe layout factor (see section 5.5.3 and Table 5.2)
3.x5	Multiply values from cells 3.x2, 3.x3 and 3.x4
3.6	Sum of all the values in column A

Stage 4 – Output emission factors (see section 5.5.4)

4.1	Subtract the value from cell 3.6 from cell 2.2

Additional rows have been included to be used if more than one radiator is used. The procedure for all radiators is the same. Therefore, the steps have been combined.

4.x2–4.x6	If an element is not required, enter 0 for all cells
4.x2	Mean water to air differential factor (f1) (see section 5.5.4.1 and Table 5.3)
4.x3	Pipe connections factor (f2) (see section 5.5.4.2 and Table 5.4)
4.x4	Enclosure factor (f3) (see section 5.5.4.3 and Table 5.5)
4.x5	Finish factor (f4) (see section 5.5.4.4 and Table 5.6)
4.x6	Multiply the values from cells 4.x2, 4.x3, 4.x4 and 4.x5 for each row

Stage 5 – Radiator selection (see section 5.5.5)

Additional rows have been included to be used if more than one radiator is used. The procedure for all radiators is the same. Therefore, the steps have been combined.

5.x1–5.x6   If an element is not required, enter 0 for all cells

5.x1   Proportion of the value in cell 4.1

Examples:

- If there is to be only one radiator in the room, then enter the value from cell 4.1 in cell 5.x1 in the 'Radiator 1' row
- If there are to be two equally sized radiators in the room, then enter 50% of the value from cell 4.1 in cell 5.x1 in the 'Radiator 1' and 'Radiator 2' rows

5.x2   Divide values from cells 5.x1 by the corresponding 4.x6 values

5.x3–5.x5   Select from manufacturer's literature and note the details of a specific radiator that satisfies 5.x2

5.x3   Manufacturer listed part number

5.x4   Manufacturer listed water content

5.x5   Manufacturer listed output

5.x6   Multiply values from cells 5.x5 and the corresponding 4.x6 values

5.16.3 Worksheet C – Water Content of System – Blank

See next page.

Worksheet C – Water Content of System

Stage 1 - Job information

Job 1.1   Page 1.2   of   1.3

Stage 2 - Heat generator

	Manufacturer and model	Rated heat output (W)	**B** Water content (litres)
Heat generator 1	2.x1	2.x2	2.x3
Heat generator 2	2.x1	2.x2	2.x3

Stage 3 - Hot water cylinder

	Manufacturer and model	Storage capacity (litres)	Water content of coil (litres)
Hot water cylinder 1	3.x1	3.x2	3.x3
Hot water cylinder 2	3.x1	3.x2	3.x3

Stage 4 - Pipework

Diameter (mm)	Length (m)	**A** Water content per metre (litres)	Water content (litres)
8	4.x1	0.036	4.x2
10	4.x1	0.055	4.x2
15	4.x1	0.145	4.x2
22	4.x1	0.32	4.x2
28	4.x1	0.539	4.x2
35	4.x1	0.836	4.x2
42	4.x1	1.233	4.x2
54	4.x1	2.094	4.x2
67	4.x1	3.244	4.x2
76	4.x1	4.211	4.x2
108	4.x1	8.68	4.x2

Stage 5 - Heat emitters

	Room	Location in room	Water content (litres)
Heat emitter 1	5.x1	5.x2	5.x3
Heat emitter 2	5.x1	5.x2	5.x3
Heat emitter 3	5.x1	5.x2	5.x3
Heat emitter 4	5.x1	5.x2	5.x3
Heat emitter 5	5.x1	5.x2	5.x3
Heat emitter 6	5.x1	5.x2	5.x3
Heat emitter 7	5.x1	5.x2	5.x3
Heat emitter 8	5.x1	5.x2	5.x3
Heat emitter 9	5.x1	5.x2	5.x3
Heat emitter 10	5.x1	5.x2	5.x3

Stage 6 - Expansion vessel selection

Total system water content (litres)	System static pressure at expansion vessel (bar)	Safety valve setting (bar)	Minimum required volume (litres)	Manufacturer listed		
				part #	pre-charge (bar)	Volume (litres)
6.1	6.2	6.3	6.4	6.5	6.6	6.7

DBSP - DHDG -V2020.0

5.16.4 Worksheet C – Water Content of System – Instructions

Work through the following steps, calculating or entering data as required.

Stage 1 – Worksheet information

1.1	Job name that the worksheet is part of
1.2	Page number of the worksheet
1.3	Total number of pages of worksheets for the job

Stage 2 – Heat generator (see section 5.9.1.4.1)

Additional rows have been included to be used if more than one heat generator is used. The procedure for all heat generators is the same. Therefore, the steps have been combined.

2.x1–2.x3	Select and note the details of a specific heat generator. If an element is not required, enter 0 for all cells
2.x1	Manufacturer and model of selected heat generator
2.x2	Manufacturer's listed rated heat output for the selected heat generator
2.x3	Manufacturer's listed water content for the selected heat generator

Stage 3 – Hot water cylinder (see section 5.9.1.4.1 and Table 5.13)

Additional rows have been included to be used if more than one hot water cylinder is used. The procedure for all hot water cylinders is the same. Therefore, the steps have been combined.

3.x1–3.x3	Select and note the details of a specific hot water cylinder. If an element is not required, enter 0 for all cells
3.x1	Manufacturer and model of selected hot water cylinder
3.x2	Manufacturer's listed storage capacity of the hot water cylinder
3.x3	Manufacturer's listed water content of the hot water cylinder heating coil; if not available, see Table 5.13

Stage 4 – Pipework (see section 5.9.1.4.1 and Table 5.14)

The procedure for all pipe sizes is the same. Therefore, the steps have been combined.

4.x1–4.x2	If an element is not required, enter 0 for all cells
4.x1	The total length of the corresponding diameter of the pipework in the system
4.x2	Multiply the value from cells 4.x1 by the corresponding value in column A

Stage 5 – Heat emitters (see section 5.9.1.4.1)

Additional rows have been included to be used if more than one heat emitter is used. The procedure for all heat emitters is the same. Therefore, the steps have been combined.

5.x1–5.x3	Select and note the details of specific heat emitters. For radiators, these can be copied from Worksheet B for each room. If an element is not required, enter 0 for all cells
5.x1	Room the heat emitter is located in
5.x2	Location of the heat emitter in the room (if more than one)
5.x3	Manufacturer's listed water content of the heat emitter (value in cell 5.x4 in Worksheet B if a radiator)

Stage 6 – Expansion vessel selection (see section 5.9.1.4.2)

6.1	Sum of all values in column B
6.2	System static pressure at the expansion vessel (see section 5.9.1.2.1)
6.3	Safety valve setting (see sections 5.9.1.2.2 and 5.9.1.4.2 and the manufacturer's literature)
6.4	Minimum required expansion vessel volume (see section 5.9.1.4.2 and Table 5.15)

Based on value of cell 6.4, select a suitable expansion vessel from the manufacturer's literature (see section 5.9.1.4.2)

6.5	Manufacturer's listed part number of selected expansion vessel
6.6	Manufacturer's listed pre charge of selected expansion vessel
6.7	Manufacturer's listed volume of selected expansion vessel